KILLA

To my beautiful daughters Elsie and Isla

KILLA

The Autobiography of Kevin Kilbane

Kevin Kilbane with
Andy Merriman

First published in Great Britain
2013 by Aurum Press Ltd
74-77 White Lion Street
London N19PF
www.aurumpress.co.uk

A catalogue record for this book is
available from the British Library.

ISBN 978 1 84513 601 7

1 3 5 7 9 10 8 6 4 2

2013 2015 2017 2016 2014

Typeset in Sabon by SX Composing DTP, Rayleigh, Essex

Printed and bound by CPI Group (UK) Ltd, Croydon, CR0 4YY

Contents

Foreword

I'm delighted to be able to write this foreword for Kevin, who I've admired both on and off the park since he first came to my notice when he was a floppy-haired teenager at Preston and I was the Republic of Ireland manager. His undoubted natural ability was plain to see and, with his power and pace, I knew straightaway that he was going to progress. He soon became a regular in the Under 21 side and once I'd given him a full international debut at the age of twenty his name was one of the first I penned on the team sheet. He became an integral part of my team and gave us the balance that made us hard to beat. Kevin was not a flighty, tricky winger but he was effective and always diligent, and never afraid put his shift in. He is a proper player. Always has been.

You'll have heard pundits, managers or players talk about who they think is the nicest man in football and I know it can become a bit of a cliché. But in the case of Kevin Kilbane it's true. He is the most genuine man you'll ever meet. Of course that's only one part of his character – there's so much more to Kevin than that. You're not chosen for your country 110 times or make more than 600 club appearances by just being a good lad. Kevin has an inner strength and determination that belies his easy-going personality. He's had to deal with some unfair criticism on occasions but he has never shied away from responsibility or tried to hide.

Some people are modest because…they have a lot to be modest about, but this couldn't be further from the truth when it comes to Kevin, who is reluctant to sing his own praises but is much admired by his fellow professionals. He is, above all, a team player, who I could always rely on and who never gave less than his all for his chosen country.

Kevin was always a joy to have around – he was extremely low maintenance and never gave me or any of his other managers a moment of trouble. I remember when Peter Reid, then manager of Sunderland, rang me when he was thinking about signing Kevin from West Brom and asked me what I thought. 'Sign him,' I said. I didn't need to say anything else. Peter replied, 'Thanks, Mick, that's good enough for me!'

Peter did sign Kevin and during his time at Sunderland Kevin played for me in the 2002 World Cup finals. Kevin is a proud Irishman, who was given the chance to play for England but chose Ireland because of his family background and because he had been raised in that culture.

I picked Kevin for Ireland and the fact that, after me, Brian Kerr, Steve Staunton and Giovanni Trapattoni all wanted Kevin in the their teams says everything about his commitment, professionalism and undoubted talent. Four international managers have picked him for sixty-six consecutive competitive matches. That says all you need to know about 'Killa'.

It doesn't surprise me at all that, following his retirement from playing, Kevin is now distinguishing himself in a new career in the media and I am so pleased that he is enjoying further success. He has also devoted a great a deal of time and energy to charity work for the Down's Syndrome Association and Down's Syndrome Ireland, to whom the royalties of this book are to be paid.

I would be proud to have Kevin as a son. That's how much I think of him.

Mick McCarthy
London
June 2013

Preface
Croke Park, Dublin, 14 October 2009

I'm on the side of the pitch, lining up with the rest of the team, and I'm in a bit of a state. I rarely get tense before games now and haven't really been anxious about an international since my debut against Iceland and the World Cup opener versus Cameroon. But for the first time in my life I actually feel petrified – although the game against Montenegro doesn't have any significance as we have already qualified for the World Cup play-offs and can't catch Italy at the top of the group. It's not the attendance of nearly 40,000 fans either – I'm used to playing in front of big crowds. It should be plain-sailing and a straightforward game for me to play in. I want today to be like any other match day in my preparation. But today isn't just another game. Whenever anyone mentions my hundredth cap I choke up. I've tried to play it down throughout the week's preparations but in reality I've been a nervous wreck. From the moment I woke up this morning every minute has seemed like an hour and I just can't wait for the referee to give that familiar blast on the whistle and for the game to kick off. I feel incredibly emotional and find myself thinking of all my past appearances. I just want to get through the game as quickly as possible. I'm so pleased that Shay Given, who is also receiving his hundredth cap tonight, is sharing this honour with me but even his calming presence hasn't eased my nerves at all.

Then my daughters, Elsie and Isla, join me on the pitch and now I'm really struggling. The tears flow. I'm trying to hide them as best I can but the occasion proves much too much for any self-control. And now comes the national anthem…I truly feel I am a 'Son of the Gael'.

I just can't believe I'm achieving something that only one other Irish player has done before and that so many wonderful and better Irish players and true Irish football legends had never been able to attain.

I feel extraordinarily lucky and proud…not bad for an ordinary lad from Preston.

Chapter One

Stand Up for the Boy in Green

'Football united the kids. You didn't have to call for your mates;
simply walking down the street bouncing a ball had the Pied Piper
effect. We could all smell a game from 200 yards.'

TOM FINNEY

'Are you okay?' I heard somebody's concerned voice and slowly opened my eyes, blinking in the half-light. I looked up to see a young woman leaning over me. She touched my arm gently as I gradually regained my senses. 'Are you okay?' she repeated. I didn't know. I had no idea what had happened. I was taking my usual route, walking through St Gregory's church grounds across Blackpool Road but had then stared at the red traffic light to my right and I had suddenly felt weak.

Now I was lying on the pavement.

'I was worried,' she said. 'You were shaking all over and your eyes were rolling.'

I sat up slowly. 'I think I'm okay,' I finally replied when I was able to speak. 'I must have fainted. I'm fine now. Thanks.'

Although this had never happened to me before and my symptoms weren't exactly those of a fainting fit, I wasn't scared. My Good Samaritan seemed satisfied with my explanation and wandered off. I was just ten years old and had been on my way to play in an Under 11s game for Preston Schools at Deepdale.

Goodness only knows how I made it to the players' entrance which was about 200 metres away from where I collapsed. Of course, other ten-year-old lads aren't going to notice if I appeared a bit pale or shaken. That's probably how we looked most of the time, so they didn't notice my demeanour. We were there to play football and that was all that mattered – certainly not the health of one of their team members. I met the boys, Chris, Mackie, Tommy and the others, and went on to play that day as if nothing had happened. When I went home I didn't tell a soul. After all, I was all right now, wasn't I? And Mum would only worry.

Home was a three-bedroom council house in an area of Preston called Holme Slack; 35 Manor House Lane, the same road where Preston legend Tom Finney grew up and within a goal-kick of Deepdale, Preston North End's famous home ground. I shared a bedroom with my brother, Farrell, who was two years older than me, and then there was my sister and the bane of my life at that time, Geraldine.

My dad, Patrick Farrell Kilbane, was no longer living with us. My mum had got fed up with his drinking and his increasingly difficult and erratic behaviour. Not that we really noticed he was absent. He worked all day as a road digger and labourer for an Irish firm and then went straight to the pub, only to return home after we were all in bed, when he would drunkenly demand his dinner. Apart from occasionally hearing him parking his van (he was banned from driving on several occasions for being over the limit) and listening to my parents' late-night arguments, his departure made no difference to my life.

The estate was in a mixed but friendly working-class community – a predominantly Catholic neighbourhood, although there was no sectarian conflict or gangs and it felt a safe environment. Preston North End, originally named Priest Town, had an unusually high number of Roman Catholics living in the town. The mid-nineteenth century saw a rapid increase in the numbers of Irish born in Lancashire, in the wake of the Irish famine and employment in the mills. Many Irish labourers worked in the post-war building boom in the 1950s and 1960s and there were also many Irish nurses and domestics living in the town.

My grandparents were part of this Irish diaspora. My maternal grandfather, James Mell, who played Gaelic football, had come over to England to find work on the docks in Birkenhead, Liverpool. He later moved to Preston where his wife, Joan, and the rest of the family eventually joined him. He was a keen football fan, originally following Tranmere Rovers, and he used to take Mum to Deepdale when she was a teenager. Sadly, I never really knew him as he died in 1981 when I was only four years old. I like to think he would have followed my career.

Teresa, my mum, was born in County Longford, which had been affected particularly badly by the potato famine. Mum came over from Ireland to finish her schooling when she was in her early teenage years. She is from a very close but extended family and has two sisters and a brother. My dad's family hailed from Achill Island, County Mayo, but, sadly, my paternal grandfather, Daniel Kilbane, whose middle name I inherited, died in 1963 when my dad was just seven years old. His widow came to England with my dad, who had six siblings.

Mum and Dad met at the Hibernian Club, an Irish meeting place in Preston. Ironically, in those days he was what was known as 'a Pioneer' (Pioneer Total Abstinence Association of the Sacred Heart), an Irish temperance movement, which encouraged complete abstinence from alcoholic drink among its members. My dad had apparently 'taken the pledge' and wore a badge proclaiming the fact. It's amazing to think that Dad was a teetotaller when Mum first met him.

I was born at Sharoe Green Maternity Hospital on 1 February 1977, and weighed in at 8lb 12oz. I was due a couple of weeks earlier and my mum was taken into hospital to be induced. It was a difficult birth because of my size and pretty painful for my mum. My dad wasn't present – according to Mum he was very squeamish and once passed out while watching some hospital drama on television! So I think she was quite relieved not to have to worry about him as well as me.

My earliest memories were exactly as you might expect; our house stood at the end of a row of terraced council houses and from the age of five my mates and I played football on a tiny patch of grass at the crossroads opposite. We would use the hedge for a goal or sometimes the cars, parked by fans attending North End matches, served as more interesting targets.

Because my dad was absent most of the time and provided very little support, my mum was definitely in charge. She was a real matriarch. Loving and devoted, but strict. She dished out the discipline and wasn't afraid to give any of us kids a real belt if she felt our behaviour warranted such action. She worked in the local launderette and later became a dinner lady at my old school, St Gregory's. (She now works as a dinner lady at a special school.) Apart from working every day, she did all the cleaning, shopping and cooking. Money was tight even when Dad was around as he pissed away all his wages. It was a constant struggle to make ends meet and Mum would often get into debt.

My brother Farrell was a great influence in my life both then and much later when we were both pursuing professional football careers. I remember Mum telling me that he walked at nine months and was kicking a ball a few weeks later! In the years that followed, he let me join in the football games with his friends and so, from quite a young age, I was kicking a ball around with boys older than me. I know that playing with them really helped me develop and made me into a better footballer.

As I said, we mainly played in the street outside our house. One night, when Mum was watching *Coronation Street*, a football crashed through the front window, giving her the fright of her life. She somehow knew I was the culprit and rushed to the door, shouting the odds. She chased me up the street, but fortunately she couldn't catch me. I don't think I'd ever run faster. 'You were as quick as Linford Christie that day,' Mum later remarked. I stayed away for as long as I could but then came skulking back for the inevitable tongue-lashing. Mum had to get some cardboard to cover the window but didn't sleep a wink that night for fear of being burgled.

Apart from playing with Farrell, we also let my sister Geraldine play when she was old enough. Of course, we always put her in goal!

I had a pretty feisty relationship with my sister. Because we were only eighteen months apart, we used to fight constantly. I loved winding her up and teased her mercilessly. I used to lock her out of the house and if we ever had any money for ice creams, I made sure I got a double scoop, with hundreds and thousands and chocolate sauce, and poor Geraldine used to get one plain scoop if she was lucky. Even then I would hide her cone behind my back and pretend I'd forgotten to get one for her.

Once, when we were pretending to be superstars of the World Wrestling Federation, Geraldine fell off the side of the bed, blood dripping from a cut on her head. I thought of likely punishments and implored Geraldine, 'Don't tell Mum how it happened!' Geraldine replied: 'Well, what am I going to tell her then?' I think I told her to say that one of her heavy dancing shoes had fallen off a shelf and hit her on the head, but I don't think it worked.

We did get on sometimes – we liked the idea of being successful pop singers and used hairbrushes as pretend microphones. Geraldine had a good voice although her real talent was for Irish dancing and my mum used to take her to displays and competitions. In fact, those weighty dancing shoes were quite handy for Geraldine as she would also use them as weapons if I went too far with my teasing.

Geraldine was, however, very supportive about me being a

professional footballer and, despite occasionally tempting me with a cigarette when we were very young, always encouraged me in the career I eventually chose to follow.

It wasn't just with Geraldine that I got into scrapes. For some reason, I was always the boy who would be dared to play tricks and, of course, I was always up for it; I remember playing 'chicken', running out at the last minute in front of passing traffic and dodging the passing cars. 'Knock a door run' was another favourite when I would bang on the front doors of unsuspecting neighbours and then run away. A similar lark was to tie cotton thread to a door knocker, then hide in bushes across the other side of the street. We'd pull on the thread from a safe distance and then, when the homeowner came to answer the door, there was no one outside. All harmless compared to some of the stuff kids get up to nowadays but it must have driven the poor neighbours crackers.

The lads and I would also get up to tricks at the local golf course; we would hide in the woods near one of the holes in which there was a large dip in the middle of the fairway. Once the golfers had driven off and had walked a hundred yards or so, they couldn't see the rest of the fairway. We would then run on to the course, steal their golf balls and then return to our hiding place in the woods. We fell about while watching the golfers searching for their balls, which they were sure they had driven 'right down the middle'! I collected quite a few balls that way and, with an old golf club I found, used to drive golf balls into wasteland at the back of the estate – that was the closest I ever got to a golf course.

Occasionally the head groundsman would see what we were doing and chase us across the course in his tractor.

My mum never had any money to pursue her own hobbies and interests but was selfless in that she would always support Farrell and me in our football careers and Geraldine with her dancing. Mum was, however, very involved in the local Irish community and, growing up, it was inevitable that I should be completely immersed in the culture of 'the old country'.

It was also a very volatile time in terms of Irish politics. I remember a friend's completely innocent father being arrested on suspicion of being involved in terrorist activities. Mum, a staunch nationalist, wouldn't allow me to wear a poppy. One day, when my brother came home from school wearing one, she immediately told him to take it off. My dad, who was known by his middle name, Farrell, rather than Patrick, because he didn't like the connotation of being a thick 'Paddy', felt exactly the same way. My parents always listened to Irish music on a battered old record player. Pat McGuigan, who had represented Ireland in the Eurovision Song Contest, was a great favourite. His son, Barry, became a famous boxer and was eventually crowned WBA world featherweight champion. Pat McGuigan's pre-fight renditions of 'Danny Boy' were the stuff of legend.

My footballing heroes were all Irish. I even won a goldfish at the local fair and named him 'Paul McGrath' after the legendary international centre-half, who was born in England but repre-sented Ireland. Although I didn't support Manchester United I had a soft spot for them because of their Irish players. One of my first memories of watching football on television was seeing Kevin Moran being sent off in the 1985 FA Cup final. I also liked Northern Ireland's Norman Whiteside.

I started attending the local Roman Catholic primary school, St Gregory's, in 1981 when I was four. My first friend there was Chris 'Boz' Borwick. We've played together in several football teams since then and he was an apprentice with me at PNE. When we began to play competitively, Chris's dad, Steve, would take me to games in his car every week and, when times were really bad, Chris would give me his trainers. I owe Steve Borwick a huge debt of gratitude: I really don't think I would have made it in football if it hadn't been for him. I remember wishing that I had a dad like Boz's. Mine never went to see any of my schoolboy games whereas Steve Borwick was always encouraging Chris. It made me resentful that my dad didn't show any interest in me.

From the school we could actually see Deepdale, the corrugated roof of the sprawling Spion Kop terrace and the four floodlight towers. St Gregory's was an excellent footballing school and by the time I was seven I was already playing occasionally for the Under 11 team in eleven-a-side games. Being left-footed helped me stake a claim at left-back or left midfield. Unfortunately, all school fixtures were cancelled during the 1985–6 season due to the teachers' strike, but when I was nine we won the Under 11 Preston Schools Cup and the final was played at Deepdale, which was a great thrill for a boy of my age. An article in the *Lancashire Evening Post*, dated 21 May 1987, reads: 'The team have won the double for the third year, winning the Preston Primary 11-a-side, the Harold Slater Shield six-a-side, Smiths Crisps competition. And they were runners-up to Blackburn in the West Lancs Championship.'

The school team colours were green and white hoops – just like those of my second favourite team...Glasgow Celtic. In fact, I played for St Gregory's in my own Celtic shirt. I had always dreamed of playing for Celtic, a club originally formed by an order of monks from County Sligo. In common with all Scottish clubs with Irish roots, Celtic adopted green and white as their colours. My favourite goalkeeper, Paddy Bonner, played for Celtic and Ireland.

Another goalie, PNE's Alan Kelly, had attended St Gregory's nearly a decade before. He went on to win thirty-four caps for the Republic of Ireland and we were team-mates in the 2002 World Cup squad. He'd also been coached by my teacher, Keith Aspinall, the manager of St Gregory's. Mr Aspinall, who was the deputy headmaster, lived and breathed football and was the foremost influence in shaping my career. It was he who recommended me and Chris Borwick to the Preston North End School of Excellence. Keith Aspinall also arranged for me, goalkeeper

David Lucas, who at the time of writing has made nearly four hundred league appearances, and was in the year below me at St Gregory's primary school, and Boz to be ball boys on match days at Deepdale. Sam Allardyce, now manager of West Ham, was skipper in those days and in the tunnel we would always be deafened by his loud bellows of encouragement as the team came out on to the pitch and he would also shout at us in fun. (In those days, the teams came out separately.) Sadly, Keith Aspinall has passed away but his son still runs the Preston Town Schools team.

The role of the Roman Catholic Church in the establishment of a strong community life among the Lancashire Irish has always been important and so, while at St Gregory's and between the ages of seven and eleven, I became an altar boy with my brother, Farrell, at the church attached to the school. Both my parents were religious, although my dad wasn't a habitual churchgoer. My mum went to church regularly and to Mass every Sunday.

I don't remember feeling very religious – I think it was more of a family tradition and an expectation from my parents. I have to say I really enjoyed taking part in the customs and Farrell and I actually had quite a giggle. We enjoyed ourselves and used to get there early in preparation for the administration of the sacraments. The older altar boys were in charge, however, and didn't take any nonsense. Although we had to attend at least one Mass on Sundays, sometimes two, and several during the week, we never felt resentful.

Although it wasn't exactly like *Monty Python*'s famous 'Four Yorkshiremen' sketch – we never had to suck on a damp cloth or eat a handful of freezing gravel for sustenance – there were times when we didn't have enough money to be able to eat. I can't even remember a single family holiday. Our priest, Father Gerald Muir, was a wonderful man. Although he liked a glass of wine, he was a dedicated and caring priest. On the occasions when we didn't have enough money for food, Father Muir would always help us out with an emergency payment from parish funds. Father Muir is now in a retirement home in Blackpool and I'm glad to say is being well looked after.

I'm afraid that, as good a man as Father Muir was, the same could not be said for one of the other priests at St Gregory's, Father Edmund Cotter, who acted as referee and coached the football team, attending every training session and playing an important role. At Preston Town Court, in August 2007, then aged sixty, Cotter admitted to thirteen counts of indecent assault. Although he had never tried anything on with me while he was teaching at St Gregory's primary school, he had abused up to ten girls and one boy while he was a parish priest at two churches in Preston from the mid-1970s to the mid-1980s. Cotter had told one of the youngsters (they were all aged between seven and eleven) that he was like God and that if she was not a good girl she would burn in hell. He used his authority to silence his victims so that they were too frightened to report his offences.

When his abusive behaviour was originally discovered, Father Cotter was transferred to another parish in Cumbria in the hope that it could be kept quiet. He was, however, duly arrested and confessed to his crimes. Father Cotter was subsequently jailed for five years and two months, put on the sex offenders' register for life and disqualified from working with children ever again. What was almost as appalling was that the Catholic Church had tried to keep his offences secret and had moved him to another parish in an attempt to prevent his crimes from being publicised. Sadly, as we now know, this was not an isolated incident and similar cover-ups have, I'm ashamed to say, disgraced the Catholic Church worldwide.

By the time I was ten, the consequences of Dad's drinking had become habitual and his teetotal pledge had long been forgotten. His behaviour became even more erratic and he became aggressive towards my mum. She finally refused to tolerate this any longer and threw him out for good. He had, after all, played very little part in our upbringing and she had been left to look after us single-handed anyway. Although I was quite young, I felt nothing when he left. I wasn't upset and I certainly didn't miss him. At least now we wouldn't be woken up at night when he came home drunk and argued with Mum. Now I realise that alcoholism is an illness and that Dad needed help, which he didn't receive. As a child I had no idea what he was going through and the torment he must have been suffering.

At the age of ten, during the 1987–8 season, I was picked to play for PNE's Under 12s School of Excellence. I suppose I always considered myself a fairly good player but never stood out as better than some of my mates and so I was thrilled to be selected. It was a moment of real pride to pull on the famous white shirt and to face other schools of excellence from Blackpool, Blackburn and Man Utd.

Preston North End, or 'Preston Knob Enders' as me and my mates used to call them, were, of course, the team I supported as a child but I couldn't afford the admission fee, although I managed to watch the last twenty minutes of the home games. In the middle of the second half, the gates were opened for supporters who wanted to leave early and I would nip in through the disabled entrance and watch the last quarter of the game. In fact, my dad took me to my first game at PNE by sneaking me through the disabled entrance before kick-off and therefore avoiding having to pay.

It was at this time that I started to suffer from epilepsy. Two weeks after I collapsed in the street outside Deepdale, I had another seizure. I was playing football out in the street with my brother and a couple of older lads. Farrell saw me collapse and start twitching and he ran into our house, calling out for my mum, who immediately rang for an ambulance. As with the initial fit, I couldn't remember anything about it. When I came to, the first thing I was aware of was waking up in an ambulance on the way to hospital. I was discharged without any follow-up or advice and told by the attending doctor: 'It was just one of those things. Try to relax when you get home.' I was naturally relieved to hear this explanation and accepted his simple advice but, in retrospect, this approach and lack of further investigation now seems more than a little negligent.

Unfortunately 'relaxing' didn't seem to help; within a short time, I had experienced a number of further fits, once when I was on my paper round and was rescued by Geraldine, who told the newsagent. Most fits seemed to be triggered by me seeing the colour red. Traffic lights on 'stop' were the most common thing to set me off and once I even had a fit while I was asleep! I dreamed of red traffic lights and lost consciousness. Luckily, my brother noticed my movements and called my mum who cushioned my head with a pillow. They both knew what to do and made sure my head was protected.

The most embarrassing seizures took place at school. Once, in the cloakroom, I regained consciousness to discover a crowd of fellow pupils surrounding me and watching my convulsions. I felt very embarrassed and, when I was taunted by some of the pupils, I wouldn't try to reason with them; my frustration got the better of me. I would lose my temper and because of this I got into quite a few fights at primary school. I just didn't want to think about how these seizures were affecting my health and tried to ignore the attacks, hoping they would just stop of their own accord. Luckily for me, my mum took my condition seriously and realised that I needed urgent medical treatment. We went to see the GP and I was then referred to Dr Tomlinson, a consultant at Preston Royal Infirmary. She asked me if I'd had any recent blows to the head. In fact, my mum had thrown a football boot at me not long before and nearly knocked me out but I either didn't want to tell her or didn't think it could have been the cause of all this.

I had an EEG (electroencephalogram) and was subsequently

diagnosed as 'an epileptic'. I was prescribed medication, which diminished the fits and eventually stopped them happening altogether. Over the next couple of years I had to go with my mum every month to a clinic in town to a sort of group therapy session with other children while my mum met parents of children with the same condition.

The trouble was that these sessions were always on a Monday evening, which clashed with Preston North End's Under 12 football training. So I didn't ever want to go to them and didn't really pay attention to what was being said because I was missing football and was worried that I'd be dropped from the team if I didn't turn up for training. Mum explained to the manager why I had to be absent every so often but I never spoke to him about it and avoided the issue. I was in total denial. I just didn't think, at that age, that my epilepsy would prevent me from leading a normal life because, in general, it didn't stop me doing things. I just wouldn't say anything to anybody and, if asked, refused to admit I had a condition. In fact, in later years I always denied that I had suffered from epilepsy; I thought it would complicate any medicals and would ultimately affect my career.

I never even talked to my friends about it. The school made an attempt to address the subject and the head teacher actually arranged a special assembly about epilepsy so that staff and pupils would know more about it. When I was about twelve I came off the medication for good as I hadn't fitted for a long time. The doctor told me she hoped it was something I had grown out of and she was proved correct. I didn't realise at the time but it was quite something me coming off medication. It would shape my future in a big way.

The natural progression from St Gregory's was to Corpus Christi Roman Catholic Secondary School. Chris Borwick moved on with me but I soon became mates with some lads who are still really close friends: Declan Hanley, Bobby Parkinson, Mark Shepherd, John Calligan ('Cal'), Tommy Taylor (nephew of world snooker champion Dennis Taylor), Paul McMenemy ('Mackie') and Andy Dixon. Most of my friends were from Irish families and the culture, beliefs and philosophies bound us together. Of course, we played football at every opportunity and at lunchtime, instead of sitting down to a proper meal, we always took a butty to the playground so that our games weren't interrupted. These games usually consisted of an England v. Ireland match with the boys from an Irish background playing against the English lads. These were pretty aggressive affairs and most games ended in fights. I considered these games my first opportunity to represent the Irish Republic!

But it was, of course, the school football team that bound us together and the team turned out to be highly successful: by year nine our team had won every competition we had entered. We won the Lancashire Schools cup twice (Under 14s and Under 16s) and were easily the best team ever to represent the school.

Two of the school's PE teachers, Fred Wilkinson and Len Devey, coached and managed our side throughout our school years. Mr Wilkinson also had a part-time job at Deepdale and would allow us to play on the actual pitch, which was, infamously, a synthetic Astroturf.

I was inextricably linked to Preston North End.

Although we weren't really cricketers, we enjoyed playing most sports and several of the football team represented the school at cricket. When I was about fourteen, Corpus Christi played a match against local rivals Ribbleton Hall. We were doing quite well until a large, athletic-looking lad came in to bat. He looked useful and had scored a few when he whacked the ball in my direction. I was fielding right on the boundary and went to catch the ball. The 'cherry' was hit with such power that it went straight through my hands, hit me slap-bang in the chest and knocked me over. To make matters worse, the ball rolled over the boundary and I was left with a very bruised rib. That lad went on to score a hundred and then to bowl most of our team out. His name? Andrew Flintoff. Not surprisingly, 'Freddie' was also a very useful goalkeeper who represented Preston Schools.

Apart from the Corpus Christi school team, I was also picked to represent Preston Town's Under 14 team, which at the time was the most successful combined schools team, playing against other Lancashire towns. The manager, John Murphy, was another influential character who helped my game to progress. The coach was Sean Haslegrave, who had played for Preston and before that Nottingham Forest, under Brian Clough. Not a bad pedigree! I played left-wing and tried to model myself on Chris Waddle. Mr Murphy helped develop my general awareness and I will always be grateful for his guidance. He – that's Mr Murphy – not Chris Waddle – later became a teacher at Cardinal Newman School, but has now retired.

I also continued playing for Preston Schools and our team, Preston Town and our Under 14 side, was arguably the best ever to represent the combined schools. We finished as Lancashire Schools champions and won the Schools Cup, beating Liverpool at their Penny Lane training ground. A year later we beat Hyndburn 11-1 in the final, with Tommy Taylor scoring five times. Tommy was a prolific striker and in one game against Chorley, one of the parents, Mrs Jackson, offered £1 per goal for the Children In Need charity. Tommy notched another hat-trick and we won 10-1. Obviously Mrs Jackson can't have seen us play before and, equally obviously, she didn't realise that we were such a free-scoring team, so it cost her a tidy amount! It was a real shame that, in later years, Tommy wasn't taken on as a trainee at Preston because in those days he was one of the best players in the town.

And in case I wasn't getting quite enough football, for a couple of years I also played – alongside Tommy Taylor, Chris Borwick and Paul – for a local Sunday team, Fulwood Colts. However, by 1991 I had signed for a side slightly more famous than Fulwood and a team steeped in footballing history. These days, lads who are registered with professional clubs aren't allowed to play with their mates in school or Sunday league teams. I can understand this from the age of fourteen, but for younger boys I think it's wrong that they can no longer play together. Before that age, I believe it should all be about enjoyment and being with your mates. Professional clubs need to take another look at this.

I had already been playing for Preston North End since the age of ten but now, several years later, I was at the age when we could sign for the club on schoolboy terms. This was a vital landmark in any young lad's progression to become a professional footballer. In my case it was touch and go as to whether PNE were going to sign me. Tommy Taylor, Boz and Mackie had already signed schoolboy forms but I was very anxious that I wasn't going to be picked up. (Paul McMenemy was later robbed of a very promising career when one of the lads drove over his foot one night after training.) I had always been a decent player growing up and usually one of the best in my year, but at Under 14 level I really improved and started to develop my game much better. Much of this was due to my two years spent with Peter Warburton at Preston North End's School of Excellence.

Peter encouraged me greatly and I learned a great deal from his coaching when he worked on my skills and positional sense. Fortunately Peter stuck his neck out for me and recommended me to Fred O'Donoghue, an ex-North End player, who was chief scout. Fred wasn't sure that I had a future in the game and wanted to let me go, but Peter stuck his neck out for me and persuaded the club to keep me on and see how I progressed in the next couple of years. So it was a great thrill when I was invited to be taken on by Preston North End on schoolboy terms.

This was the first time that I really thought about the possibility of becoming a professional. Although I continued to play for Preston Schools and Sunday league teams, Preston North End were really now my team and I was proud to be able to represent them at this level. For the next two years I did nothing but play. I was involved in five or six matches a week – sometimes two games on a Sunday. We enjoyed all the amenities of a league club and played against some very good sides such as Crewe Alexandra, famous for their successful youth teams, and I remember being pitched against future England star Danny Murphy. It was brilliant working with youth team manager Walter Joyce in the Under 15s season. His son, North End's first-team captain, Warren, would sometimes take training, coach us and would even manage the team for some games.During those two years nothing in life mattered apart from Preston North End and I really made the most of the coaching and facilities. With all the physical activity, I grew leaner and developed a bit of pace and my game improved vastly. All I thought about was football. I'd practise with my mate Cal (John Calligan) every night at Deepdale on the plastic pitch and we were allowed to play until 10 p.m. The pitch was rented out to local teams to train on and would generally be split into quarters. Cal and I would occupy the space behind the small hockey-style goals and practise shooting into the back of the nets. A lot of the time the ball would miss the target and go on to the pitch, disrupting the teams playing on the main pitches. We were threatened with being beaten up loads of times by the furious players but that wasn't going to stop us and we still carried on.

We would even go on Sundays or Bank Holidays when the ground was shut. We had discovered a way to get in by scaling a ten-foot wall at the back of the town end. The goals still had the nets on them (there weren't many pitches with nets in Preston) and it was brilliant to crack the ball into the goal and hear that sound of it rustling in the back of the net. We could stay as long as we wanted without anyone throwing us out. I would practise my crossing while Cal worked on his heading and finishing. We would be there for hours in the silence of the stadium, and would imagine we were playing for Ireland in front of a capacity crowd at Lansdowne Road. Cal had played for Ireland at schoolboy level and, although I was proud of him I was also very jealous as I wanted to play for Ireland so badly. It was always Kevin Sheedy (me) whipping balls in for Tony Cascarino (Cal) to head home.

My first trip to Northern Ireland was in 1991 when I was fourteen and we played in a competition called the Milk Cup. This was an international tournament and included select teams from the Irish Republic, Iceland and the USA, and club sides Coleraine, Heart of Midlothian, Nottingham Forest, Newcastle United, Middlesbrough and Norwich. We boarded a coach at Deepdale, drove to Scotland and then crossed the Irish Sea at Stranraer, landing at Larne. We then took the coach to Portstewart.

We had an excellent side. I remember I wore the No. 14 shirt and only played in several of the games. It was exciting to be in Ireland and playing against teams from other countries. We lost to Newcastle in the quarter-finals and Norwich went on to win the tournament. Incidentally, the Under 16s competition was won by Manchester United, hardly surprising when you look at some of their team members: Paul Scholes, David Beckham, Nicky Butt, Gary Neville and Robbie Savage.

We stayed in the Windsor Hotel in Portstewart on the North Antrim coast. It turned out that the hotel belonged to Harry Gregg. Although I knew he had been Manchester United's goalkeeper and had represented Northern Ireland twenty-five times, I didn't realise he was such a legend and later wished that I had talked to him about his career and, perhaps, about surviving the Munich air disaster of 1958. In fact, it's only recently that he has spoken about his experiences and, in a remarkable BBC TV documentary, *One Life*, Harry revealed the raw emotion of that fateful day. Although he was far too modest to claim any credit, it became clear that Harry Gregg saved several lives in the ensuing chaos after the crash.

I, meanwhile, was still playing for my school team, Corpus Christi. PE teacher Fred Wilkinson was a great coach, a real football man, and had played semi-professionally for Bishop Auckland and Blyth Spartans among other teams. He was involved in an FA Cup tie for Spartans and Mr Wilkinson, whose position was full-back, found himself up against one of my idols, Chris Waddle. Mr Wilkinson once reminisced about the match and how it felt to play against the flying winger: 'I thought I'd show him the outside. I did…and he was past me in a flash. Okay, then I'll force him inside. I did…and he was gone. The third time I thought my only chance was just to whack him! I did…and he was gone…but this time into the hoardings.' I don't think they make PE teachers like that any more!

Later on, Len Devey, who was head of PE, took over the running of the team. He and Mr Wilkinson worked together for thirty-two years. Len later became a scout for North End. The Corpus Christi school team enjoyed great success, winning two league titles, and we won the Schools Cup four times in five years. This was at a time when the British game was being more and more influenced by foreign coaches, who were now starting to make their mark on the English game with a more sophisticated approach to fitness regimes and particularly dietary requirements.

Before a game, players were encouraged to eat carbohydrates and so, instead of tucking into chicken and chips – the favoured pre-match meal of 1970s footballers – pasta was now on the menu. So, before one Schools Cup final, four of us lads went around to Chris Borwick's house where his mother filled us up with huge platefuls of spaghetti bolognese. By the time we returned to the school we could barely move and felt queasy at the thought of the approaching game. We were terrible in the first half and Chris and Tommy Taylor were actually sick during the opening twenty minutes. By the start of the second half, however, we had digested the grub and luckily went on to win easily!

When we were sixteen and in our last year at Corpus Christi, we went on a week's retreat to Castlerigg Manor, Keswick, in the Lake District. Catholic schoolchildren from all over the country would travel to this gathering, arranged to mark the end of their schooldays. We were supposed to spend the days walking and climbing in the magnificent Lakeland scenery, conferring with nature and thinking deep thoughts. It was supposed to be a rite of passage, a spiritual experience to prepare us for life beyond the educational institution and entering adulthood. Well, I suppose it was in one way: I was caught in one of the girls' dormitories and had to wash dishes as a punishment.

I shared a dorm with Boz, Declan and Mackie. Alcohol was banned so naturally we trooped into town and bought some cans of Diamond White cider, which was cheap but potent. By our reckoning we would only need to smuggle in about ten cans as it was so strong. As soon as we had finished a can we would throw it out of the window on to the road. Big mistake. One of the lads chucked a can out of the window just as a car was coming along and it hit the windscreen. The aggrieved motorist stopped the car and made a complaint. The next morning one of the centre workers had collected the cans and dumped them all in the middle of our dorm until we owned up to 'the crime'. Fred Wilkinson pretended to be outraged at our behaviour and threatened to send us home but he knew we were just having a bit of fun. He was more upset that we hadn't had the nous just to hide the cans.

For much of my final year of school, while I was studying (I use the term loosely) for my GCSEs I was also being considered for a place on the Youth Training Scheme at Preston. Football, and progressing to a professional career, was all that mattered. I was really distracted and showed little interest in my studies and put very little work into my exams. In addition, there was hardly a tradition of academic achievement in our family and neither Mum nor Dad particularly encouraged me at school. It wasn't their fault; they just weren't from that sort of background and I suppose they didn't see the need for someone like me or my siblings to achieve academically.

When I did get my results that summer they were pretty disappointing. I had passed nine GCSEs, but only three of them (Maths, English Literature and Language and IT Studies) at grades A–C. I really should have done much better. I remember going to school to collect my results and then returning straight back to training. Although I regret it now, it didn't bother me then that I hadn't done well. In the scheme of things, it just didn't seem important at the time.

A number of people have asked me: 'What would you have done if you hadn't been a footballer?' When I was at Corpus Christi, I went to Preston bus depot for a fortnight's work experience. I assisted with breakdowns and helped fix and maintain buses for the whole of Preston. I remember that the lads at the depot laughed when I told them I wanted to be a footballer. They said I had no chance and that I should apply for a job with them. I suppose I must have done all right there; had the football not worked for me I might well have become a bus mechanic.

Fortunately, though, I was now playing regularly for Preston North End Under 16s and would occasionally get a call-up for the youth team on a Saturday morning. Walter Joyce resigned when John Beck took over as manager of the club and Sam Allardyce took over as manager of the youth team and the Under 16s. When I was growing up, Big Sam was a hero of mine as he had played a huge part in Preston's promotion to the Third Division in 1987. He once visited our primary school with Osher Williams (former PNE player and now at the PFA) for a question and answer session with our class and I was selected to ask one of the questions.

It was thus Big Sam's decision as to whether I would be offered a YTS traineeship and also whether the next stage of pursuing my dream as a professional footballer would be realised. If this wasn't going to happen, I would be leaving school with, I imagined, few qualifications and an uncertain future – probably without football.

It was a nerve-racking experience. We were called to Deepdale one evening and a group of nervous lads and their parents waited in Preston's Guild Club (The Players' Lounge). My mum came with me and we sat anxiously waiting to be called into Sam Allardyce's office. Finally, my turn came and I entered the room and sat down opposite him. Sam made a short speech and said that I had done well: 'I've been impressed with your performances. You've made good progress.' I was waiting for the 'but'…but there was no 'but' and Sam continued, 'and so we'd like to offer you a place on the scheme.'

I'd made it. I was in. I'd made the grade. I mumbled an excited 'Thanks!' and went outside to tell my mum, who was thrilled. I had a future – well, for two years at least – at Preston North End, my home-town club.

In April 1993, I received an official letter from Sam Allardyce:

Dear Kevin,

The Manager (John Beck) and Coaching staff of Preston North End Football Club are pleased to offer you a place on our Youth Training Scheme which runs for two years.

I will be in contact with you and your parents as soon as possible to arrange a meeting to complete the formalities.

I hope this is the start of a bright future for you.

Chapter Two

Proud Preston

'The more contact I have with humans, the more I learn.'
ARNOLD SCHWARZENEGGER, *THE TERMINATOR*

The trainee agreement was for two years and sorted me out careerwise until the beginning of April 1995. The contract stated: 'The player agrees to play to the best of his ability in all football matches in which he is selected to play for the club and...shall play football solely for the club. The player shall be entitled to a minimum of four weeks' holiday per year...and shall not participate in competitive football during his holiday.'

And, of course, I would be paid...although I had a paper round when I was young and earned £3 a week, the YTS money was my first proper pay packet. My first payment, which I received from the Government, was for £29.50, which seemed like a fortune. My 'wage' went up to £31 and then on my seventeenth birthday it rose to £37 per week. I augmented my money by claiming a £20 a month bus pass from the club, which was meant to fund my travelling to training and the ground – even though I lived within spitting distance of Deepdale!

This was unbelievable: I was actually being paid to play football. I was so proud of myself and gave my mum £10 a week for board and lodging. At that stage I had no need to have anything to do with banks and so I was paid in cash until I opened an account. Apart from my rent, most of the money was spent in the snooker club behind Deepdale, where I honed my skills as the next Dennis Taylor.

It was a brilliant time and, although the money was a bonus, it was the fact that I had been taken on by PNE, who felt I had a future as a professional footballer, that was so exciting. Most of my mates had also been taken on, but the really bad news was that one of my closest mates, and someone I still see, Tommy Taylor, had been refused a place on the YTS. I felt really sorry for Tommy and was very disappointed on his behalf. He had always scored goals for whichever team he had played for, had been highly regarded and tipped as a future professional.

Chris Borwick and Cal also signed pro terms and, although they both played in lots of reserve games, they never made the first team and both were released by the club after their first year. The fact that Boz never played for the first team amazed me. He was always the best player in any team we played in together and I'm sorry that he never made it as a professional. I'm pleased to say he's still a very good mate.

Cal came from a very tough background and we knew it would be hard for him to knuckle down to a life outside football. I really felt for him and for the other lads whose dream it had been to play professional football but for one reason or another hadn't made the grade. It was heartbreaking, even at this early stage. Within two years, Cal went off the rails and ended up in Lancaster Farms Prison, where I later visited him.

Cal's story was a salutary lesson – our backgrounds weren't that dissimilar and I've often wondered if I might have drifted into some dodgy stuff if things hadn't worked out for me as a professional footballer. I've often been asked what I would have done if I hadn't been a professional footballer. I always liked Peter Crouch's response when asked the same thing: 'I'd have been a virgin.'

Anyway, I was lucky enough to be taken on by PNE and like many apprentices before me I had to clean the professionals' boots. We were each responsible for one or two pairs and I had to make sure that they were softened with Vaseline and highly polished. Surprisingly I never used to moan about it and loved being at the club so much that it never seemed a chore. This and other jobs also created a feeling of camaraderie – we were all in it together and were surprisingly supportive of each other. If one of the lads still had a task to complete, such as cleaning the dressing room, and the rest of us had finished our work, we would all pitch in.

One of the first tasks that I had to undertake, however, had very little to do with an aspiring footballing career: we had to paint the dressing room. I also remember having to clean the stands regularly after match days. On match days themselves, we were also asked to sweep the Deepdale Astroturf pitch. Ten youth trainees would be mobilised with huge industrial brooms to brush like mad until the majority of the sand came to the surface. We couldn't understand why until we realised that this was done on purpose to suit Preston's long ball tactics. The sand would stop the ball from skidding off the pitch when the ball was hoofed into the corners or penalty areas.

The North End manager, John Beck, had all sorts of other interesting strategies for unsettling the opposition: apart from the sand trick, before matches he also used to get us to soak the practice balls in salt water in a bath before they were allocated to the away team in the pre-match kickabout. I really can't think what the method behind the madness was – other than to make the balls so heavy that the opposition were worn out before the match kicked off. The apprentices also had to make tea for the away team and I remember being told to put huge amounts of sugar in their tea before the match. John Beck was apparently under the impression that, as a result of all the sugar, the opposition would be full of energy for the first half but then fade in the second.

For Mr Beck it wasn't exactly whether to play inverted wingers, the diamond or the Christmas tree formation – it was more a matter of coming up with different ways to nobble the opposition with a simple combination of salt, sugar and sand!

John Vaughan, now a goalkeeping coach, was at PNE when I was a trainee and reminded me about another of John Beck's unusual coaching techniques; he wanted to make sure that his goalkeepers were strong and fearless, particularly when it came to cutting out crosses. To help them prepare he had the trainees standing by with bags full of footballs; when the crosses came in from the wings, we had to hit the goalies with the bags. In this way during the actual game the men in green would think nothing of Joe Jordan-type challenges. Of course we were a bit timid about it as we didn't want to hurt the keeper – especially as the Astroturf was like concrete if you fell on it – but if John Beck saw us being timid he would scream at us: 'Hit the keeper harder!' Immediately John Vaughan, a tough Londoner himself, would respond by issuing half-whispered, blood-curdling threats that if anyone dared hit him harder with the bag, he would see them after training. Talk about Hobson's choice…

Another task that didn't seem to have much to do with our development as professional footballers was the cleaning of the manager's car. As the job was to clean inside the vehicle as well as outside, John Beck gave us his car keys. Big mistake by the gaffer. We used to practise driving at speed, skidding, handbrake turns in the car park for a while before we got down to any washing. In fact, I'd say it was probably then that I learned to drive properly!

It wasn't all roses, though. There were times when you wanted to be anywhere but mixing with the pros. It was quite scary on occasions – we used to have to come into the dressing room and the first team were 'invited' to comment on how the trainees had performed their various tasks. They would take great delight in telling us in graphic detail whether we had been up to the job in question. If the boots hadn't been cleaned properly the trainee or youth team member would have to undergo some sort of punishment, which might be something as embarrassing as having to run around the pitch naked – much to the mirth of the other lads.

Although some of this was 'a laugh', and supposed to be a bonding experience, it was also nerve-racking and, while I wouldn't call it bullying, there were times when things got out of hand. Sometimes, after a call of 'lights off in the boot room', 'friendly' fights would break out and some hefty punches were thrown. Some of the pros clearly enjoyed this physical intimidation, but luckily others were more kindly and approachable. David Moyes, now manager of Manchester United after a number of years at Everton, was one of the regular first teamers and was already a large presence and an influential voice in the dressing room; he would later become assistant manager at Preston. It may be surprising to some people that at Preston Moyesy was a practical joker: he would be the lad most likely to cut up the socks of various team-mates or pull various stunts in the dressing room. Scottish winger Kevin Magee would always come in and have a joke with us. I used to make the tea, knock on the dressing-room door, rush in, set the tray down and exit quickly so as to avoid any stick from the lads.

There was also the inevitable initiation ceremony for the apprentices or trainees. I decided to sing 'Stand By Me'. Luckily I have quite a good voice (my mum always said jokingly that I could have been a crooner if I hadn't been a footballer) and I actually received a standing ovation for my rendition of the Ben E. King song.

Our responsibilities sometimes lay beyond the immediate environs of Deepdale. One good idea of John Beck's was to take a trainee to every away league game. Our role was to help the kit man and also to make snacks and tea for the first team, but it was a great experience to travel on the coach with the professionals and feel part of the first-team squad. My first trip was to Lincoln City.

I was responsible for making the tea on the coach and all I can remember doing is running up and down the bus trying to cope with all the lads' demands. There was a toaster that would only brown one side of the bread and because it took so long, and the lads got impatient, I would butter one side only and hope they didn't notice! Striker Tony Ellis always did, however, and used to give me a hard time. But I was only sixteen and it was brilliant. We stayed overnight and I roomed with Lee Bamber (part-time goalkeeper) who was drafted in at short notice to provide emergency cover. He later became a goalkeeping coach at Old Trafford and then at the Australian football club, Perth Glory.

Nowadays academy players don't have those sorts of experiences; they aren't expected to work as odd-job men or gofers and the first team doesn't train with the youth teams. Although some of the practices I've described would now be considered non-PC, I do believe that having to perform some of the menial tasks helped with team bonding and creating a feeling of togetherness. The game has changed so much that if some of the younger lads today were asked to help out with boots or kit or clean up, they would be appalled. Current pros simply do not command the respect that they were automatically given when I started playing. I believe that if a number of the more cocky lads in youth academies today were forced to undertake some of the activities we did, it might provide them with a little more humility. That said, I just can't imagine some of the teenage wannabees of the Premiership knuckling down to such practices.

Every other Friday members of the first team would play against the youth team and some of the banter in the dressing room would be transferred to the pitch. These half-hour, nine-a side matches were played across the width of the Astroturf pitch and involved players from the first-team squad not playing in the following day's match as well as assistant manager, Gary Peters, and John Beck and Sam Allardyce. Those players on the fringe of the first-team squad were frustrated not to be playing every Saturday and would sometimes take out their frustrations on the youth team players. Some of the lads would also on occasions take the opportunity to smash John Beck in tackles! It was sometimes pretty vicious and quite often fights would break out after over-enthusiastic flying tackles on the Astroturf surface, whose surface could easily cause burns on unprotected flesh. I remember Sam Allardyce's advice at the time, which was short and sweet: 'If the pros kick you in training, kick them back...harder!' Despite this, I really enjoyed the ultra-competitive nature of these games. They were tough, but I got more out of them than any of the youth team games.

My brother, Farrell, was a trainee at Cambridge where John Beck was manager before he came to Preston. When Beck came to Deepdale, he offered Farrell a professional contract so I often used to face my brother in these training sessions. Farrell, a fiery character on the pitch, would soon let me know who was boss. He tried to clean me out in the matches but I was usually too quick for him. Farrell was a terrific player at either right-back or centre-half. If I played against him, our right-back used to hang the ball up over Farrell's head and I would go over the top of him. In later years, David Weir did the same for me at Everton and I would bury the opposing full-back. This always amused Farrell!

When Farrell was a teenager, quite a lot of professional clubs were interested in him. He played at centre-forward in those days and was sought after for his prolific goal scoring. I learned a lot from my brother – playing against him and his friends certainly toughened me up. He enjoyed a really good non-league career, turning out for, among other teams, Southport, Barrow and Stafford Rangers before, ending his playing days at

Burscough FC in Division One of the Northern Premier League.

I started well although I was not yet a regular in the youth team. However, mixing and playing with the first team brought my game on no end and, to my delight and surprise, I made my reserve team debut in August 1993 in the first game of the season at Barnsley. I was just sixteen. My home debut against Blackpool followed soon after and I scored twice.

There was another, even more significant development during this period. Towards the end of the 1993–4 season, my first year as a trainee, we played a game at Marine to win the youth team league. After the inevitable dressing-room celebrations, Sam Allardyce called the whole team together and announced that one of our number had been called up to the England Under 18 squad.

I looked around, wondering who he meant. We had some good lads but I couldn't work out who it might be. Maybe Jamie Squires or even Chris Borwick? Then Sam looked in my direction and announced: 'It's you, Kevin. Well done. Congratulations! I'm pleased for you.'

I was shocked but not excited. Quite the opposite, in fact. I should have been honoured, but my heart sank. I wasn't happy. I was Irish after all. My entire upbringing had been shaped by Irish culture and lifestyle. If I was good enough to play international football, there was only one team I wanted to play for…and that was the Republic.

I didn't know what to say or do. I couldn't refuse the offer in front of the whole team: to turn down the chance of playing for England at this stage in my career would appear incredibly arrogant but I knew this was what I would have to do. But not here. Not now. I mumbled something inaudible and left as quickly as I could.

I hardly slept a wink that night. I knew I had to be honest with Sam but I didn't know how or when to say anything. After further fretting, I realised that I would have to tell Sam as soon as I could bear to face him. I went through training the next day with a heavy heart. I knew this couldn't go on any longer. At the end of the session, and after I had finished my YT chores, I plucked up the courage to talk to Sam. You see, I had a lot of respect for him – he was great with us lads and was a brilliant coach. He had helped me become the player I now was and I owed him a lot. He was obviously very proud that one of his protégés had done so well and I didn't want to disappoint him.

I knocked tentatively on his door. Perhaps sporting my Celtic shirt wasn't the most tactful thing I could have done in the circumstances, but, then, wearing it always gave me confidence. And, boy, did I need that now. Initially Big Sam was all smiles and thought I'd come to talk about the England offer, which of course I had – but not quite in the terms he had envisaged.

I came straight out with my decision. 'I'm sorry but I don't want to join the England squad.'

Sam's jaw dropped. 'What?'

I continued nervously, 'I can't take up their offer.'

Sam started to go the colour of the Anderlecht home kit. 'What the fuck are you talking about?'

'My parents are Irish. My heroes are Irish. I'm Irish. I want to play for Ireland.

Sam was furious. 'Fuck off, Kevin. I was a professional foot-baller for twenty years and I never got the chance to play for my country and you're turning the chance down! Now, get out of my office. I don't want to have to look at you any more. Fuck off!'

I did. Quickly. I was a bit shaken but greatly relieved.

An hour later, Sam approached and asked me to go into the referees' dressing room. He apologised for getting so angry and said he understood how I felt. He did suggest, however, that I go and train with the England Under 18s at Lilleshall. It would be a good experience and it didn't commit me to anything in the future. Although my heart wasn't in it, I agreed for Sam's sake.

I went down to Lilleshall reluctantly and joined the lads, who included such players as Kevin Davies, Danny Murphy and Lee

Bowyer. I still gave it my best, as I always have done, but it just confirmed that I didn't want to be part of the England setup. I still hadn't played in the first team for Preston and I was turning down England. Like I said before, it wasn't out of arrogance, it was just...being Irish.

I had always taken my career seriously, even as a teenager, and had hardly ever touched alcohol. I had seen the results of overindulgence in my dad. My contact with him was minimal once he had left the family home, although I remember, on my seventeenth birthday, having to spend the night at a psychiatric hospital while he went cold turkey to try to get him off alcohol. He was hallucinating and trying to break down the doors of the ward. It was a horrible night and one I'll never forget. I had a youth team game the next day but for once I realised football wasn't always the most important thing in the world. I've never drunk much alcohol and, interestingly, can't touch whisky, my dad's favourite tipple.

But in November 1994 I did overdo the drinking and it got me into all sorts of trouble. Although very influential in my career, David Moyes had once given me some advice that had nothing to do with football: 'Always drink half-pints on nights out so that anyone who recognises you won't think you're a big drinker and spread rumours.' I think it might have given me licence to down lots of halves of lager without feeling guilty. Somehow I don't think he meant for me to do this and on this particular occasion I really overdid it.

I went for a night out with my mates and ventured into a few of the usual spots in town, ending up at Tokyo Joe's nightclub. Afterwards several of us were hungry and we called in at the local fish-and-chip shop. I didn't have enough money for a fish meal as well as sharing a taxi home. I was starving so I decided to have something to eat at the chippy and then walk home – a few miles away. It turned out to be a very bad decision.

I started walking home with my mate Bobby and Mark,

a friend of Farrell's. They didn't have any money either. While passing nearby Preston prison, we decided to try and get into a car, hoping that the spare set of keys would be in the sun visor and that we would get home for free and quickly. We'd seen it being done in *Terminator 2: Judgement Day*, so why not now? It felt like a great idea at the time; we were underage drunks, none of us could drive and we were going to steal a car. What a plan.

We tried loads of cars along the way but they were all locked. We finally found one car door that opened and so we all climbed in. We had a quick search, checked the sun visor – no sign of any car keys: the owner obviously hadn't seen *Terminator 2*. We looked in the glove compartment, but there was nothing of interest there either. For some reason I then just yanked at the stereo which came clean out of its socket. It wasn't like the sophisticated stereos in cars nowadays and it came out without too much trouble. I don't know why I did it. It wasn't that I even really wanted the thing. It was just pure vandalism and I thought I would get a laugh from the others.

Leaving the scene of the crime, we carried on walking along the Deepdale Road, me with the stereo under my arm. Within a couple of minutes three police cars came roaring into view from different directions, lights flashing and sirens wailing. (Someone had been suspicious about what we were up to and had alerted the police.) Mark shouted, 'Run!', but it was too late to flee. We were done for. I immediately chucked the stereo into a nearby hedge and waited while six policemen got out of their cars. I think they realised we weren't master criminals and didn't give us too hard a time. They did handcuff us though and took us straight to the police station in separate cars.

I was in one car with two of the coppers. They asked me all sorts of questions about whether I had been in trouble before, my address and my age. When we arrived at the station, Bobby was sitting in reception but I didn't know where Mark was. The policemen wouldn't let Bobby and me talk to each other and so I was put straight into a cell on my own and left there for a few hours. If I had been drunk in the first place I sobered up very quickly and didn't sleep a wink. I was left to ponder on how stupid I'd been. I thought I might go to jail for a long time. I even believed my football career might be finished – before it had even properly started. An officer checked me every so often to make sure I was all right but I wasn't taken out of the cell and questioned until the morning. I had mug shots taken and fingerprints done.

I admitted that I had taken the car stereo, which was wrapped in a plastic bag on the desk in front of me. I told the policeman exactly what had happened and didn't leave anything out. I knew I had to be honest and didn't want the other lads to get the blame for the theft of the sound system. I signed a statement and was told I could go. I was advised to expect a letter, informing me what would happen next.

When I got home I really didn't want to explain to my mum what had happened and so I told her that I had spent the night at my mate Declan's house. From then on I was convinced that every letter that dropped on to the mat would seal my fate. I was looking at a future away from football, languishing in some penal institution. Ridiculous really when looking back, but the longer it went on the more my imagination ran riot. Weeks later, I still hadn't heard anything from the police or received a court summons.

Then Bobby was told to report to the police station for further questioning. It appeared that they thought it was him who had taken the stereo. He protested his innocence without grassing me up and so they let him go. I had already admitted stealing it, and had signed a statement, but it seems that they wanted to nail Bobby. As soon as he told me what had happened, I rang the police and told them it was definitely me they wanted!

I was ordered to the station to speak to one of the higher

ranking officers and received the longest bollocking of my life –
and I've had a few. But this was different. He asked what job I
did because I hadn't been asked that when I was initially arrest.
I told him I was a footballer but I'd not yet played in the first
team and so he obviously didn't know who I was. He said I was
stupid to risk everything just for 'a bit of fun' and told me that
I was heading the same way as a number of good young players
in the past. I had been given an incredible opportunity and I was
putting it all at risk. If I didn't sort myself and start living the
right way I would look back on my life with regret, etc, etc. I
felt about one inch tall by the time he'd finished with me but I
knew he was right. I had never done anything like that before.
I had never stolen anything. I'd never been tempted despite the
fact that we never had much money. But stealing was wrong –
I had received a very strict moral upbringing. The worst thing
I had ever done up until then was once not paying for my train
ticket on a day trip to Blackpool.

In February 1995, I received an official caution. Luckily the
club never knew about the incident as it might have caused me
some problems, and the ticking off from the copper did help me
get my head down and to apply myself. I was also pleased that
my mum never found out about it either; she would have been
horrified. It was only recently that Bobby admitted to me that he
had stolen a bottle of Tippex from the car that night. Perhaps he
was just thinking of covering his tracks...

Later, after I signed as a professional, I was asked to present
some trophies at a PNE function. Coincidentally, the very same
policeman who'd admonished me was also attending the function. Once I'd realised that he wasn't there to arrest me, I was
pleased that he was able to see that his stern words had had the
desired effect on me.

PNE were then in the Third Division (the equivalent of today's
League 2), and to ensure that the first team were used to playing
on grass for away games they had to find somewhere to train;

sometimes they ended up on local park pitches or at the playing fields of the local agricultural college that had some decent pitches. Up until 1994 home games were played on Astroturf, which was then ripped up after the famous Torquay semi-final play-off at Deepdale. The club had done a sponsorship deal with Baxi Heating, a prosperous local company that had promised to invest £10 million in restoring PNE to its former glory.

Attendances had also increased at Deepdale under John Beck's stewardship, but in December 1994, when North End were third from bottom of the Third Division, Beck was sacked. His assistant and good mate Gary Peters took over, which I believe caused some friction between them as John felt that Gary had shown a lack of loyalty by accepting the manager's job. Despite some of John Beck's eccentricities, I thought he was a good coach but I suppose Gary Peters' less direct tactical approach suited my game better. He recognised that the team's tactics under Beck had been predictable and that opposition teams were starting to cope easily with his one-dimensional approach. There had been no plan B under John Beck. Gary Peters certainly allowed us more freedom to express ourselves and there was less of the long-ball approach. Before long, I had good reason to appreciate his appointment as manager.

In the spring of 1995 I attended a Preston North End dinner held at the Preston Guild and Rotary to raise funds for the School of Excellence. There were more than a hundred people present and it was one of the largest events I had ever been to. At the dinner, Gary Peters announced that two lads from the youth team, managed by Chris Sulley, had done particularly well and would be offered professional contracts. He continued, 'So please put your hands to together and congratulate Chris Borwick and Kevin Kilbane.'

Although I knew that the decision was due to be made shortly, I had no idea that this was how it would happen. It was totally unexpected and incredibly exciting. I was really pleased for Boz, a great lad and a fantastic player.

In July 1995, I signed professional terms for Preston North End. I was offered a one-year contract on £100 a week and told that I had twelve months to prove I was good enough to be a professional. There was no agent or representative of the PFA to negotiate on my behalf and it certainly felt like a 'take it or leave it' offer. However, this was a dream come true and I wanted to snap their hands off when Preston proposed these terms. I was still living at home and walking to training.

I was playing regularly for the reserves and one game still stands out in my memory: a Tuesday afternoon at The Cliff, Manchester United's training ground. In January 1995 Eric Cantona had been sent off at Crystal Palace after a kung-fu kick aimed at Palace fan Matthew Simmons. The Frenchman's actions led to him being fined and banned from all football for eight months by the FA. (A two-week prison sentence for the offence was reduced on appeal to 120 hours of community service.) Manchester United arranged a series of games behind closed doors to keep Cantona fit during his long lay-off. Preston took a team down to The Cliff where we faced a United team comprised mainly of youth players and reserves. There was no official referee and one of United's coaches took charge. Eric Cantona barely moved and certainly didn't deem to run around very much, but his imposing presence was unforgettable and the quality of his touch and control was simply extraordinary. I was in awe of him and couldn't believe I was actually on the same pitch as this legend. It was just another game for him but for us it was very special.

Preston started the 1995–6 season brightly and, after a good run early on, were already favourites for promotion from the old Third Division. I had been playing well in the reserves and was included for the first time in the first team squad for an away match at Torquay and was told that I would be on the bench. Travelling down to the West Country was brilliant and when we arrived in Torquay the seaside resort was bathed in sunshine. This was the first time I'd been a substitute and the manager had said to me just before kick-off, 'Make sure you're ready to come on if I need you.' So naturally I made sure I was prepared to join the action from the first whistle and I can remember spending most of the match running nervously up and down the touchline just in case I was called on.

With fifteen minutes to go, Gary Peters sent me on, replacing Graeme Atkinson. We were either three or four nil up, which was a great time to come on. I was really anxious but my team-mates tried to get me into the game as quickly as they could. I don't remember touching the ball very much but when the final whistle went I was overjoyed. We ran out 4-0 winners. It was brilliant to have such a good win on my debut.

We returned to Preston immediately after the match and, by the time I got home some hours later, the house was in darkness and everyone was asleep. There were no celebrations that night but I was sure that this was just the start.

I grabbed my first goal in professional football when I again came on as substitute against Wigan, two days after my nine-teenth birthday. With twenty minutes to go, Lee Cartwright sent over a cross and I headed it in at the far post. It turned out to be the winning goal and I was naturally ecstatic. I made sure that, on the following Monday evening, I watched the game on *Granada Reports*, a local news programme which broadcast highlights of local Lancashire sides.

The gaffer, Gary Peters, had quite a pedigree. He had played professionally with Wimbledon in the Crazy Gang era and had also worked with George Best at Fulham and David Beckham, who he had brought on loan to PNE the previous year from Manchester United. Gary liked to play attacking football and I played left-wing, hoping to emulate Chris Waddle. But Gary – and I am grateful for this – wanted to make me into more of an all-round player and, while I was beginning to make my mark in the first team on the wing, played me in the reserves at left-back. He felt that this would give me a better tactical understanding of the game and would improve my defensive qualities. He didn't want people to think of me as a 'flimsy' left-winger; he was of the opinion that if things were going wrong, it was invariably the wingers who got substituted most often. Gary Peters always wanted to produce teams that could play good football but, equally, wanted to ensure that all the players possessed a degree of defensive awareness.

The manager liked the fact that I played instinctively and believed I was better when I had to act spontaneously. He encouraged me to go past players and knew I would usually deliver a decent cross. Fortunately for me, he liked to try out young players and followed the Matt Busby maxim – 'If they're good enough they're old enough.'

Within a couple of months of signing the professional contract I was playing well enough to be considered as a future asset and was offered a three-year contract on double my current wages. As before, I had no one to advise me and there were no negotiations. I was told: 'Take it or leave it.' I took it.

Another few months down the line and I was called into Gary Peters' office again. This time I was offered £300 a week for five years but again there was no bargaining and this time it was in the style of Don Corleone – I was made an offer I couldn't refuse: I should have sought advice but didn't. Club skipper Ian Bryson was annoyed when I told him about the contract and said he would have gladly helped me if he had known about it.

Unfortunately, early in 1996 I twisted my ankle badly in a reserve game. Mick Rathbone (nicknamed 'Baz' after Hollywood film star Basil Rathbone) was the club's physiotherapist and had been a cult figure at PNE since his playing days when his reputation for incredible fitness and fearsome tackling – even on the Astroturf – was still talked about. Baz had been working in the outpatients department of Blackburn Infirmary when Gary Peters asked him to join the club in 1995. Anyway, Baz carried me down the tunnel to the medical room, assessed my injury in his role as physiotherapist and then, because he still turned out for the reserves, donned his shin pads and took my place!

I was out injured for six weeks. I was really gutted because I was playing very well, but there was nothing I could do other than be patient and take time to recover. I came back for the reserves at Grimsby. I felt I did all right after a long lay-off, but Gary Peters slaughtered me in front of the team: 'Just because you've signed a new contract with the club doesn't mean you've made the big time!' Baz told me afterwards, 'You didn't have that bad a game – he's just trying to keep your feet on the ground.' At the time it seemed Gary was really going unnecessarily over the top, but in retrospect I have to say it made me stronger and I became even more dedicated to the game.

Baz was always great with me and I owe him a lot. He was always positive and supportive at times when I was struggling with form or confidence. I was often insecure about my abilities and never really believed that I was good enough to be a professional footballer. Self-doubt has been a nagging concern for much of my career and I found it difficult to believe managers or coaches when they gave me positive feedback. It may sound strange but I felt more at ease with abuse than praise. It seemed more real. Praise was somehow disingenuous – something to appease me and make me feel better. No matter how many times I was told I was a decent player, I never believed what I heard. I've always found it difficult to accept praise. This was especially true in my formative years. I'm not sure why this is; perhaps because I never received any praise at home, positive reinforcement has always been a bit alien to me and my character. The fact that I've been more comfortable with abuse has certainly helped me at various times in my career – although there have been occasions when this has become personal and not a reflection of my playing.

A couple of months into 1996 the team was going through a flat spell and we needed a kick up the backside. Gary Peters needed some help and the club appointed Steve Harrison as first-team coach. Steve, or 'Harry' as we called him, had been part of the England setup when Graham Taylor was national manager and had built up a fantastic reputation. Not only was Harry tactically astute, he also made training enjoyable by mixing up the routines and making them as fun as possible. He certainly raised the levels of confidence in a squad that was wobbling a bit and he was one of the reasons why we improved enough to gain promotion. Club captain and assistant manager David Moyes was also a great influence and he and Harry used to give me extra training sessions in the afternoons, working on crossing and my positional play. David was playing in nearly every match at the time and on occasions must have been knackered. I'm sure it was the last thing he wanted to do, but he was always there to encourage me.

I was keen to learn and, looking back, it is amazing that at the age of nineteen I had two such incredibly committed and devoted football men giving that extra time to aid my development.

Harry immediately made a personal impact on me – he was a great influence, not only on my playing skills but also my attitude. From the outset he made it clear that I had a big future in the game but only if I knuckled down and worked hard. I had great respect for him and was delighted that a coach of his pedigree had come to Preston.

When I returned to the first team I became a regular fixture in the starting line-up. The lads were playing well and were riding high in the Third Division throughout the season. We had some really good players and characters. David Moyes marshalled the defence, Ian Bryson was captain and we had Andy Saville and Steve Wilkinson up front. We ended up winning promotion at Orient with a 2-0 win.

David Beckham had been on loan at PNE a year earlier and

was already establishing a bit of a name for himself at United. He came down to Brisbane Road to watch us and was in the dressing room before the game and celebrated with us in the players' lounge afterwards. He was unassuming and friendly and I remember him saying that he had an old Golf VW that he wanted to get rid of as it wasn't fast enough!

The following week we clinched the title with another 2-0 away win, this time at Hartlepool. We were in high spirits on the coach back to Preston and 'Don't Look Back In Anger' by Oasis, our favourite track on away games, was blasting through the speakers. I still love that song: it reminds me of a brilliant season and fantastic times. Moyesy's choice of Motown Classics was also regularly requested…mainly by Moyesy…

The drinks flowed on the journey home and we naturally continued the celebrations by going out on the town and drinking far too much champagne. Chris Borwick and I got completely hammered, as a result of which I was arrested for being drunk and disorderly. I was spotted by a policeman, who witnessed me kicking out at a taxi. I really cannot remember anything about it but it was stupid of me to commit such an offence. Luckily there was no damage to the cab (I must have used my right foot) but it was enough to earn me a night in the cells.

I was released the following morning, thinking once again that I had put my career at risk. First thing on Monday I went to Gary Peters' office and told him exactly what had happened. When the boss had stopped pissing himself laughing, he told me that he wasn't very happy about my behaviour but realised that everyone does something wrong in their youth. 'I'm not condoning your behaviour but it's not the worst thing in the world. Just as long as it doesn't happen again.' He stressed the importance of protecting the players from the press and publicly showing support at all times.

I was advised that I would have to appear in court at some future date. I was naturally very worried that my previous caution would be taken into consideration and that this time I would definitely be sent down. I was even anxious that my career would then be threatened and, looking back, I realise I got myself into quite a state. The lads gave me a lot of stick and enjoyed ribbing me about not being able to hold my drink. I didn't really think it was that funny. To make matters worse, the whole incident was front-page news in the *Lancashire Evening Post* with the banner headline:

PNE STAR FACES DRINK CHARGE.

The report continued, 'Promising young Preston North End star Kevin Kilbane is to appear before a court to face allegations of being drunk and disorderly. He and team-mate Chris Borwick were taken to Preston police station in the early hours of the morning where they were both quizzed by officers. Both players were later charged with being drunk and disorderly outside the Tithebarn Street club. They were bailed by police and are due to appear before Preston Magistrates Court on May 20th.'

I felt really bad about the incident and decided to apologise to the court before the hearing. I wasn't very confident about composing a letter to this effect and so asked Ann, a girl who worked in the snooker hall, to help me write a grovelling letter in an attempt to mitigate my circumstances. My main line of defence was that I had been carried away by events on the pitch, that I had never drunk champagne before, and because of that it had gone straight to my head. All of which was, in fact, true.

I had naively hoped that on receipt of the letter the magistrates would take pity on me, dismiss the case before I had to appear and let me off completely. No such luck. I had to attend the court and, on my way in, was snapped by a photographer from the *Preston Evening News*. It's still the closest I've come to being caught by the paparazzi! To make matters worse, the embarrassing letter also later appeared in the press.

During the court appearance, one of the three magistrates

declared himself to be a North End season ticket holder and so had to withdraw, but the other two acknowledged my admission of guilt and issued me with a caution. I was lucky not to have been given a more serious punishment and decided that this was to be the last time I would get into trouble. I wouldn't go out drinking and would devote myself to my profession. There would not be a third court appearance.

The final match of the season was the following Saturday at home to Exeter City. The ground could have been sold out several times and thousands of fans were locked out. The atmosphere in the ground was joyful and the best I had yet experienced. The pressure was off as we had already won the title and I played one of my best ever games. The match ended in yet another 2-0 win and it meant so much to all of us that we finished the season on such a high and with a great performance. Afterwards we were presented with the Third Division trophy, which we then paraded around the pitch. It was a brilliant occasion for the lads, the club and the town.

It was a great time for the football club altogether and, we all hoped, the start of a revival of the club's fortunes. We were in the bottom tier, or certainly the bottom two tiers, for too long. It was always up and down and something needed to be done and it seemed from that season onwards that the club was really going places. For me in my first season, to win the Third Division championship was unbelievable really. It is still the only medal of any significance that I have won in my career. Winning a medal like that in your first season, you begin to think that you are going to get that every season, but I found out it was not quite that easy to be winning championships, no matter what level you were playing at.

Of course, there were further celebrations that night and, although I joined in, I was very careful not to overdo it. On the following Monday we toured the city in an open-top bus. The skipper Ian Bryson later wrote, 'Team spirit played a big part in

North End's success that season. I would not say we were the greatest team in the world, but we gelled together really well. As a team out on the pitch we were really together and that really made the difference come the end of the season...They were a terrific bunch of lads both on and off the pitch...we really stuck at it, we did the jobs that we had worked on during the week in training. We won games, we kept plenty of clean sheets and in the end I think we deserved the championship.'

I could not have been happier at the end of my first season as a professional. I was also able to pursue my dream of buying a car. As soon as I had reached the legal age to drive, I had some driving lessons, but had to give them up as I couldn't afford to continue. When I was eighteen I resumed them and passed my test. At the end of the season, I received a promotion bonus of £2,000 – the biggest cheque I had ever received in my life. I spent £1,200 on a Vauxhall Astra and the remaining £800 on my insurance. Expensive, but then I suppose an eighteen-year-old footballer is a good source of income as far as insurance companies are concerned! I was the last of my mates to get a car and soon became the designated driver, which also put paid to any drinking.

Chapter Three

Taking the Plunge

*'There's no need to fear the wind if your haystacks
are tied down.'*

IRISH PROVERB

I had no idea that during my first professional season at Preston
– and after he had recovered from my decision to reject England
– Sam Allardyce had contacted Mick McCarthy, then manager
of the Republic of Ireland senior squad, and told him that I
wanted to play for Ireland. It was quite a shock when, towards
the end of the season, I was called into Gary Peters' office to
learn that a fax from Mick McCarthy's assistant, Ian Evans, had
arrived at Deepdale informing the club that I had been selected
to join the Irish Under 21 squad for a friendly against Russia in
Drogheda.

I couldn't believe it and I had to read the fax a few times to
take it in. I was just nineteen and my dream to play for Ireland
had moved a huge step closer. Preston's secretary, Audrey
Shaw, arranged my travel arrangements with the FAI (Football
Association of Ireland) and I was then told to report to the Forte
Post House hotel at Dublin airport. I was still pinching myself
when I boarded the plane.

Always ready with advice, David Moyes had told me to
travel in a suit (still not sure if it was a joke) and make the right

impression. When I arrived at the hotel I looked so out of place because the rest of the lads were sporting tracksuits or wearing jeans and trainers. Luckily, none of them knew who I was but I recognised a few of them sitting around having coffee. Some of the lads were already established players in the top league: Stephen Carr and Kevin Maher were both at Spurs, Gareth Farrelly was at Everton and Dominic Foley at Wolves.

I couldn't quite work out why so many of the players were hanging around the reception area until I realised that, as is the case in most airport hotels, there were lots of air steward-esses around – also with time to kill. Mick McCarthy was also in reception when I arrived, with a few members of his staff. I didn't know any of the coaches and nobody seemed to know who I was. Once I had registered at the desk, the receptionist called out my name to Eddie Corcoran, who was employed as the squad's player liaison and travel coordinator.

Eddie then introduced me to Ian 'Taff' Evans and we exchanged pleasantries. Taff, a retired Welsh international, had been with Mick at Millwall and was now part of the Republic's setup. While we were talking, Mick McCarthy approached and asked how everything was at Preston. I was amazed he knew anything about me. I was totally in awe of him. Whenever I talked to him in those early days, all I could think about was the celebrated block tackle during Italia 90 that sent Paul Gascoigne somersaulting over the top of our 'Captain Fantastic'.

The game was to be Taff's first in charge of the Under 21s, a role he fulfilled as assistant to Mick McCarthy with the senior team. In this way there was continuity between the Under 21s and the senior squad and Mick attended all the Under 21 matches so that he would get to know all the up-and-coming players. But when it came to managing the Under 21s, Taff was very much in charge. He was a no-nonsense type, but always very fair.

We trained at the AUL sports complex just near the airport and I was surprised to discover that the pitches were very poor

– certainly no better, if not worse, than we had at Preston. And at North End we didn't even have our own training ground!

I was lucky that there were a lot of other new faces in the squad, which definitely helped me settle in quicker, and I'm sure that was also the case for the other lads. Every player was desperate to make an early impression on Taff – no one was certain of a starting place as he was also trying to get to know us all and find out what we were capable of.

I was amazed at the tempo of the training games and the technical ability of the lads. I had probably had more experience than most of them in terms of games played, but there were some very gifted footballers among the group. Taff put us at our ease by making training enjoyable. He made a big impression on us all with his professional but calm attitude and, despite a hip injury he had suffered during his playing days, he always made an attempt to participate in the matches.

The few days we had together went so quickly and I was fortunate that I was one of the only left-footers in the squad. Mick had adopted a 5-3-2 formation with the senior team immediately on his appointment as Irish manager and wanted the Under 21s to play a similar system. I was thus chosen to play left-wing-back – a position I had never played before and so I had to adapt quickly to a new approach. In fact, it suited me quite well as the three centre-halves provided more defensive cover and I could attack from further up the field than if I was playing at full-back.

I made my debut for the Under 21s against Russia in Drogheda. It was an amazing buzz when I pulled on the Irish shirt for the first time. I couldn't have been more excited. It was also the night before Mick McCarthy took charge of the senior team for the first time. Early on, we won a corner and so I made my way into the penalty area, hoping to get on the end of the set piece, but I couldn't go just where I wanted. A tough-looking Russian defender was intent on stopping me and paid no attention to the ball. He grabbed me around the waist, tugged hard on my shirt and made sure that I stayed rooted to the spot. I turned to the referee to complain, but he simply ignored me. I had never encountered anything like it. In my youth teams, school teams, even playing league football with Preston, no one had ever just grabbed me or my shirt in any area of the pitch to prevent me from getting the ball. It was something I later found I would have to get used to at the higher level – particularly against Eastern European sides and especially those from the former Yugoslavia, who were notorious for their rugged defending.

I followed up my Under 21 debut with appearances against Northern Ireland and Scotland in Mayo; this was particularly satisfying as not only did I skipper the side but it was also the county that my dad hailed from.

All in all, I turned out eleven times for the Under 21s. I became a bit of a spokesman for the lads if they wanted to raise any issues, because I seemed to have Taff's ear. After one game in Romania I was elected to approach Taff and ask if we could go out for a drink. Unlike some of the other lads, I seemed to be able to get round him. Anyhow, Taff agreed to let us all go and have a drink in the bar, from which, of course, we took full advantage. We then continued the party in our hotel rooms. The following day, very much the worse for wear, Peter Gain, then an apprentice at Tottenham, couldn't get himself out of bed and missed the plane home. The senior team were playing that night and so Peter had to remain with them, watch the game and fly back with the senior squad. As punishment, Peter had to sit between Mick and Taff on the flight home! (I reminded him of this when we met in a League 1 fixture in 2011, when I was playing for Huddersfield and Peter was playing for Dagenham & Redbridge.)

That summer, during Euro 1996, I went with some of my old school mates on holiday to Malia in Crete. As soon as we arrived, the guys all went to get drinks and something to eat. I headed straight to the hotel pool and lay in the blazing sun until

I dropped off. A few hours later, when my mates came to find me, I was still fast asleep – and bright crimson.

They woke me up and I was in terrible pain. I felt awful, but received little sympathy from my so-called mates; all they said was that they thought I had joined Manchester United, such was the colour of my skin. I went to bed for the afternoon and missed England losing to Germany. But when I woke up a few hours later I naturally wanted to join the others on our first night out in the resort. I started out but I was dehydrated and suffering from sunstroke. I was dizzy, disoriented and stumbling about and other holidaymakers clearly believed I was drunk. I fell over a couple of times and sat down in an outdoor restaurant until the owner threw me out, thinking I was pissed. I went back to bed where I remained until the following day. Towards the end of our holiday I met a woman firefighter from Nottingham – sadly it was too late for her to do anything about my burns.

I hadn't had much experience with girls up until then and, although I was certainly interested in them, a relationship never seemed to go beyond a first date – and that was usually at my instigation. There was one girl, however, who did appear to pay me more attention than I wanted. She lived locally, always seemed to be around and used to come to the house all the time. My mum knew the family and, according to her, she was a very nice girl but quite obsessed with me and would follow me about. So, at the age of seventeen, I had a stalker and didn't quite know what to do about her. She was no 'bunny boiler' but this fixation did develop into her becoming a nuisance. She used to blag her way into the players' lounge and her mother actually used to encourage her behaviour. The pair of them would even come to church and sit behind us. I wasn't at all interested in her, but my mates thought it was hilarious and used to encourage her because she had a bevy of good-looking girlfriends. Fortunately, the stalking stopped as suddenly as it started.

I returned to pre-season training in the summer of 1996 and I couldn't wait to get started in my second season. I badly wanted to improve my game and establish myself as a regular in the first team.

A pre-season tour to Scotland had been arranged, which I was really excited about. David Moyes' dad used to work at Ibrox and he took us around the ground. Being a Celtic fan, I just didn't feel right being there and remember being surprised by a photograph of the Queen in the dressing room – something I'd never seen before. I felt much better when we also did a tour of Celtic Park in the afternoon!

We played several games north of the border at the end of July and the beginning of August. I was a substitute against Partick Thistle, when we were one nil down, and was called on about ten minutes from the end. The Preston historian, Ian Rigby, wrote, in a later programme, 'Kilbane replaced the injured Brown and, in his first run, Kevin made the long trip northwards worthwhile, as he cut in from the right-wing leaving several defenders in his wake. He let fly and found the bottom left-hand corner of the net to give North End a much deserved equaliser.' I wish I could remember that – sounded all right!

Things went very well at the outset: on our return home, we played First Division West Bromwich Albion at Deepdale, the game ended in a 2-2 draw and I made both goals. A week later, I played in another pre-season friendly against Blackburn Rovers at Deepdale. It was a particularly special occasion for all of us as the match also marked the opening of the new Tom Finney Stand. I had a particularly good game, despite being pitched up against Norwegian international Henning Berg, and was voted man of the match. Ray Harford was then the manager of Blackburn and there were rumours going around that he was interested in signing me, although Blackburn already had Damien Duff and Jason Wilcox on their books, both left-sided midfielders.

One of the earliest encounters of the season was against Premiership opposition, Tottenham, in a League Cup tie, in those days played over two legs. We drew 1-1 in the first leg at Deepdale, but in the return Spurs tonked us 3-0. Not surprising when you think that their team was full of world-class players such as Teddy Sheringham, Darren Anderton and Sol Campbell. Still, I loved playing at White Hart Lane in front of 35,000; it was the biggest crowd I'd ever played in front of, and it's still my favourite Premiership ground.

I've already mentioned how much I admired Steve Harrison and how influential a coach he was in my life. Apart from his experience and talent, Harry brought to the club something else that was to have an even greater affect on my life…or should I say someone else…his daughter Laura, who I first met in the autumn of 1996.

The funny thing was that Harry had always warned his daughters about dating footballers. He had very little time for footballers on a personal level and had told Laura that they were mostly selfish, immature womanisers. Can't think where he got that idea from! There wasn't much of a build-up and at first Laura was reluctant to go out with me. In defence of footballers everywhere, I have to say that Harry had been equally disapproving of Laura's previous boyfriends, who weren't footballers. It didn't augur well.

However, Harry seemed to like me – he had coached me for about six months before I first met Laura – and fortunately had told his family that I was a decent lad. In the end he actually encouraged Laura to go out with me, which she thought was hilarious.

The Harrison family, Steve's wife, Christine, Laura and sister Sally, were still living in Watford while Harry rented a house in Lytham St Annes when he got the Preston job. Laura had been to a few games and I have to say she had caught my eye straightaway when we met in the players' lounge. She was eighteen, petite, brunette and very pretty. I had never been very successful with women. I'd always been a bit shy and a lack of confidence meant I never seemed to know what to say. I certainly couldn't seem to charm them. Looking back, I was a bit of a dead loss with the opposite sex.

I was too nervous to invite Laura for a date but I discovered that one of the team, Michael Holt, was going out with a friend of hers. So I asked 'Holty' to ask his girlfriend to ask Laura if she would go out with me! Bit cowardly, but it worked and the four of us went out on a double date after a first round FA Cup tie against Altrincham. We had a league game later that week and Gary Peters had announced that he didn't want any of the players going out on – or being seen in – the town. But I was determined not to miss out on the opportunity of a date with Laura and so we all went to a nightclub in Liverpool where we thought we wouldn't be discovered. I actually asked Harry for permission to take Laura out, and his reply was, 'Ask her yourself – she is eighteen!' Because of Gary's instructions, my request put Harry in a bit of a tricky situation, but I told him that we were going to the cinema rather than a nightclub because I really didn't think he would approve. It was a shame that our first date took place amid such subterfuge but that was the way it had to be and I suppose the secrecy made it all a bit more romantic. From the first date I was smitten. (I like to think that Laura also brought us luck as we won that league match 4-1.)

I was still a bit wary of Harry and used to ring Laura for a chat when I knew he wouldn't be around. As part of his club duties, he always used to attend North End's reserve home games, which usually kicked off at 7 p.m., and so I would ring at 6.55, knowing that he would be at the ground and so I could avoid any awkward conversations before talking to Laura.

It was in the early stages of our relationship that I discovered I needed glasses. Playing in an evening game at Bloomfield Road, Blackpool, I completely lost track of the ball in the glare of the floodlights and realised that I really needed to do something about it. Out of pure vanity I didn't want Laura to think she was dating Mr Magoo and stupidly tried to hide the fact from her by wearing contact lenses. Eventually I admitted to her that I had difficulties with my eyesight and some years later underwent laser treatment.

In 1997, when I was called into the full Irish squad, it was becoming apparent that I might be of some commercial value to someone in the future. A number of agents were now circling and some even contacted my mother, hoping she could influence my decision as to who I might sign with. Among these were solicitor and football agent, Mel Stein, whose partner Ian Elliott later admitted mishandling the financial affairs of Stewart Downing when he was secretary of the England international's company. Shay Trainor, who also worked for Mel Stein, was attempting to sign me up with the organisation and asked if I had any footballing heroes. 'Chris Waddle' was my immediate reply. Shay picked up the phone and dialled a number. He said a few words and then passed me the instrument, 'Here, Kevin, have a chat with Chrissy.' What better way of impressing a young lad?

In fact, various characters were in touch with me about representation at that time. Sam Allardyce, who had been sacked as manager of Blackpool in May 1996, suggested a meeting with Mark Curtis, his own agent. I was still very much in awe of Big Sam and highly likely to heed any recommendation of his, so I agreed to meet the two men at the Tickled Trout hotel in Preston, just off the M6.

Naively, I couldn't work out why Sam was so keen for me to sign with Mark Curtis. Mark produced a pre-written contract and I think he expected me to sign there and then. However, it didn't feel right to commit myself so quickly and I told him I wasn't sure about it. It felt awkward but part of me didn't want to let Big Sam down. Mark seemed surprised but said, 'Go away and think about it and we'll meet up again.'

I did just that and, when I looked at the contract more carefully, I realised that by signing the paperwork not only was I agreeing to his fees, but also to handing over a substantial percentage of my earnings for the length of the contract. Looking back, I should have enlisted the assistance of the PFA or at least sought advice from David Moyes. Mark Curtis rang me again a few days later, pressing for another meeting.

We met again at the Tickled Trout. This time I took my brother Farrell to support me and provide a bit of muscle. Curtis placed the contract in front of me and again expected me to put pen to paper. I told him, 'No thanks, I don't think I need an agent at the moment.' He was naturally disappointed, but accepted my decision without too much of an argument. And I was grateful that in the following weeks he didn't try to hassle me. I had no further contact with either Mark Curtis or Sam Allardyce although our paths have crossed occasionally and Sam has always wished me well.

In fact, soon after, I acquired Paul Stretford as my agent. Paul had set up Pro-Active Sports Management with Irish international Frank Stapleton. He had been recommended by Mark Rankine, one of the lads at Preston, and also, more crucially, Harry, who knew of Paul through his association with Stan Collymore.

The Tickled Trout – where else? – was the venue yet again for my meeting with Paul Stretford and I immediately felt comfortable in his company. He was very straight with me, didn't give me any bullshit, told me that success wasn't guaranteed and that I would have to work hard. I took a liking to Paul and for the following eight years we enjoyed a good relationship when he negotiated my transfers to and contracts with WBA, Sunderland and Everton.

Towards the end of my second season as a professional with North End, I had heard rumours that a couple of clubs in higher divisions were after me. However, I didn't really think anything would happen because it seemed too early in my career to be moving upwards; and in any case I just couldn't see myself leaving Preston at that particular time. Although we had only finished mid-table I was very happy with my home-town club and had no reason to think of leaving.

This all changed when I was called into a meeting with Gary Peters. As was usual after the final fixture of the season, every player had his customary end-of-season chat with the manager. He would normally tell each player what he thought of their overall performance during the season. It actually coincided with a period when I wasn't playing that well. I was troubled by a hernia problem that had been niggling me and had only just undergone surgery a few days earlier.

Gary started by saying how I'd started the season well but didn't really give me any more positives than that. Short and sharp. He went on to say that I'd underperformed for the last few months. I agreed. He said I was no longer guaranteed a place in the team and that I would probably start the next season on the bench as there were other players better than me.

I tried to say that I had been playing with the groin injury since Christmas. I had struggled on, never missed training and, although I realised that it wasn't the only reason for my poor form, the injury had certainly contributed.

Gary was less than sympathetic and I was totally unprepared for the bombshell that was to follow. As I was about to get up and go, he told me that the club had accepted an offer for me from West Bromwich Albion and I was to go down and talk to them over the next couple of days. I felt lower than a snake's belly. My immediate reaction was to say I didn't want to go. I wanted to stay at Preston. He told me that the club would not be offering me a new contract and that was all there was to say about it.

It's a man's game and now I was in no doubt about it. I know now the reasons why Gary said what he did in the meeting but I still don't agree with the way he did it. Previously, I had been offered improved contracts very quickly, but I was now being treated very differently.

I went out of Gary's office and straight to the treatment room where a few of the lads had gathered: skipper Ian Bryson (Bryce), Simon Davey and Ryan Kidd were there with a few others. I told them what I had just been told and they were great – especially Bryce. He said to go home and think about it and not to be pressured into a quick decision. But they did all agree it was a great opportunity to move to a great club like WBA, who were in Division One (what is today the Championship). I didn't really see it like that.

The following day I set off for West Brom and it had been arranged for me to meet my agent's assistant, Jonathan Stanger, at Knutsford services on the M6. (Paul Stretford himself was away in Barbados – great timing!) When I arrived at Knutsford, David Moyes was there to greet me. Moyesy confided to me that Gary Peters, who knew I was meeting my agent, had sent him along to make sure that I signed a transfer request. Moyesy was really decent – he still had a foot in the players' camp and was great with me. He told me I should refuse to sign such a request. As far as he knew, the deal had already been done between the two clubs and my putting in a transfer request would make it appear that the club was doing all it could to keep me at Deepdale and that Preston really didn't want to sell me.

Jonathan Stanger turned up soon after. Gary Peters then called Moyesy on his mobile and asked to speak to me. He told me that I should put in a written transfer request and give it to Moyesy. I told Gary that I wouldn't be signing any such document. Gary hardly let me get a word in.

I told him that would suit me fine, that I was very happy to stay at Preston and in any case I didn't feel comfortable with the move. Although I couldn't deny that my wages would be much increased, I was still learning my craft and I was sure there would be other opportunities. The tone of his voice changed immediately. He then said I should at least go down and speak with West Brom boss Ray Harford and that everything would be okay.

I later discovered that when Ray Harford had made an inquiry about me when he was at Blackburn, he had been refused permission to talk to me. Now that he was at Albion, he was interested in signing me and was prepared to offer some serious money. In retrospect, I could understand why Gary was keen for me to give it some thought. From the club's point of view, it was a very substantial offer that would benefit Preston and Gary knew that I was likely to move on at some stage.

After much thought, and realising that I didn't really have a future under Gary at Preston, I agreed to talk to Ray Harford and a deal was struck with regard to a fee. Personal terms had yet to be agreed, however, and as I wasn't happy with a couple of things in the contract, before I signed anything I met up with Paul Stretford and Steve Harrison at the Thistle Hotel near Haydock racecourse.

On the way back, Harry gave me a forty-five-minute lecture about the move to Albion. 'This is a big move. Don't let it go to your head or get carried away. You're a young lad. Don't get your head turned. You must knuckle down and work hard.' I really appreciated his concern and I'm sure he understood that I wasn't going to receive such advice from my own father. In a way he was acting as a substitute dad. And I've no doubt he was thinking about his daughter's security as well as mine! Harry got so carried away dispensing advice that before long we realised we had been travelling the wrong way down the M6 and found ourselves in Wolverhampton instead of Preston!

Gary was keen to conclude the deal – in case something went wrong. He wanted me to sign the contract straightaway and have it all done and dusted without delay. But I still didn't want to rush into it. I told Gary that I would sign the paperwork on my return from Lanzarote, where I had planned a holiday with

Laura. It wasn't that I was being arrogant or difficult – I just didn't see the urgency.

As Laura and I were waiting to board the plane at the airport, having already checked in our bags, Jonathan Stanger suddenly appeared! He'd been asked by Paul Stretford to explain that the move to West Brom would now definitely *not* take place unless my written transfer request was signed.

In the end, although I felt manipulated, it was clear that I had no choice; not only would the move be off but, more importantly, I wouldn't be very popular with the club or the gaffer, and that would obviously affect my future at Preston. So, after much soul-searching, I actually wrote out a transfer request in the airport terminal. It's still one of my biggest regrets that I agreed to this: I felt I was betraying the club that had nurtured me from the age of seven.

It's also fair to say that Harry wasn't too pleased with the way I'd been treated and felt that Gary was putting too much pressure on me. The two of them fell out and there was no doubt that Harry was also being protective towards Laura as the move affected her too.

While all this was going on I received a call from Mick McCarthy, who wanted me to join the senior Irish squad; but because of my hernia operation I couldn't join them. I was gutted. Talk about the highs and lows of being a professional footballer!

While on holiday in Lanzarote I asked Laura to marry me. It was 30 May and coincided with Laura's nineteenth birthday. I hadn't planned to ask her – it was all incredibly spontaneous. We'd been out for a romantic dinner and were walking back to the hotel when I was overtaken by my feelings for her. I went down on one knee by a stone seat overlooking the beach and popped the question. She agreed and we started making plans immediately and talked about living together on our return from holiday.

We were very young; looking back, perhaps too young. My

home life had been pretty disruptive and insecure and now I was moving away from friends and my home town in what was a huge career move. I was probably looking for some security, which I felt Laura and her family could provide. I liked my future in-laws and Harry was the father figure I had never really had. At the time it felt right.

When we returned from holiday, I thought I'd better do the right thing; I wanted to ask Harry for permission to marry his daughter, although I'd already asked her! On the day we returned from Lanzarote, we arranged to see Harry and Christine. I told Harry that I had something important to speak to him about and we went into their lounge and closed the door behind us. Laura and her mum remained in the kitchen.

Harry gave me 'a fatherly chat', in which he told me of his expectations, how much Laura meant to him and that I should look after her at all times. He ended by telling me, 'I'm delighted to welcome you into the family.' It felt important that Harry had given us his blessing. I had and still have a lot of respect for him both as a man and a coach. He helped me a lot while I was at Preston and I'll always be in his debt.

I also went home to see my mum and tell her the news. 'Sit down, I've got something exciting to tell you.' Mum's immediate response was, 'You haven't got Laura pregnant, have you?'

I ignored that and told her, 'Laura and I are going to get married!' She didn't exactly jump for joy. Rather than the expected congratulations, she replied: 'I've lost you.' I know that mothers can be possessive – particularly Irish mothers – but I was surprised by her response. I genuinely thought she'd be pleased, but in any case I was so excited about my future and tried to put her reaction out of my mind. There were also lots of other things going on.

On 13 June 1997, I joined West Bromwich Albion for a club record fee of £1.25 million. At Preston I had been earning £350 a week, but at Albion I was now going to receive a basic salary of £1,250 a week. With bonuses and various extras, I would be earning about £100,000 a year. I had always considered myself pretty level-headed, but this was a huge move and I was only twenty years old. It was now time to work hard and prove myself. Harry's words, 'Make the best of yourself!', echoed in my ears.

I had made over fifty appearances for Preston North End in my two years as a professional and, although I was sad to leave my home-town club, I was moving up a division. At the time, Gary Peters' explanation to the media about my transfer confirmed his public protestations at wanting me to stay: 'Kevin Kilbane signed a four-year deal with us about four months earlier and then, as changing-room gossip goes, he was advised to get an agent. The agent comes in to advise Kevin and realises he can't get him a deal. Then he comes in and attempts to get him a move.'

The first thing to do was to get up to the Hawthorns to complete my medical, which I still hadn't done. To be honest, the medical was a bit of a joke and probably the least testing one I've ever had in my career – all I remember having to do was touch my toes and run a mile!

I was a bit surprised by the setup at West Brom. I was sure the training facilities would be a great improvement on what I had been used to at Preston, but I was in for a shock. The club didn't own its own training ground – the grounds were rented from Aston University and we shared the pitches and changing rooms with the students. The showers were really crap – they were grubby and there was seldom any hot water. The ten pitches were situated on a sloping stretch of open ground and the ones at the bottom of the dip were often waterlogged – it was like playing on marshland. The university ground staff were responsible for allocating pitches and we didn't seem to have priority over anyone else for the better playing surfaces. Things have moved on at the club since my day and Albion now have state-of-the-art amenities – some of the best in the country.

Still, I couldn't wait to get started, although there was a lot of pressure on me as I was Albion's first million-pound player. I hadn't realised at the time that the transfer was such a big deal. Although my arrival couldn't exactly be described as 'a marquee signing', for a club that was struggling financially to invest over a million pounds on a player made front-page headlines in the Black Country. There was belief in manager Ray Harford and, by all accounts, the fans felt optimistic to the extent that season ticket sales rose steadily.

John Trewick was appointed as Ray Harford's assistant and was quoted in the press soon after my signing: 'Kevin Kilbane will be one of the babes of the squad. He is a very quick player and he has achieved a lot but everyone has to remember he is only twenty. He has to be given time to settle in. The set-up at Albion is a lot different from Preston.' Although I didn't exactly feel like 'a babe', I was grateful for his support when I started training in the first week of July, a week earlier than the majority of the squad as I was still recovering from the injury that had delayed my signature in the first place.

I made my debut for the club on 6 July 1997 as a substitute in a pre-season friendly at Hednesford and got on the score sheet in a game at Kidderminster a couple of weeks later. I also played against a Chelsea team that included Gianluca Vialli and Dutch international goalkeeper Ed De Goey. I didn't particularly shine in these games and it was another new boy, Lee Hughes, who seemed to settle in more quickly at the club and showed what he was capable of in these games, particularly against Chelsea when he proved himself a bit of a handful.

Lee had signed for Albion from Kidderminster Harriers for £200,000 – a record fee for a non-league player – at the same time as me and it was good to have another 'new boy' in the camp. We got on well and used to spend quite a lot of time together. He was daft in those days and would do anything for a laugh, which naturally made him very popular with the lads. Lee was a local lad, born in Smethwick, a lifelong supporter of Albion, who sported a WBA tattoo and whose dream had always been to play for the club. As has been well documented, nearly seven years later Lee was involved in a fatal car crash for which he went to jail for causing death by dangerous driving and his contract was cancelled. I tried to ring him in prison but I regret that I never visited him. Although I knew he had done wrong and had caused untold misery to a family he had never met, I knew he was rightly feeling very guilty and must be suffering too.

The build-up to my West Brom league debut was a bit of a nightmare. When I first signed, the club had put me in a room at the Moat House hotel in West Bromwich. The night before the game I hardly got a wink of sleep. I went to bed early to make sure I got enough rest but I ended up having a terrible night. First, some joker started the fire alarm at midnight. There was also a disco in the hotel and the music thumped away until 2.30 a.m. It was the worst possible way to prepare for a match. Then, on the morning of the match, I discovered that the tyres on my car had been slashed. I thought that at least the vandal couldn't have been an Albion fan because they hadn't seen me play yet.

Anyway, I took to the field against Tranmere Rovers on 9 August and any fatigue was obliterated by the adrenaline coursing through me. I was also pleased that my mum and her sister were sitting in the stands cheering me on and hoped they were proud of me. We won 2-1 and I marked my first Division One appearance with a goal and the man of the match award.

In the second game, we were 2-1 down with five minutes to go but managed to snatch a 3-2 win thanks to Lee. Although only two games had been played we were joint top and we followed our great start with a 1-0 victory over Black Country rivals Wolverhampton Wanderers. Despite this bright beginning, my initial months at Albion were disappointing and I didn't play with any consistency. I was desperate to make an immediate impression and to prove that I was worth the money Albion had splashed out. It took me a while to settle and I was concerned about the expectation of the fans. I was nervous before and during games and, I suppose, still a bit naive. Looking back, I realise that this was the establishment of a bit of a pattern: I found that I often took more time than I would have liked to settle into a new club. I'm not sure why this should be – perhaps I did sometimes try too hard and too quickly to make my mark playing for a new team and this could sometimes prove counter-productive.

I had been flattered that a coach as accomplished as Ray Harford wanted me at Albion. Ray had built his reputation as one of England's top coaches in a career that included being Kenny Dalglish's number two in Blackburn's Premiership-winning team of 1995. Ray's experience and sensitive man management were a great support and I remember him telling me, 'Don't worry about the transfer fee – it's the club that decided the amount. Not you. Just relax and try and enjoy yourself here.' This was music to my ears and I really appreciated that he understood how I was feeling.

I was still living at the Moat House hotel in West Bromwich, where Laura joined me, and in September we bought our first house together and moved into a property in Edgbaston, Birmingham, near the cricket ground. Goalkeeper Alan Miller had also just joined the club and was still living in the Moat House. When he saw our house he liked the street so much that he decided to buy a house in the same road. At the time he was going out with *Brookside* actress Clare Sweeney and she and Laura used to go to games together. In fact, both Alan and Clare were really supportive of us, a young couple just making it out on our own in the world, and we were very grateful for their kindness.

Laura initially started working at one of the Body Shop outlets but then, in the New Year, found a job at a children's nursery, which suited her better. She's wonderful with children and this job was much more fulfilling. Laura's parents moved back to the city when Harry was appointed assistant manager to John Gregory at Aston Villa in February 1998.

To maintain some continuity and stability I joined the congregation at St Chad's Roman Catholic Cathedral in Birmingham and became friendly with one of the priests, Father Patrick Daly. I got to know Father Patrick pretty well and would go and have a cup of tea with him at the presbytery. He was a lovely man who knew little about football, but was very keen to learn about the game and what it was like for me to be a professional. Although he seemed to be much older than me and we led quite different lives, I was grateful for the time I spent with him in what he described professionally as a pastoral relationship – one of spiritual guidance.

Chapter Four

Plastic Paddy

'I'll tell you a riddle. You're waiting for a train, a train that will take you far away. You know where you hope this train will take you, but you don't know for sure. But it doesn't matter. How can it not matter to you where that train will take you?'

MAL COBB, *INCEPTION*

In August 1997, I received another call-up to the full Irish squad in the form of a fax from the FAI to the club, and my confidence was further boosted by Mick McCarthy in a newspaper interview in which he was quoted as saying, 'Kevin has done very well at his new club. We always realised he had the talent to make it at the highest level.' I had been so disappointed at having to withdraw previously when I was recovering from my hernia operation and had a nagging fear that maybe I had missed my chance. I never took it for granted that I would get another chance and so I felt on top of the world. I thought back to my days in the playground and our schoolboy 'pretend' internationals. But this was the real thing. It had been my ambition for as long as I could remember and my decision to turn down Big Sam's advice to join the England squad had been vindicated.

I boarded the plane for Dublin at Birmingham airport and one of the first people I saw was David 'Ned' Kelly, a prolific goalscorer then playing for Tranmere Rovers, but born and living

70

in Birmingham. He was a big Albion fan, so he recognised me and invited me to sit next to him. I sat between him and Andy Townsend, who, on the other hand, had no idea who I was! Fortunately, Andy, who had just joined Middlesbrough from Aston Villa, soon made me feel welcome with his quick-witted humour. Andy was a legend in Irish football and had captained the 1994 World Cup team. Both David and Andy were what were described as 'Plastic Paddys' – lads who were born in the UK but had chosen to play for Ireland. Although I wasn't crazy about the label, I hoped I was about to join their ranks.

We met up with the rest of the international squad in Dublin at the airport hotel. I was welcomed by Mick McCarthy who told me that the lads were going out for a drink that evening and that I should join them. We went to Copper Face Jacks in Harcourt Street, where I felt a little in awe of the company. I've got to say that a few beers relaxed me.

The following afternoon (we needed the morning to recover from the session the previous night) we took a bus to the training ground. I looked around the coach and it suddenly hit me. I had to pinch myself to prove that this wasn't all a hoax or a dream. I was surrounded by my footballing heroes, players like Roy Keane, Steve Staunton, Ray Houghton and Tony Cascarino. I had watched some of them take the field in the World Cup and European Championships.

As with the transfer to Albion, I felt under terrible pressure to prove myself and was extremely nervous when I trained with the squad. On the first day of training, we performed some of the usual routines and I remember an exercise involving some of the lads forming a circle and a couple of them in the middle trying to get possession of the ball. The lads forming the circle would make one-touch passes to each other. They had to be quick and sharp. But whenever the ball went to Roy Keane he would belt it at me at about 100mph. It was impossible to control, the ball ended up miles away and, of course, I always ended up in the circle. The other lads all fell about but Roy would remain stony-faced. I later discovered that this was some sort of initiation ceremony, albeit of a footballing nature, in which Roy would test the mettle of newcomers to see how they reacted.

I was a substitute in a testimonial for Eoin Hand against the League of Ireland Select XI on 3 September 1997. Eoin had previously managed the national team but had undergone serious surgery earlier in the year. The match, which was played in Dublin, unfortunately didn't attract a large crowd, which was disappointing, but the game provided me with an opportunity to make my first appearance for the full team. Although this wasn't a competitive international, when I came on in the second half I couldn't have been more thrilled. I was also excited that Preston legend Brian Mooney, who I used to watch from the terraces, was playing for the Select XI. I was quite pleased with my performance and, having had a taste of playing at this level, couldn't wait for another opportunity.

After the game, a young lad from the League of Ireland team came into the dressing room, wanting an Irish shirt from one of us. Unfortunately for him, by the time he approached us most of the lads had gone and only Roy Keane and I were still getting dressed. Roy couldn't oblige because he had already offered his shirt for a charity auction, and as it was my first senior appearance in an Irish shirt I obviously wanted to keep that particular shirt. I felt sorry for him but there wasn't much we could do. Physiotherapist Mick Byrne saw our dilemma and, not wanting to see the lad disappointed, hunted in the used kit skip and chucked him a pair of dirty, sweaty socks. 'There you are, son, enjoy these!' Not exactly what the youngster was hoping for but there you are.

I must have done enough in the testimonial to impress Mick McCarthy because, the day before the World Cup qualifier against Iceland in Reykjavik, Mick informed me that I would be making my international debut. This was the ultimate accolade both for me and my Irish family. I had stayed with my cousin, Paul Smyth, in Dublin the year before and he had taught me the words of the Irish national anthem. I was ready to sing them out loud and proudly.

I can remember the date of my debut only too well – Saturday 6 September 1997 – because it coincided with the funeral of Princess Diana. Like the entire nation I had been shocked by her death and was in Birmingham, preparing to fly out to Dublin that day to meet up with the Irish squad, when I heard the news about the car crash in Paris.

We flew to Reykjavik a couple of days before the match and trained on the stadium pitch the day before. We watched a video of Iceland's previous matches. Nowadays there is a wealth of material available on the internet, but then we would have viewed some sort of compilation. Of course, there was much less material in those days and attendance at such a video viewing wasn't mandatory. Mick would give his team talk, which would address tactics and individual responsibilities. He tried to keep it simple and always trusted his players to know what was expected of them. Most of the work had already been done on the training ground.

The following morning, we had a gentle stroll. Kick-off was at 3 p.m. and I followed my usual routine. I'm not one of those players who performs a series of pre-match rituals. I'm not superstitious – touch wood. We devoured a light brunch of scrambled eggs on toast at about 11.30 a.m. and then took a coach to the ground from our hotel. We went straight into the dressing room where the kit had been laid out in readiness. Mick Byrne would announce the allocation of the shirt numbers – mine was No. 11, which I have worn for most of my career. I looked through the programme briefly, mostly at the pictures (not because, as the old joke goes, footballers can't read but because, not unnaturally, the programme was printed in Icelandic). We'd then put on our warm-up shirts, shorts and socks about forty-five minutes before kick-off and I'd strap up my ankles, which I had done throughout my career. Some of the lads would have massages or anti-inflammatory injections if required.

The pre-match international timetable is prescribed by FIFA regulations and there is usually a printout on the dressing-room wall, which indicates the times of the warm-up, the presentations, the national anthems and, of course, the kick-off.

Mick and Taff would take the warm-up before returning to the dressing room where we would don our match shirts. Music was an important element pre-match. In the coach, we would listen to Irish rebel songs, usually played by the Wolf Tones, the Dubliners, Paddy Reilly or the Fureys. Once in the dressing room it was U2 and the album, *Joshua Tree*. The first three tracks, 'Where The Streets Have No Name', 'I Still Haven't Found What I'm Looking For' and 'With Or Without You', were blasted out at top volume and Mick Byrne would invariably be rocking around and playing air guitar. Mick was brilliant in the dressing room before matches, hopping about like a demented leprechaun, full of mischief and fun, in an attempt to alleviate some of the pressure and nerves. No matter what it took to relax the players, Mick would do it!

Despite his antics, the banter and the excitement, I felt much more tense than at any other game I had played in. This was different. This was a World Cup qualifier for my country. The final words before we went out were delivered by Mick McCarthy in which he reiterated what needed to be done, how we could win the match and in a calm, assured way, would motivate the team.

We took to the pitch, met the dignitaries, the heads of the respective international associations and sang our national anthem, which I always felt was important. But I just wanted to get on with the game. I'd never been as nervous. Unfortunately, in the end, it was all a bit of an anti-climax once the game started.

I played in left midfield and was up against Stoke's right-back, Larus Sigurdsson, who clattered me early on. I'd better get used to this, I thought. We took the lead through David Connolly but Iceland equalised just before the break.

I never got into the game and when we trooped in at half-time, with the score at 1-1, I came off the field feeling very disappointed about how I'd played. I knew I could and should have done better but maybe the occasion was just too much for me. As soon as we got into the dressing room, Mick said he was going to make a couple of changes for the second half. I knew I was going to be dragged off at half-time, which is horrible for any player. He didn't criticise me or make it personal, but I knew I'd let myself and the team down. Despite the best efforts of Mick Byrne and kit man Johnny Fallon to cheer me up I felt really low and alone. The backroom staff were incredibly important members of the setup and it had been instilled in them how they could help create harmony within the squad and establish a bond with the players.

In fact, Johnny stayed with me for a while in the dressing room to help gee me up and I remember him saying to me, 'When you have got your hundredth cap, you'll be able to look back at this and laugh.' I certainly didn't feel like laughing then and although I was grateful for his words, Johnny was clearly talking rubbish! I showered and changed and the game had already restarted by the time I took my seat on the bench to watch the rest of the match. In the second half, Roy Keane notched two goals and my replacement, Mark Kennedy, scored towards the end and the game ended in a 4-2 win. Interestingly, Larus Sigurdsson was sent off halfway through the second half!

The squad travelled to Lithuania for a game on the following Wednesday but I knew I wasn't going to feature. I thought that maybe I had completely blown my chance. Perhaps forty-five minutes was to be the extent of my senior international career. Not even a one-game wonder – just a one half-game wonder. But I have to say the lads were brilliant with me and, when we were in Vilnius the day before the game, Roy Keane made sure he spent a lot of time talking to me and lifting my spirits. I remember being amazed by his encyclopaedic knowledge of the game – and not just international or Premiership. He had an astonishing grasp and awareness of players and teams in all the leagues. Anyway, I watched the game from the sidelines that day and we beat Lithuania 2-1 with two goals from Tony Cascarino.

I was therefore still pretty devastated after my disappointing international debut and my inconsistent club form continued for another couple of months. I hadn't been playing well and despite Ray Harford's kind words the fee was weighing heavily on my mind. I felt that I was letting the fans down...some of them let me know how they felt and were questioning my ability. I've always had my knockers – something I've had to deal with throughout my career – but I've found that experience and age have helped me to withstand criticism. When I was a boy my mum used to hand out some pretty fierce treatment at times, and when you've had 'the hairdryer' treatment from Gary Peters and John Beck as a young lad you can cope with most things!

I had yet to convince some of the West Brom supporters when I first arrived. A joke in one of the fanzines went as follows: 'There's no truth in the rumour that when in Iceland Kevin Kilbane bumped into the greatest living Icelander, Magnus Magnusson, he was asked by the *Mastermind* host, 'What do you do?'

'Er...pass,' replied Kevin

'That's not what your team-mates tell me,' quipped Magnus.

There was even some criticism of my running style and the suggestion that I was lazy – something I've never been accused of. However, the majority of the Albion fans stuck by me and I was grateful for their support.

At the time, the manager played a 4-5-1 formation with two holding midfielders; although it has been adopted widely these days it was, at the time, an unusually defensive formation, designed to stifle the opposition. Richard Sneekes and I were the main midfield support players for the front man, who switched between Bob Taylor, Andy Hunt, Paul Peschisolido or Lee Hughes. All great forwards.

Dutchman Richard Sneekes, who had begun his career at the Ajax Academy, was a very skilful, attacking midfielder and scored lots of goals. He sported a mane of blond hair and became something of a cult figure at the Hawthorns, where lots of fans took to wearing long blond wigs as a form of hero worship. Richard, who pretty much kept his own counsel, had an eye for business and could invariably be found reading the *Financial Times* on away trips.

Fortunately, I started to settle into the team by the end of November. I remember playing against Middlesbrough in particular, although we lost 1-0, I had one of my best games in front of 30,000 fans. My other abiding memory of that game is witnessing one of Paul Gascoigne's 'red mist' moments when he committed a wild foul on Sean Flynn and was lucky to receive only a yellow card.

Sadly, I only worked with Ray Harford for a few months. His public demeanour was sometimes a bit cold and he was never completely at home with the media, but in private he was warm and much more affable. He was tactically astute and studied the game in depth. Although we were doing quite well and were riding high in the table, Ray was having problems combining home and family life as he was still living in Berkshire. (I later found this to be a common problem for coaches, who were expected to work long hours and often lived some distance from home and family.) Not only did Ray want to be back in London and nearer to home but he was also constrained by serious financial pressures. In December 1997, Ray was appointed as manager of Division One rivals Queens Park Rangers.

It was a real shame because Ray was one of the best coaches I've ever worked with. He was especially good for me because he liked to use wingers and insisted that we get plenty of crosses into the box. There is a sad postscript to this story: five years later, while at Millwall, Ray Harford was diagnosed with lung cancer and within a year had passed away. He was only fifty-eight. A much respected and lovely man.

After Ray's departure, Ritchie Barker took over for a month, but Albion duly appointed Denis Smith as manager. Denis had a reputation as a tough, uncompromising defender (notably with Stoke City) and I must admit I wondered how he would view me and if he'd even pick me. Fortunately, Denis wanted me in the team and asked me to play in several different positions, something I was always happy to do if it meant keeping my place in the team. He changed the formation and we played a more standard 4-4-2. I scored in his first game at Reading. Denis also made Lee Hughes first-choice striker. Under Smith, the side would include a minimum of four attacking players and, unlike under Ray, when we had a tendency to lose 1-0 against the top teams, we always had a chance of scoring more goals.

I know that Denis Smith thought I should have scored more goals at the back post as I was good in the air, and he also felt I should have been more aggressive, but he has since told me that he admired the fact that I was a team player and read the game well. He definitely got me playing with more freedom. My only criticism of Denis was that he liked us to play eleven versus eleven matches in training and there wasn't much variety in the training methods. This can have an adverse affect on the players because, when training becomes repetitive, they get bored, which, in turn, can be detrimental to squad morale.

In fact, my form really picked up when Denis took over and felt I was beginning to pay the fans back for their loyalty – not to mention a little bit of the transfer fee! I started 1998 well and was man of the match against Stoke in the league and followed that up with a headed goal against them in a third round FA Cup tie when Mick McCarthy was in the crowd.

We didn't fare so well in the next round at Villa Park, when we were trounced 4-0, but before the game I was actually interviewed on the coach by a local journalist. You can see it on YouTube now, and almost as embarrassing as the result that day is my spotty skin and droopy hairstyle. Although I appeared confident, I admitted that the game against Villa was going to be the biggest club game of my career.

Although we played well in parts for the rest of the season we failed to win enough games and ended up in a very disappointing tenth position – particularly so as we had been third when Denis took over. One notable victory, however, was at Bramall Lane during penultimate game of the season. We hadn't scored more than three goals in any game all season, but this time we ran out 4-2 winners and I found the net in a move that was voted WBA's goal of the season. Picking up the ball on the touchline, just past the halfway line, I outstripped two opposition players before veering inside and from thirty yards unleashed a right-foot rocket which fizzed into the net. Even more satisfying was the fact that the despairing keeper was none other than Irish international and ex-Preston goalie Alan Kelly, who had attended my old school, St Gregory's, a few years before me. Alan Kelly – currently goalkeeping coach to the Ireland team – still moans about it, saying he was only beaten because my shot was deflected!

My international career had been equally mixed during the season. I had been called into the squad for a play-off game against Belgium for France 98 at the Heysel Stadium in Brussels in November 1997 but I didn't play. We had drawn the home leg 1-1. Mick McCarthy sent Ray Houghton on as a substitute for Alan McLoughlin after forty-nine minutes and ten minutes later Ray scored his last ever goal for Ireland, which brought us back on level terms. Unfortunately, Luc Nilis scored the winning goal and Belgium qualified for the finals in France. I remember Shay Given being in tears after the game and Ray Houghton, who was about to retire, getting more and more pissed on the plane home.

Although I was devastated that we were out of the tournament I was greatly relieved that I was in the squad as I thought my international days were over before they'd really begun. My second cap didn't come until March 1998, when we lost 2-1 to the Czech Republic in a friendly in Olomouc. There were a number of international debutants that day, including a precocious seventeen-year-old striker from Wolves by the name of Robbie Keane, who made an instant impact off the field as well as on it. Robbie was the best seventeen-year-old I have ever seen – and I played with Wayne Rooney when he was that age.

Robbie played with natural ability; he didn't need to be coached and absolutely loved playing. He had just moved to England and completely bypassed the Under 21s, going straight into the senior squad. Whereas it took me a while to settle in, Robbie felt at home straightaway with all his heroes in the Irish team. He was also great fun off the pitch – confident, likeably precocious and possessing the Dublin charm. I remember playing a lot of Pro Evolution with Robbie, Lee Carsley and Richard Dunne to kill the long hours in hotel rooms.

Damien Duff was another lad playing for the first time in the senior green shirt. I had known of Duffer when he turned out for the Blackburn youth team; even then there was a lot of talk about his ability and he was already building something of a reputation. Although left-footed, Duffer could play anywhere across the park and in training could beat four or five players at will. We became great friends and often shared a beer. Duffer loves his music, another interest we share. In those days teetotaller and modern Renaissance Man Kenny Cunningham became our designated driver. Kenny is a good counterpoint to the unfair suggestion that footballers' interests outside football only stretch to fast cars and girls. We might not all be that well educated but that doesn't means we're all unintelligent or oafish.

I gained my third international cap on 22 April 1998 in a 2-0 defeat to Argentina in a friendly in Dublin. Despite the disappointment of losing, I was excited about playing in my first game at Lansdowne Road. When I was growing up, some of the international games were played on midweek afternoons due to the lack of floodlights and my woodwork teacher, Mr McGeoghan (thank goodness for all the Irish in Preston), used to let us listen to the games being broadcast on the radio. I couldn't believe I was now playing at this iconic ground. Robbie, who had only played a handful of games for Wolves at that stage, showed what a pro he was going to be. Playing in his home town, the crowd took to him straightaway. The Argentine team featured such stars as Juan Sebastián Verón, Gabriel Batistuta and Diego Simeone, but it was Ariel Ortega who took my eye – he was fantastic and as good a player as I've played against in my career. I did okay, but was replaced by that legend Denis Irwin at half-time.

Back at Albion, we finished a creditable tenth in the First Division and by now I had made over fifty appearances for the club, scoring six goals. Despite only having been at Albion a year, there was already some interest from other clubs. Nottingham Forest and Sunderland made enquiries but it was Premiership club Middlesbrough, managed by Bryan Robson, that actually made a bid of £2 million – news of which was reported in the Irish newspapers. My agent Paul Stretford informed me of the possible move and even told me that Bryan Robson had been quoted as saying I shouldn't expect to be on the same terms as stars such as Gazza and Andy Townsend! That didn't bother me at all – I was just flattered that a Premiership club were interested in me. In the event, Denis Smith wanted to keep me at the club and turned the bid down.

I didn't mind too much about the transfer falling through as I had no real desire to move. I was now enjoying my football and very happy at West Brom; I also felt a debt of loyalty to them for showing some faith in taking me from a lower division. Paul Stretford had suggested that, to ensure a transfer, I should ask for a move, but no way was I going to do that. You learn from experience: after what had happened at Preston I decided I was never going to put in a transfer request again.

Due to Irish Under 21 commitments, I only had a short break at the end of the season and was then back in training with Albion at the beginning of July for the 1998–9 season. Due to lack of funds there was no European pre-season tour and the furthest we travelled was to Cardiff, with other games at Worcester, Bromsgrove and Halesowen.

Denis Smith was trying to build a new, younger side and he signed centre-half Matt Carbon from Derby and James Quinn from Blackpool. Both Bob Taylor and Andy Hunt had gone, as had ex-Liverpool midfielder Steve Nicol who'd come in on loan under Smith but preferred to move to America rather than stay. My old hotel mate and neighbour Alan Miller was also out of favour.

I started my second season determined to continue where I had left off. We had a good side and the general feeling was that we would consolidate our position in mid-table from the previous season and be challenging for promotion. We won three of our first four games but then came unstuck in the next couple, although against Bolton, at the Hawthorns, I scored the goal that still remains my favourite strike. We were 0-2 down when I picked the ball up some distance from goal, beat one player and then exchanged a one-two. The Trotters' keeper, Jussi Jääskeläinen, rushed out to narrow the angle but I chipped it over him into the top corner. A lovely moment and a goal that didn't go unnoticed elsewhere.

The following week I went to watch Aston Villa play, my father-in-law Harry having been there as John Gregory's assistant since February. In the players' lounge after the match, Mr Gregory tapped me on the cheek and said, 'If you keep scoring goals like that [referring to my goal against Bolton] we might give you a chance to play for Villa.' I found that pretty patronising but didn't want to say anything out of turn and just answered: 'Thanks, but I'm very happy at Albion!'

I was combining well with Lee Hughes and was being noticed by other clubs. Transfer rumours started early in the season, although I had no thoughts of leaving Albion. As the defeats continued and financial problems became more evident, there was lots of media whispering. An editorial in a fanzine in September 1998 struck a resigned note: 'Kilbane deserves praise for keeping his thoughts to himself but I fear it is inevitable he will leave...the Board have shareholders to answer to and holding an unhappy player to his contract makes for unhappy balance sheet reading. Firm "nyets" from our hierarchy are, I suspect, aimed more at talking the price up than an outright determination to keep Killa come what may. The more realistic option is to extract the maximum price possible and to have a replacement lined up.'

Despite all this talk I didn't feel unsettled at all and was quite happy plying my trade at Albion. At this time, the influence of Sky TV was really starting to kick in – four Saturday home matches were moved to accommodate their broadcasts. I didn't really concern myself with the fact that these matches were watched live by a few million viewers. I was just delighted to be playing regularly and, of course, we had no idea that Sky coverage would be as far-reaching as it is today.

We started the league season fairly well with a draw and three wins before suffering defeats to Grimsby and Bolton. We recovered but then, on 29 September, there was a particularly upsetting 3-0 defeat at Oxford United – Denis Smith's old side. A few weeks later there was a game I remember vividly. Although the 2-2 draw at Swindon wasn't a dramatic scoreline, the match was played in driving rain and 70mph winds! The gusts were so strong that our goalkeeper conceded a corner from his own goal-kick! Virtually all the away supporters were obliged to stand on an allocated terrace wearing plastic raincoats, even though there were thousands of empty seats. At half-time, St John Ambulance staff had to treat some of the Albion fans for exposure. I was brought down in the box with two minutes to go but we were only awarded a corner. Both teams were desperate to get off the pitch at the end of the game and happy to settle for a draw.

I've never exactly been a prolific goalscorer, but I have managed some stonkers during my career. In November 1998, I scored one such cracking goal, one of my best ever, against Wolves in a 2-0 win. We had a free-kick just outside the area and one of the lads dummied as if to hit it with his right foot, only to back-heel the ball to me, which I duly crashed into the net with my left. We had tried it a few times before, without any success, but on this occasion it worked beautifully.

However, my main memory is of playing against Dean Richards, a resolute and skilful centre-half, who had represented England at Under 21 level. 'Deano' was loved wherever he played, both on and off the pitch. Following a prestigious move to Spurs via Southampton, his career was cut short by illness. Although I was only watching on television, one of the most moving sights I've ever witnessed at a match was before the Premier match between Wolves and Tottenham in March 2011 just a week after Dean's tragic death from cancer at the age of thirty-six. Deano's partner and two small, bewildered sons took to the Molineux pitch to receive the overwhelming plaudits of the crowd. It was an extraordinary occasion befitting the great man.

Denis Smith wanted to bring in some new players, but there were no funds and a season that had promised much fizzled out in mid-table mediocrity and we ended up twelfth. Lee Hughes scored thirty-one goals (more than any other player in the Football League or the FA Premier League) but we leaked too many goals and weren't consistent enough. The manager ended the season under a lot of pressure and I felt sorry for him. But I was still enjoying myself, happy that I was playing regularly for such a great club. There was stuff going on behind the scenes that would inevitably shape my future. The club was, as I have said, in dire financial straits and just about surviving.

After a year's absence from the international scene I was also back playing for the Republic senior team and gained my fourth cap in a 2-0 win against Sweden in a friendly at Lansdowne Road. I was initially on the bench but came on and played much more effectively than in my previous three outings. Mick was introducing younger players into the squad and the whole team was developing a new look.

I was selected again for the Euro qualifier against Macedonia, also in Dublin, which took place on 9 June 1999 and which we won 1-0. I'd been injured before the game and was on the bench, but was called on again. It was an important victory and one that gave us much reason to feel triumphant. Although it was a very important day, there was another date a couple of days later that was even more personally significant and another reason to celebrate...Laura and I were getting married.

I tried to keep the event as quiet as possible as I knew I would take some stick – but inevitably there were a couple of stag nights during which I got hammered. I had a night out with my old mates from Preston and another locally in Birmingham, which my brother, Farrell, attended. We started off at Perry Bar dog track and ended up at Legs Eleven strip club. Not sure I told Laura about that...

The actual wedding took some organising – there were lots of backstage dramas involving my family. We could only have fifty guests at the reception, which suited us as we didn't want a huge affair, but I have loads of relatives whereas Laura comes from a much smaller family and there was much discussion, and subsequent strife, about guest lists.

We were married in St Chad's Cathedral in Birmingham by Father Patrick Daly. Farrell was best man and Laura's sister, Sally, and her cousin, Rose, were bridesmaids. Although it was a fairly low-key event, I felt more nervous than if I'd been playing in front of 50,000 at Lansdowne Road!

I think Mum might have wanted me to marry an Irish, or at least a Catholic, girl. She may also have thought we were too young – I was twenty-two and Laura a year younger. Dad did come to the wedding, but kept himself to himself and didn't get too involve in the occasion. As long as he had a pint to occupy him he was happy. I suppose he must have felt a bit of an outsider as he hadn't devoted much time to us as kids and my mum had pretty well brought us up single-handed. I later discovered that he had also fathered another child, a half-sister I've yet to meet. Mine was a pretty chaotic family.

Laura and I honeymooned at an all-inclusive resort in Antigua, where there were lots of other 'just married' couples. It was brilliant, but I was always aware of not overdoing the food or drink too much because I had to be back and ready for pre-season training a fortnight later.

Behind the scenes at the Hawthorns, Albion's major share-holder, Paul Thompson, was unhappy about the way the club was being run and the lack of progress under chairman Tony Hale, and there followed a campaign to relieve Hale of his duties. The chairman claimed that he had been given 'irrevocable pledges of cash from unnamed contacts' and that he would be putting more of his own money into the club. He also insisted that Denis Smith would remain at the helm. In fact, neither happened.

On the pitch, there was a pre-season tour to Denmark (thanks to a link-up with a well-funded amateur side, Greve, near Copenhagen). About 150 supporters followed us there and we played a couple of games – the first a 4-0 stroll against Greve, in which I scored two goals and then a 2-1 defeat to Odense. Our accommodation was unusual; we were billeted four to a room in an old school and were only let out on one night. During the trip, four of the lads were told that they were being placed on the transfer list. Not an ideal way to start the 1999–2000 season!

We continued our pre-season preparations in July with a testimonial game for defender Paul Raven against Sheffield Wednesday. Unfortunately, the turnout was very poor, which was such shame for him. He had been such a good club servant and deserved more. It made me think about what happens at the end of a career and how often loyalty goes unrewarded.

We lost the game and played pretty poorly but we weren't prepared for the aftermath. This result, although of no real significance, seemed to be the final straw for the club's board, who felt that the team weren't going to improve. They sacked Denis Smith soon after the game, but it was us, the players, who should have borne the responsibility. We had underachieved and I felt we had let Denis down. He is a good man and I felt sorry for him. The league programme was due to start in just eleven days' time and, as far as I know, it was the first time a manager had been dismissed following a poor performance in a testimonial! It's never great timing to lose your manager just before a new season is about to start.

Aston villa legend Brian Little assumed the manager's mantle. He'd been a great player and we got on well. He was quiet, never raised his voice and had a calm presence. He was extremely knowledgeable about the game and I continued to grow as a player and played well for West Brom while he was boss. In fact, Brian is one of the nicest men in football – perhaps too nice to be a successful manager. He appreciated me and gave me confidence to express myself. I remember a couple of goals, including two against Blackburn in September – one when I dribbled from the halfway line to equalise. Lee Carsley, who was then playing for Rovers and is now my best mate, still maintains that he could easily have brought me down but had heard I was about to be transferred and didn't want to be responsible for the deal being scrapped. All rubbish, of course. I was very happy at Albion and in any case he could never match me for pace!

The squad was strengthened by Andy Townsend, who had

retired from international football and was already beginning to make a name for himself as a pundit on ITV. He was brilliant to me, good to have around, and he always gave me good advice, especially about any possible moves: 'Take your time, don't get rushed into anything.' I was still only twenty-two and it was great to have that kind of experience to draw on, both on and off the field. Unfortunately, apart from Andy, because of the club's continuing financial problems there were no new signings and consequently no real ambition to improve our league position. We should at least have been aiming for a top-six finish, but we were expected just to plod along and somehow get through the season without any major disasters. We started unexpectedly well and won 2-1 at Port Vale in our first away game, a game in which I scored after a one-two with Lee Hughes. We were playing really well and our first defeat came after ten games.

Meanwhile, I had been called up again into the Irish squad and participated in three Euro qualifiers. It had taken me two years to settle into the international scene, to not feel intimidated by the senior players, to become accustomed to playing alongside my heroes and now I genuinely felt part of the setup. Gary Breen, Kenny Cunningham, Lee Carsley (Carso), Robbie, Ian Harte and Duffer were all starting to establish themselves. It was a great period.

I wasn't sure that I was going to play against Yugoslavia, but I did start and played well in a 2-1 win at Lansdowne Road on 1 September. Three days later we were beaten in Zagreb by Croatia, but went on to beat the group's whipping boys, Malta, 3-2 in Valetta. I was on the bench for the fateful game against Macedonia in Skopje a month later. We had advanced through the group and a win, in this the final group match, would clinch top spot in the group and an automatic qualifying place in the finals.

Niall Quinn opened the scoring after eighteen minutes and we held on to the lead without too much difficulty for most of the action. With about five minutes left on the clock, and to waste a little time, Mick replaced Mark Kennedy with some fresh legs in the shape of Keith O'Neill, who would also give us more attacking options. Mark turned to me and said, 'We're in the Euros!' Unfortunately, his prediction proved premature. Macedonia were awarded a corner in added time. One of the lads asked the referee how long there was to go. The man in black replied, 'When you clear the corner, I blow.' Unfortunately, we didn't clear the ball – Keith hadn't tracked his runner and Goran Stavrevski scored from the corner. We were devastated. It was absolutely heartbreaking that we had thrown away the game at the death and in the dressing room afterwards Mick was furious. He was desperate to qualify for the finals and felt terrible for some of the lads with whom he had previously played. I had never seen him so angry.

It was particularly ironic that Keith O'Neill was culpable as before the game he had been going around, in his customary manner, ranting and raving and trying to motivate the players with soul-stirring outbursts. The calm and unflappable Denis Irwin, who had recently won the European Cup with Manchester United, was tying up his bootlaces when Keith shouted at him, 'But do you want it, Denis? Do you really fucking want it?' I remember Denis peering over his shoulder and quietly saying, 'Get him out of my fucking face.' I think that was Keith's last appearance for Ireland; he retired at the age of twenty-seven with a chronic back injury.

Apart from the obvious – two play-off games against Turkey – there was another legacy from the game against Macedonia. From then on, after every training session the lads would secretly vote for the player who had performed the worst. At the next session, the unfortunate player then had to wear a specially designed training shirt with the slogan 'I had a Macedonia' across the chest. I had to wear this on regular occasions – it was really smelly, as if nobody had ever bothered to wash it. Later on, the Macedonians found out about this and were said to be insulted, although it was actually more of a slight against us than them.

It was also around this time that Liverpool's Steve Staunton approached me and told me that Gérard Houllier had asked 'Stan' to ask me if I would be interested in signing for Liverpool. 'Of course,' I said. Who wouldn't be? I was very flattered. There were apparently talks between WBA and Liverpool, but unfortunately nothing transpired. It's quite normal when international players meet up – the lads bring messages from managers and there are a few whispered conversations.

The first leg of the Euro play-off against Turkey took place on Saturday 13 November 1999 at Lansdowne Road and my appearance was the first in a run of sixty-six consecutive competitive games I was to play for the Republic (a record that lasted until 2011).

It was an evening kick-off and following our customary pre-match walk on the beach at Malahide and an afternoon's rest, the coach left the hotel at about six o'clock. There was already a buzz around the city and the atmosphere in the ground was electric, which galvanised us. We started brightly and I went close with a couple of long-range efforts. Robbie opened the scoring with about ten minutes to go after great work from Denis Irwin and David Connolly but four minutes later Carso fell in the area as he tried to clear and the ball rolled off his arm on to his chest. Turkey equalised from the penalty. The game ended 1-1 and the Turks had a crucial away goal.

The return leg was a few days later in Bursa. We discovered then why the Turks had chosen the town for their home venue at the end of a horrendous journey. It was a deliberate ploy to exhaust us before we had even stepped out on to the pitch. The trip began with a four-hour flight to Istanbul where, at the airport, we received a 'lively' welcome from Turkish fans – a sign of things to come. We then had a short coach ride before undertaking an hour-long ferry trip across the Bosphorus, linking Europe to Asia, which was made in total darkness. It was incredibly rough and lots of the lads were throwing up. It makes me laugh now to recollect that all Irish trips abroad were arranged by ex-Republic international Ray Treacy, who was himself frightened of flying and could get seasick in the bath!

We had another eighty minutes in the coach before we reached our hotel. We could also see signs of the damage and destruction caused by the recent earthquake and hundreds of plastic shacks, temporarily erected for families who had lost their homes. The plight of these poor people certainly put our own discomfort in the shade.

The Atatürk Stadium, named after the first president of Turkey, was both an intimate and intimidating atmosphere, and the importance of the match, the state of the pitch and the cold and blustery conditions did nothing to create a quality game. Robbie was suspended, but we were boosted by Niall Quinn passing a fitness test shortly before the game. Although we started well, we didn't manage a shot on target in the first half, whereas Dean Kiely, who was making his international debut, was called into action a couple of times with good saves. Stephen Carr was stretchered off with a leg injury after six minutes and was replaced by Jeff Kenna.

We played much better after the break and threw everything we could at the Turks, especially in the last ten minutes, when we put them under real pressure, but they defended as if their lives depended on it. The crowd were whistling long before the final whistle and the six minutes of stoppage time that was added. We just couldn't score and the game ended 0-0. We went out of the tournament on the away goal rule.

When the final whistle went, Turkish players and officials surged on to the pitch. As Tony Cascarino approached the tunnel, the Turkish full-back threw insults at him and, when Cas flicked out a boot, the Turk hit him with haymaker. Tony got stuck in and then a brawl broke out all around us.

I remember the Turkish riot police coming on to the pitch and whacking players with their truncheons as we left the field. Tony took refuge in the dressing room where Mick Byrne provided some ice for his swollen lip. It was sad that this turned out to be Tony's last international appearance and he later wrote that he felt guilty about initiating the brawl – although no one blamed him for reacting the way he did.

We had failed to qualify again for the Euros and felt devastated for ourselves, our fans and the nation. It was a desperate end to the campaign: we had been expected to qualify for the finals in Belgium and Holland but it wasn't to be. We sat in stunned silence on the coach and on the ferry journey and endured further hassle at Istanbul airport, before flying home via Frankfurt.

Back at West Brom, things weren't much better. Brian Little was unable to revive the team's fortunes (he was eventually sacked in March 2000 after just eight months in charge and replaced by Gary Megson) and we were languishing fifteenth in the league. I played in a 2-0 defeat at Crewe Alexandra on 7 December 1999 and, unexpectedly, this turned out to be my last game for Albion. We were due to play against Grimsby in another away game a few days later.

The night before the game, I received a call from Paul Stretford to say that talks were taking place between West Brom and Sunderland. On the bus the next day Paul rang to tell me that West Brom had accepted the bid. I asked Brian Little what was going on. He told me he didn't know anything about it. The journey up to Grimsby was miserable – the team weren't in the best of spirits and it was freezing cold and bucketing down with rain. We had travelled early and arrived at our hotel at lunchtime. We had a rest in the afternoon and then I attended the team talk, which took place at 4.30 p.m., about three hours before kick-off.

I was then informed that a deal had been agreed and I was immediately withdrawn from the playing squad. I sat in the stand and watched the first half before Paul Stretford arrived at Blundell Park, picked me up and we headed for Wearside. It all happened so quickly that I didn't even get a chance to say goodbye to the lads. In some ways it was easier than having a long-drawn-out goodbye. They can be emotional.

Apparently Brian Little wasn't happy about the transfer but the club needed some money quickly. Although I knew we were struggling financially, I hadn't realised that Albion had to raise funds to pay off a pressing loan, and that if I hadn't been sold there was a risk that the club could be put into administration, with the possibility of being docked points.

Some of the Albion fans were angry that I had been sold and, although the deal was valued at £2.5 million, other fans who didn't mind me going thought the fee was less than what I was worth. One of Albion's most established fanzines, Gorty Dick, summed up the mood of the fans: 'The sad tale of Kilbane's abrupt bargain departure is unfolding, accompanied by a raw anger, an emotion up there with other infamous events of recent years...where has the money gone? You know, if Albion are losing thousands then frankly it's the clubs fault with their appalling PR plus inflexible and unrealistic ticketing prices. Don't blame us. Having a fine tradition is not enough.'

Following my departure, the Albion chairman resigned and it was stated in the press that I hadn't been interested in extending my contract. In fact, I had no idea of the negotiations going on behind my back and I was never offered another contract. Just as had happened at Preston, WBA wanted it to appear as if they had done everything in their power to keep me.

This was another huge career move. Sunderland were in the Premiership. I was rapidly climbing up the leagues. This was surely going to be the most exciting time for me but for some reason I had doubts about the move.

Chapter Five

Wearside Woes

'May your blessings outnumber the shamrocks that grow and may
trouble avoid you wherever you go.'

IRISH BLESSING

The following morning I trained with the Sunderland lads although I still hadn't signed a contract. Looking back, I dread to think what would have happened if I'd been injured in training. Who would have been responsible? Albion, I suppose, as no forms had been signed, but they certainly wouldn't have been very happy about it. In any case, my future team-mates were very welcoming, the facilities were superb and I have to admit the money on offer was brilliant. The medical was much more stringent than the toe-touching at Albion and I spent most of the day at a local hospital where I had a full assessment and scans on both knees and ankles. All seemed fine…and yet, for some reason, I had my doubts about the move. I couldn't say what it was – a gut feeling that something wasn't right. I couldn't understand why my mood didn't reflect the circumstances. Inexplicable. I spoke to Paul Stretford again and then I telephoned Steve Harrison, 'I'm not sure about this, Harry. Something isn't right.'

My father in-law was brilliant and listened patiently to my ramblings. The trouble was there was no real reason not to sign.

He reassured me and reminded me that this was yet another step up. Sunderland were a great club, steeped in history and with fantastic fans. The team was sitting pretty in third position in the Premiership. This was an opportunity I had to grasp. Maybe I was daunted by playing for such a famous club, but I wanted to prove myself at the top level and I might not get another chance. By the end of the conversation I was convinced that this was the right move and one I had to seize.

By the time I had signed the four and a half year deal later that day I felt strangely elated and couldn't understand why I had felt so ill at ease earlier in the day. I had now experienced a complete change of heart and a total emotional turnaround.

Peter Reid, ex-Everton and England midfielder and Sunderland's manager, was the man who paid £2.5 million for me and I was delighted that such a legendary player as Peter wanted me as part of his team. He had been appointed late in the 1994–5 season and managed to keep the club from being relegated into the Second Division. The following year Sunderland were promoted to the Premier League, but were relegated back to the First Division at the end of the 1996–7 season before finally regaining Premiership status.

I was also very grateful to Niall Quinn, who had encouraged Peter Reid to add me to the Black Cats' squad. We were also international team-mates and Niall was convinced that I was ready to step up and play in the Premier League.

My first day at Sunderland came soon after Niall had won 'North East Player of the Year' and we had arranged a night out, which coincided with the award celebrations. We started in the Shakespeare pub, a well-known Durham haunt, and then moved on to the Dun Cow, reputed to be one of the oldest pubs in Durham, for a long night of drinking – quite an interesting beginning to life at my new club. It was during this evening that I met *Daily Mail* journalist Colin Young for the first time. He and I have become good mates, partly because he started reporting the Republic of Ireland matches at roughly the same time as I began my senior international career in 1997. Niall and I also became close friends – we ended up playing together at Sunderland for two and a half years and roomed together when we played for Ireland.

My first game was three days after I had officially joined the club – against Southampton at the Stadium of Light. There were nearly 50,000 fervent fans in the stadium, something I had never experienced before. I could see straightaway that this was going to be a whole new experience. I didn't start, but came off the bench and crossed the ball for Niall to head down for Kevin Phillips to score. It struck me as strange that during the match Peter Reid was getting stick from some of the crowd and yet we were third in the table.

On my way home after the first game I was mobbed by supporters on the train. Everyone welcomed me and was incredibly friendly. It was brilliant and it was only just beginning to dawn on me what a huge, high-profile club Sunderland was. The fans lived, breathed and died football and there was no escaping their attention.

Initially, Laura and I moved into a very comfortable club apartment in the Sunderland Marina. It was a great flat and we enjoyed living by the sea. The only problem was that I was sometimes the centre of attention for enthusiastic supporters and shopping at the local supermarket always took much longer than usual, especially when we were stopped for a chat or an autograph. I really don't think I was prepared for such interest but I never resented it and nor did I see it as intrusive. It's just that I wasn't used to such attention and I'm the sort of person who likes to keep things private. Their passion was extraordinary and I was full of admiration for their total commitment to the club.

Not long after I'd signed, on New Year's Eve, Laura and I were having dinner in a restaurant when a fellow diner left his wife at their table and joined me for a long football chat. After about half an hour, with Laura getting really fed up and our fellow diner ignoring the increasingly angry gestures of his wife to return to their table, I asked him if we could get on with our dinner. I hadn't wanted to be rude and really let the conversation go on much longer than I should have. He eventually rejoined his own, very pissed off, wife!

It was funny but I never really thought of myself as being 'in the limelight'; it was just a part of the job, but I didn't enjoy being watched and followed around. Things didn't change that much when we bought a house in the centre of Durham. Although we were less visible than in the centre of Sunderland, I used to get followed around the supermarkets in the cathedral city. It became a little easier for us to lead normal lives when I had been at the club for a little longer and, to be honest, I wasn't exactly the darling of the fans for very long!

After a great start to my Sunderland career, which couldn't have gone much better, it all went downhill very quickly and the love affair with the fans was very short-lived. I had made my full debut at Goodison Park, playing up front, and we got hammered 5-1. (We didn't win again until we played Everton at home at the end of March 2000.)

I started to get stick fairly early on at Sunderland. My arrival coincided with a long run without winning and supporters started to boo as soon as my name was announced. I thought it unfair that I was being blamed entirely for the inadequacies of the team and the poor results, but fans didn't agree. The kit man, John Cooke, once remarked, 'I wasn't liked here when I was a player. In fact, there's only one man who is less popular than me. And that's you!'

The more the fans booed me the more I wanted to do better. The choice I had was either to make myself scarce and not get involved or I could look for the ball and try to prove myself. The fans probably wished I had hidden – preferably in the dressing room – but I decided to take the latter approach. But to no avail. The more I tried the more mistakes I made and the worse I played. I grew increasingly frustrated by my form and the reaction of the fans. They must have seen I was trying, but I could also understand their behaviour. Sunderland had paid a lot of money for me and I wasn't delivering. But aiming abuse at me wasn't going to get me to play better. I scored at Wimbledon and vented my aggravation with an 'up yours' gesture, aimed at no one in particular but born out of frustration and unhappiness.

Surprisingly, we still finished seventh in the league – the best ever in the club's history and narrowly missed getting into Europe – mainly thanks to the proficiency of Kevin Phillips who notched thirty goals, making him the country's top goal scorer that year. He was actually the highest league scorer and therefore won the Golden Boot Award.

At the end of the season it was a relief to join the Irish squad, where I felt much more comfortable. I had played in several friendly internationals against the Czech Republic, Greece and Scotland, but as a result of not being involved in the Euro finals we were invited to participate in the US Cup. This was a competition, sponsored by Nike and organised by United States Soccer Federation, which was initiated in 1992. This year there were four teams in a 'round robin' tournament: the USA, South Africa, Mexico and us. This was actually Ireland's third appearance in the tournament which was arranged to raise some money for the FAI and which Roy Keane described as a 'Mickey Mouse' cup.

Our first game, on 4 June, was at Chicago's Soldier Field against Mexico, which ended in a 2-2 draw and attracted over 36,000 spectators. We hadn't been allowed out during our stay in Chicago and so, by the time we arrived in Boston, the lads were a bit stir crazy as we hadn't had a night out…in days. We were desperate to sneak out even for a pizza or a burger, never mind a drink.

The second match took place at the Foxboro Stadium in Boston – this time against the USA – and was also drawn. The conditions were terrible and we played the match in torrential rain. The attendance was about half that of the Mexico game and these were mainly Irish, based in Boston, or of Irish origin. As well as being played in a driving rainstorm, we suffered a power cut (or 'power outage', as the Americans describe it) for ten minutes because of the storm. The USA were awarded a goal by the Mexican officials that was blatantly offside and some of our officials hinted at a conspiracy: if we'd won that match, we would have won the tournament!

Because of the numbers of Irish expats in Boston, lots of the team had friends and family coming to see the game and the lads had arranged a night out in Boston afterwards. So we weren't best pleased when Mick told us that we weren't allowed to join them and refused us permission to leave the hotel. The party was cancelled, but surprisingly no one tried to sneak out and we all knuckled down to yet another night in the hotel.

The following morning we boarded the coach to New York, arriving at about 2 p.m. Mick then announced that we could have some time off but that we should be back at the hotel, which was on Lexington Avenue, in the middle of Manhattan, by seven the following evening for dinner. This was music to our ears. O'Neill's Irish bar was situated near Grand Central Station, just a few blocks from our hotel, and we headed there straightaway. The drinking was interrupted briefly by a short visit to a local nightclub, but we swiftly returned to O'Neill's where the atmosphere was much more to our taste. Ridiculous when you think we had the entire vibrant city of New York to explore and yet we spent nearly all our time in an Irish bar! We were out until about 5 a.m. – even Richard Dunne and Stephen McPhail, who were only twenty and were supposedly prohibited from imbibing alcohol in New York State until they were twenty-one!

I stumbled back to my bed and what seemed like only seconds later I was rudely awoken with a slap on my head by my room-mate, Niall Quinn, at about 10 a.m., telling me that we were all going back to O'Neill's for another session. He went round all the lads' rooms, banging on their doors and ordering them to be in the bar by eleven.

We spent the whole of the afternoon boozing and in the middle of proceedings Gary Kelly took Quinny's cowboy boots and threw them into the middle of a busy Manhattan avenue. On our return to the hotel some hours later, the boots were still exactly where Gary had thrown them and Niall put them on as if nothing had happened. We arrived back in time for dinner, as Mick had instructed, but everyone was totally bladdered. I can't remember much about it but I know we behaved badly. Food was being thrown everywhere – it was like a scene from *Bugsy Malone* – and bread rolls were being lobbed across the dining room. One hit Father Paddy O'Donovan directly on the noggin, but he didn't seem to mind. Father O'Donovan was an Irish priest, based in New Jersey, who accompanied the Irish team when we were in the USA, providing pastoral care and saying Mass for us on Sundays. I suppose we should have spent some time in the confessional box after that sort of behaviour.

After dinner we went straight out again, only this time the curfew was midnight and we all stuck to it – just as well: alcohol poisoning was a real possibility by that stage.

The following day we embarked upon a short ride to some playing fields in New Jersey, where we were supposed to 'train'. I use the term loosely. It has to have been the most chaotic training session I've ever seen or participated in. The boys were falling all over the place, throwing up and collapsing with exhaustion and nausea. Unfortunately, a group of students from New York University had come to watch us and study our technique. I remember they carried clipboards and were furiously taking notes. I dread to think what they must have written down or what they thought they were learning from the experience. It was a disgrace!

Although the end of the tour must sound shambolic, it was a brilliant trip and, in retrospect, Mick handled it perfectly. The time we spent together in the USA really cemented the team's spirit and the camaraderie we all enjoyed was fantastic. It was the making of the team that was to perform so well in the coming years. The final game took place on 11 June at the New York Giants Stadium, East Rutherford, New Jersey, when we beat South Africa 2-1.

Father Paddy O'Donovan is an interesting character. Following his ordination, he went to work for the Diocese of Paterson, New Jersey, and in 1994, like many Irish Americans, got caught up in the World Cup being staged in the US. By force of circumstance he was asked to advise on training facilities for the Irish team and became a sort of ecclesiastical gofer, personal valet for various members of the FAI and some team members, arranging dinners, golf and other social gatherings. He told me, 'I was on top of the world in those days, like a child in a playpen, quite a large playpen!'

He was also called into action before my time and our tour. In June 1996, the lads had beaten Bolivia 3-0 at the Giants Stadium and returned to the Madison hotel in Morrison. Mick McCarthy asked Father Paddy if he could arrange a place for the boys to go and celebrate. Paddy takes up the story: 'It was a Saturday night and so I checked out a local Irish pub. The owner rightly made me aware that most of the boys were under the legal age (twenty-one) for drinking in New Jersey and he could not risk losing his licence. I then put plan B into effect, and steered the jubilant players to another American establishment. We had a great time and the boys were in the best of form. Close to midnight I decided to leave as I had early Sunday Mass to celebrate.'

The following morning, Paddy received a call from Mick. 'Paddy,' he said, 'we have a problem. One of the boys got in a spot of trouble last night. We are flying today and this lad has a court date to deal with.'

Apparently one of the players decided to continue with the celebrations and 'accidentally' kicked a potted palm tree outside a club. The bouncer demanded $200 in cash and if the money was not immediately forthcoming he would call the police. The international told him to 'be fruitful and multiply' – although not in those words – and the police were duly called.

Paddy offered to talk to the newly appointed state prosecutor to see what could be done. In between the Sunday Masses, Paddy tracked down the prosecutor, who told Father O'Donovan to collect the summons from the player and he would do his best to deal with the delicate incident. Paddy recalled, 'It truly was an international affair that was kept away from the press. That was a kind of coup for us back then. These were teenagers out for a good time, and it seems they had one to remember. In getting to be part of the hospitality afforded the Ireland team when they visited America, I got to know such wonderful men who represented Ireland. As an immigrant I took great pride in reaching out to them and offering a "cead mile failte".'

In the summer of 2000, at the beginning of my second season at Sunderland, left-winger Julio Arca joined the club and I moved into right midfield. Julio was one of the most popular players to represent Sunderland and, although hailing from Buenos Aires, he embraced Wearside completely. On one occasion the squad had a day out at Roker Beach and Julio got stung by a jellyfish; one of the lads had to pee in a cup and pour the contents on Julio's foot.

After the summer break, I had returned to training with Sunderland determined to do better and prove my critics wrong. I still thought I had something to contribute and despite my onfield problems didn't feel I had made a mistake in joining this great club. There was no doubt, however, that club form simply didn't match my international performances, leading to

Peter Reid's throwaway remark, 'For your sake, I just wish that Sunderland played in green.'

In those days Peter didn't spend a huge amount of time on the training ground. His assistant, Bobby Saxton, and coach, Adrian Heath, took most of the sessions although Peter liked working on set plays.

I agreed with Niall, who said that Reidy exhibited a great belief and trust in his players. If you gave him everything you had and were totally committed, he would always be loyal to you. If the effort wasn't there, he could lose his temper. Peter Reid was definitely a match-day manager. He came into his own on the morning of the game and was a great motivator. He treated each player as an individual and knew their strengths and weaknesses and made sure any advice was tailored to their personality. He always made a point of giving final instructions before we left the dressing room and we all listened because we trusted him.

I was in the Sunderland team at the start of the season and I thought I was playing well. My involvement in the World Cup qualifying games in the autumn really helped my confidence. I played one of my best games for the Republic in a 2-2 draw in Holland, followed up by a 1-1 draw against Portugal in Lisbon and a 2-0 victory in Dublin against Estonia.

I was involved in a number of internationals during the season. Apart from a friendly against Finland, the other five matches were World Cup qualifiers for the 2002 tournament. I remember the game against Cyprus in Lefkosia, which we won 4-0 thanks to an inspired performance from Roy Keane, but I recall it mainly for the fact that Mick McCarthy's Irish father, Charlie McCarthy, died in Yorkshire and Mick flew back to Barnsley for the funeral. He then returned to Cyprus for the game which Roy Keane took by the scruff of the neck, scoring twice.

I scored in the 3-0 victory over Andorra, which was played in Barcelona. Although I'd netted in a friendly against Finland at Lansdowne Road, this was my first competitive goal for my country and I got on the score sheet again in the home game a month later in which we ran out 3-1 winners. I've always liked playing against Andorra. Make of that what you will. There were two further World Cup qualifiers in June. We drew with Portugal and beat Estonia in Tallinn a few days later.

I loved being part of the squad. Mick was great to play for and, apart from what happened on the pitch, there was the craic and lots of music. Mick arranged for Finbar from the Fureys folk group to play at our hotel one night. I couldn't believe how much booze Finbar put away – he must have had about twenty pints and whisky chasers, but still managed to perform brilliantly. We also had other legends such as Patsy Watchorn, previously with the Dublin City Ramblers and the Dubliners, doing a set for us. Whenever we were on the coach, we would listen to classic Fureys' songs like 'The Green Fields Of France', 'When You Were Sweet Sixteen' and 'Red Rose Café', and other great favourites were Paddy Reilly, Christy Moore, the Wolf Tones, Luke Kelly, the Dubliners and, of course...the Pogues!

Mick's successor, Brian Kerr, also liked to try and get singers or groups to perform for us and had Irish rock group Aslan play a full set for us one night. That was a massive highlight. Andy Reid would always play guitar after games and the lads would always have a good singsong together. U2's drummer, Larry Mullin, who used to attend every home game, once came into the dressing room with his offspring. The kid had very long hair and I assumed she was Larry's daughter. I don't know who was more embarrassed when I was told he was Larry's son!

In other times, in the long hours in hotels, I have really fond memories of get-togethers around ten o'clock at night when we would congregate for tea and toast. There was always plenty of chat and Kenny Cunningham used to like initiating discussions on every subject under the sun. Everyone would get involved and it was always brilliant fun.

We also used to occupy ourselves by playing board games such as Who Wants to be a Millionaire? Scrabble (Alan Kelly always won) and Trivial Pursuit. I remember one game of Who Wants to be a Millionaire? in which Stephen Carr had to answer the question: 'In what street does the British Prime Minister live?' Stephen had the option of four answers but replied, 'Quality Street'. The lads were hysterical with laughter – particularly as Stephen's an intelligent lad. He's never lived that down.

I started the 2001–2 premiership season brightly, but unfortunately I picked up an injury in the match against Manchester United in September. I had experienced minor difficulties with my left ankle but this was my right one and a little more serious. I was expected to be out for at least four weeks, which made me doubtful for the first of the two World Cup qualifying play-off games against Iran in November. I spoke to Mick and said I was determined to be in the frame. He was great and just said: 'If you're fit, you'll play.'

I worked hard in rehab to get back to full fitness with the Sunderland staff, but Mark Leather, the Sunderland physiotherapist, was pretty pessimistic from the outset. There was an away game at Leicester ten days before the game in Dublin, which we didn't think I was going to make, but he was also convinced that I wouldn't make the game in Dublin. I think he really wanted me not to play at all for my country and to return to club duty having given my ankle a good rest. I understood that Sunderland's interests were his only concern, but I was desperate to represent my country in such important games. I hadn't really had any difficulty before with Mark, but I thought he was being deliberately unhelpful.

I told Peter Reid that I thought the Leicester game was going to be too soon for me and he told me he quite understood about my need to play for Ireland. We worked hard at getting me back to full fitness, but it was bit of a struggle as my ankle was still painful. Three days before the Leicester game, Mark had me trying to balance on a beam and jumping off a trampoline on to my bad ankle, which really wasn't up to such exercise at this stage. It was too early.

The following day we did some ball work with fitness coach Gerry Delahunt. Gerry rolled the ball to me and Mark was behind me, as if marking me. Every time I received the ball, Mark would kick me on the calf or the back of my bad ankle. This went on for a while and I just couldn't work out why Mark was doing this. It got to the point where I got so fed up with him that I gave him an elbow to get him to stop.

The day after, Mark suggested a two against two game of hockey with Gerry and Michael Reddy, who was also recovering from an ankle injury. During the game, Mark kept catching my ankle with his hockey stick. After a few times and much pain I finally snapped, and I gave him a left hook and decked him, leaving him with a fat lip and a very surprised look on his face. I went straight to see Bobby Saxton, the first team coach, and told him what had happened. Bobby was quite sympathetic when I explained the circumstances and understood my desperation to get fit as quickly as I could. He realised the sort of behaviour I'd exhibited wasn't me – it just wasn't in my nature to hit a colleague. Bobby said he would tell Peter Reid what happened, but I never heard another word.

I later apologised to Mark Leather but was disappointed that he didn't reciprocate. Things were never right between us personally after that, although we didn't let it interfere with our professional relationship.

I actually watched the Leicester game from the stands – this was the game in which £5.5 million striker Ade Akinbyi, who had gone fifteen games without a goal, finally scored and celebrated by removing his shirt to reveal a ridiculously muscular torso!

I was fit to play in the first of the two World Cup play-off games against Iran, the first on 11 November 2001 in Dublin.

The Iranians packed out the North Terrace with nearly four thousand fans, most of whom were based in the UK and had travelled over for the weekend. They certainly made themselves heard and there was little for our fans to cheer at the beginning as we tried to get the ball, route-one style, to target man Niall, but without much success. The Iranians were quite composed and patient, waiting to hit us on the counter-attack. We managed to put a bit more pressure on the Iranians as the game progressed, but my main memory was of the slapstick Iranian keeper, Ebrahim Mirzapour, who punched every ball clear and stayed on the ground after every save, clutching different parts of his anatomy as if mortally injured. The referee seemed to be fooled by the keeper's antics and failed to punish him for blatant time-wasting.

We went ahead in the first half thanks to an Ian Harte penalty and started the second much more confidently, playing with better rhythm, and, within six minutes of the restart, Robbie Keane had doubled our lead with a half-volley into the roof of the net. I had a couple of shots saved, but the Iranians came back at us strongly towards the end of the match. We ran out 2-0 winners thanks to another outstanding performance from Shay Given, who was voted the man of the match.

The return leg took place in Tehran, a few days later.

Unfortunately, we saw nothing of the sights and culture of Iran; in fact, the only scenery we saw was on the trips between the airport and the training ground and the hotel. We weren't allowed out of the hotel and security was incredibly tight with armed guards in reception and at the end of every corridor.

The match was played in the ugly, concrete cauldron of the Azadi Stadium in Tehran where 120,000 spectators started filling the terraces seven hours before the game kicked off. The stadium shook with the timed chanting, drums and fireworks and the dramatic blaring of the Muslim call to prayer, just a minute before kick-off, fooled Steve Staunton into clapping the cacophony enthusiastically, thinking it was the Iranian national anthem.

Mick decided to be positive and, in the absence of the injured Niall Quinn, started the match with David Connolly and Robbie Keane in attack. We were on the back foot for most of the match, but thanks to some strong defending and yet another immense performance from Shay, Iran failed to score until the final minute of normal time when we conceded a corner, resulting in a headed goal for Iran. By then thousands of their supporters had departed and we managed not to concede another goal.

As soon as the final whistle went, we were ushered off the pitch and into the dressing room where we immediately cele-brated our place in the World Cup finals. We had to make do with Lucozade and water because of the Islamic ban on alcohol, but it didn't matter – we had made it to the finals in Japan and South Korea! All the backroom staff and squad members joined us. Physiotherapist Ciaran Murray had enrolled with the Under 21 setup at the same time as me and he was really excited. We couldn't believe how far we'd come. Mick gave a short speech saying how proud he was of our achievement and what it meant to him. Only one photographer, Dave Maher, was allowed in the dressing room to record our triumph.

There was another fascinating cultural consequence of the match in Tehran. Women had been banned from Iranian foot-ball stadiums after the 1979 revolution but for our match the mullahs relented and gave special dispensation for forty Irish women to attend the crucial World Cup play-off. Irish fan Nicola Byrne wrote a brilliant article in the *Observer* a few days after the match in which she described the anger of the Iranian men at the presence of women at the match – even though they were veiled and dressed modestly.

Some of the male Irish supporters also donned veils, which didn't go down very well, and, as the game progressed, Nicola described the scene: 'Stones, pieces of concrete and smoke bombs rained down as it became increasingly obvious that it was Ireland and not Iran who would be going to the World Cup next year. Holding aloft burning programmes, thousands of Iranians proceeded to pool the flames, creating bonfires all around. Under an enormous mural of the late Ayatollah Khomeini, Iranians ripped out and set fire to seats, tore down banners depicting images of the country's senior mullahs and trashed the windscreens of several hundred cars outside. Riot police were quickly deployed.' We were unaware of all that going on, but were certainly noticed the flares and fires!

For the journey home, Leeds United actually arranged a private jet for their players (Ian Harte, Robbie Keane and Gary Kelly) in order for them to return more quickly than the rest of us. The Leeds manager, David O'Leary, was keen to get them home early so that they could prepare for their league match a couple of days later against…Sunderland at the Stadium of Light.

On our flight, the champagne corks started popping as soon as our chartered plane took off and we Sunderland players (Jason McAteer, Quinny and myself), as well as the other lads, were on the lash for the next forty-eight hours. The funny thing was that, despite this not being exactly the best way of preparing for an important game against Leeds, it didn't seem to do us any harm: we beat our Yorkshire rivals 2-0!

That game was one of the few victories we enjoyed during a 2001–2 campaign that brought us little joy. It was a relief that we narrowly avoided relegation, although we were the lowest scoring team in the Premier League (twenty-eight goals), ending the season in seventeenth place. We were knocked out of both English cup competitions in the first round. It was a season to forget and so I was delighted to join up with the Irish squad for the World Cup finals in Japan and South Korea, which I'll write about in the next chapter.

After holidaying in Dubai with Laura, I returned to preseason training at Sunderland. It turned out to be dramatic…

The club went on a pre-season tour of Belgium and during a match against Genk in Antwerp in August 2002 I let my frustrations get the better of me. I'd even got slaughtered during the warm-up when our fans let their feelings be known: 'Fuck off, Kilbane, you're shit', and 'You should have stayed in fucking Japan' were among the milder taunts.

The abuse really affected me and so, by the time the game started, I wasn't feeling my most confident. The season hadn't even started, for goodness' sake, and I was already a target. Anyway, I was playing on the right down by the touchline and tried to cross the ball to the near post. I mishit it completely and the ball sailed over the bar and into the crowd. I didn't mean to mess up the cross; if anything, I was trying too hard. A number of the Sunderland fans gave me a typical tirade of abuse and I just lost it. I just wanted to get them off my back so I gave the fans the V-sign and the crowd erupted. I'd created an even more vitriolic reaction. One supporter tried to get on the pitch to have a go at me but luckily he was restrained by stewards. I knew I shouldn't have reacted like that but I had had enough. Peter Reid, who had also been a target of the three hundred travelling fans, was totally sympathetic and took me off straightaway. I watched the rest of the game from the bench – but even then a couple of irate 'supporters' tried to get at me and Peter, causing the referee to stop the match for nearly ten minutes.

I honestly thought I had played my last game for the club after the match, but the following day I made a contrite statement: 'I want to offer my sincere apologies to the supporters. They travel a long way to the games and spend their cash and I deeply regret what I did. It was a moment of frustration and things just got the better of me. It was my first game back, I was tired and things just boiled over. I am devastated by the whole thing because it is always my aim when I go on the pitch to try my best for the supporters. I just want to give my all, which is what I have always tried to do, and what I will do in the future.'

Both the manager and skipper Michael Gray came to my defence. Peter Reid was quoted as saying, 'You cannot react the way Kevin did, but he is a model pro, a sincere fella and he has just made a mistake.' Michael stated, 'Kevin could not be more popular in the dressing room and we all see his ability on the training pitch. He has just struggled to produce for the first team. He knows what he did during this game was wrong, but frustration just got to him. I ask the fans to stick with him because he has a lot to produce for the club, and we will never see it if they get on his back.'

It was stated in the press that I had been fined a week's wages, but this never actually happened. Peter Reid was always very good at protecting his players.

I started the opening game of the season against Blackburn, but I was booed when substituted near the end of the match. It wasn't the best way of starting a new season and I sat out the next game, a 1-0 home win over Everton. I was disappointed but understood why I had been omitted – perhaps an appearance at the Stadium of Light in front of thousands of fans might have been difficult so soon after the incident in Genk. Although I was in the squad, once again I didn't make the bench. All I wanted to do was play and Reidy told me, 'If you get your head down, work hard, I'll put you in the team.' But I knew that I couldn't be in a situation in which I was going to be left out for home games and played in the away game the following week. It was totally unrealistic.

I felt that I had always suffered at Sunderland, when I first arrived, by having to replace Allan 'Magic' Johnston, who had been a darling of the fans and was quite a different player from me. Allan was more flamboyant and a crowd pleaser, but had been sent out on loan to Birmingham and Bolton Wanderers when he failed to renew his contract, wanting to secure a move to Glasgow Rangers. Maybe it would have been different if I had made an immediate impact on the team.

The Genk incident provoked a lot of interest in the local press and there were lots of calls for me to be sold. According to some supporters, I wasn't fit to wear the Sunderland shirt, which hurt me a great deal. I spoke to my agent Paul Stretford and told him I was desperate to get away. I was prepared to go anywhere but the problem was that I wasn't playing well and now I was getting a reputation for falling out with my own fans, the kiss of death for most professionals. Paul put the word out that I was after a move. I was very unhappy and sure that my future on Wearside was coming to an end. I'd heard through compatriots Dean Kiely and Mark Kinsella that Alan Curbishley was interested in signing me for Charlton Athletic, who were in the Premiership. I would have jumped at a move but it never happened.

Peter Reid stuck by me, even though he was under a lot of pressure and had beer thrown over him after one game! He told me not to worry and said he wanted to keep me. I didn't actually ask for a transfer – I had vowed never to do that again and the club, to my knowledge, didn't try to sell me.

My professional difficulties were also affecting my married life: Laura was hurt by the abuse I was receiving and the whole situation was making her very unhappy. She probably found it harder to accept than I did and was often reduced to tears. There was a story in the local press that she had asked me to request a transfer, which of course she never did, and the paper had to retract the story; they sent her a bouquet of flowers by way of an apology. Laura wouldn't come to games as she couldn't bear to see me humiliated and it reached the point where I didn't want to leave her on her own at home.

I was really pleased, then, when I became friendly with Gavin McCann (Preston and Blackpool together, at last!!!). Gavin and I shared a number of interests, particularly music, and we used to go to quite a few gigs together. I remember a *New Musical Express* tour of up-and-coming bands that included Manchester Indie band Alfie and Irish group JJ72. I remember crowd-surfing at Newcastle University Students' Union where Northern Ireland outfit Ash were playing.

And, of course, the abuse didn't just come from Sunderland fans. I once had to leave a nightclub in Newcastle for my own safety. Laura and Laura's sister, Sally, were in Baja's. It was still quite early and we hadn't been there long when a Newcastle fan recognised me and said, 'Go back to your own city, you Mackem twat!' He obviously spread the word that I was in the club and soon the mood became quite intimidating with a number of other clubgoers threatening me. We left after one drink. It was very unfortunate and I felt sorry for Laura and Sally. It's ridiculous that football partisanship should become so personal.

The squad was strengthened on deadline day in August by the signings of Tore Andre Flo and fellow striker Marcus Stewart. Peter Reid paid a club record £6.75 million for the Norwegian striker from Rangers, and the total cost of the transfers amounted to £10 million. Tore had struggled in Glasgow, but Reidy obviously felt that he was a natural replacement for Niall, who was struggling with a long-term back injury. Niall played his last game for the club on 19 October 2002 against West Ham before retiring from football a month later.

Niall was a huge loss to the club. Apart from his obvious abilities, he was a great influence in the dressing room. Everyone in the North East loved him, regardless of whom they supported, and tribal loyalties were mainly set aside when it came to the charismatic Niall, who still draws people to him. Bright, easygoing and charming, and always approachable, Niall was great fun to be around and always supportive of me.

Although Tore scored in his debut match, a 1-1 draw with Manchester United, he never made his mark and was a very different player from Niall and not nearly as strong in the air as Quinny. Tore never really settled and he took my place as the butt of the fans' abuse. I was sorry for him but I have to admit it was a relief for me!

The Sunderland hierarchy finally lost their patience with Reidy and he was sacked in October, following a league victory over Aston Villa. I thought it was a bit harsh but the club wanted him out. Mick McCarthy had left the Irish job the very same month and there was talk of him coming in, which would have been brilliant for me, but in the end the Sunderland board chose Howard Wilkinson.

It wasn't the most popular of appointments. The Sunderland fans didn't want Howard – he was considered a bit dour and uncharismatic and he didn't have a very good relationship with the media. It was probably a mistake to have Steve Cotterill as his number two as Steve had been manager of Stoke – albeit briefly – and probably found it difficult not being in charge. Also, the two of them had never worked together before although Howard obviously thought that Steve's reputation as a highly qualified coach would be helpful.

Training was different under Howard Wilkinson. It was much more structured and there was much more talk and planning. We discussed team shape, set pieces and watched videos of opponents. I felt this was needed and a number of players welcomed his approach, although a few of the lads found it all too tedious. There was, however, some concern that some players were losing their fitness as the training wasn't so physical and so some of us did extra to maintain our levels. Howard played me in central midfield and I found myself in the team every week. Although things weren't going so well for the team, the fans were actually much better to me and there was very little stick.

Sadly, we only registered two league victories under the new management team and both Howard Wilkinson and Steve Cotterill were sacked after just twenty games in charge and six successive Premiership defeats left us facing relegation. On 12 March 2003, Mick McCarthy was appointed manager. Unfortunately, the damage had already been done early in the season and we played the rest of the campaign under huge pressure and the threat of relegation. The team was performing poorly, morale was low and we actually lost every match under Mick's stewardship, conceding lots of late goals. Our final result of the season, a 4-0 defeat to Arsenal, established us as the worst Premier League team ever with a record low of four wins, nineteen points and twenty-one goals.

Fortunately, Mick kept his job, the blame for our relegation being placed on the two previous administrations. It was a horrible feeling to be relegated nonetheless – we'd let everyone down and our terrible record was evidence of how badly we had performed during 2002–3.

Laura and I couldn't get away quickly enough at the end of the season, and on our return from Majorca we found out that she was pregnant. We were both thrilled – we had always wanted children. I was delighted at the prospect of being a dad.

I was pretty convinced, too, that I'd soon be on my way out of Sunderland as, at the end of the season, lots of the playing staff moved on. The club had massive debts and was forced to recoup money on transfers and reduce the wage bill.

On the 2003–4 pre-season tour Mick called me into his hotel room to say that the club had accepted a bid from Southampton. Gordon Strachan was keen on signing me and I agreed to the move. In fact, nothing more happened and it was frustrating because I wanted to return to the Premiership. In the end the Saints signed another left-sided midfielder player, Neil McCann from Glasgow Rangers.

So, surprisingly, I started the new season as a Sunderland player, although I was in the last year of my contract. And despite all the difficulties, I was happy to knuckle down and try and get Sunderland back in the top flight. Despite being relegated, there had been some rebuilding and I felt we had a good squad and should be able to achieve a play-off place.

Unfortunately, the campaign got off to bad start with defeat at home to Nottingham Forest, quickly followed by a home defeat to Millwall, thereby creating a record of sixteen league defeats in a row. Luckily, we stopped the rot at Deepdale, of all venues, and had a couple of wins in quick succession – the second one being at Bradford City, where we ran out 4-0 winners. This was to be my last game for Sunderland: the following morning I received a telephone call from Paul Stretford. I discovered that David Moyes had inquired about me going to Everton.

The transfer window closed the next day and so a deal needed to be sorted pretty quickly. At first I was advised that a fee had been agreed for a permanent transfer, but then Everton had decided they wanted to take me on loan. I agreed to this if it could be done in time.

For most of Sunday night there seemed to be a stand-off between the clubs while Paul Stretford tried desperately to broker a deal. Lee Carsley rang me and asked what was happening: 'Everyone's talking about your transfer! Are you coming or not?'

Laura hadn't been at all well during her pregnancy and had been sick pretty much all the time, or so it seemed (in fact, this was hyperemesis gravidarum, the same condition that Kate Middleton suffered from during her pregnancy), and she had been staying with her parents in Wynyard, County Durham. Harry had been appointed assistant manager at Middlesbrough by Steve McClaren, and he and Laura's mum had followed us to the North East. Pretty lucky, really, as Laura had moved in with her parents so that her mum, Christine, could look after her while she was ill. Laura had continued to work for a modelling agency for a while, but gave that up when she started to feel unwell.

Mick McCarthy rang me at the Harrisons to tell me that the permanent transfer was now back on as he had refused to let me leave Sunderland on loan, and that I was in the clear to talk to Everton. I met Paul Stretford who was already at Everton's training ground, Bellefield, sorting out another loan deal for a player who was going from Arsenal to Everton.

It was a slightly unusual arrangement in that a fee of one million pounds was agreed but Everton would take on the responsibility for my existing Sunderland contract, which had nearly a year to run, and I would thus be on the same wages. There was also an option for another year if all went well. I went to the training ground at Bellefield to meet my old team-mate David Moyes who was unequivocal in his welcome: 'There are no guarantees while you're here. You've got until the end of the season to prove yourself.' It was just what I wanted to hear.

Again, the deal had been done prior to any medical having taken place but Mick Rathbone, my old physiotherapist from Preston, had since joined Everton and the club was confident in his knowledge of my medical history and that he could vouch for the fact that I had never had any serious injuries. In any event, Baz took me to a local Liverpool hospital for a complete medical.

Most of the deadline day was spent trying to sort out the deal. Everton's chief executive, Michael Dunford, processed the paperwork seconds before the 5 p.m. documentation cut-off point. The deal was done and dusted just before the deadline.

Despite the problems, I mainly enjoyed my football at Sunderland. They say that what doesn't kill you makes you stronger and I hoped that I was now more robust from my experience. Playing at the Stadium of Light had been an interesting experience. Despite the passion of the fans, there was sometimes a lack of atmosphere in the ground when we were playing sides who the fans felt we should be beating easily. The place really came alive, however, when we were up against some of the bigger Premiership teams and the fans really got behind us and the famous 'Roker Roar' was heard at the Stadium of Light.

I gave an interview to the press at Dublin airport and was reported as saying, 'Funnily enough, when it came to it I didn't feel desperate to leave Sunderland although I know lots of the fans were keen to see me go! I felt things were picking up under

Mick and I was looking forward to the challenge of trying to help them achieve promotion.' Recalling this statement now, I realise I was being disingenuous, that I was simply unable to speak my mind at the time. Although I was happy playing under Mick, I really wanted to leave and to be back playing in the Premiership. And I wasn't the only one: I was actually the sixteenth senior player to leave after Sunderland were relegated.

Chapter Six

A Spot of Trouble

JOEY: Look, I know you're hurtin' now, but in time you'll realize
what you've achieved.
JIMMY: I've achieved nothing!
JOEY: You're missin' the point. The success of the band was
irrelevant – you raised their expectations of life, you lifted
their horizons. Sure we could have been famous and made
albums and stuff, but that would have been predictable.
This way it's poetry.

THE COMMITMENTS, 1991

As soon as the 2001–2 season ended I was involved in Niall Quinn's testimonial match between Sunderland and a Republic of Ireland XI at the Stadium of Light, which was to take place on 14 May, just a few days before we were due to fly off to the World Cup finals. Naturally, there were no appearance fees, but each player received a letter from a sick child, which seemed wholly right and was very touching. Both Quinny and I played for each side and I actually scored against my own club ten minutes from the end.

The game and testimonial events raised about a £1 million, which was to be divided between two hospitals – the Royal Infirmary in Sunderland and Our Lady's Hospital for Sick

Children in Crumlin. The absence of Roy Keane caused a stir in the media although we thought nothing of it, especially in light of what was to come.

Roy told Quinny and Mick that he had suffered an injury and been told by the Manchester United doctor to travel to France for treatment and that he would not make the match. In the press it was reported as a snub, which infuriated Roy and only confirmed his opinion of certain journalists. There was some suggestion that he should at least have gone to the game as a spectator, but he didn't think this would benefit the occasion in any way and in any case he was about to be away from his wife and kids for a month at the World Cup finals.

Following the testimonial, we flew to Dublin for a friendly against Nigeria which we lost 2-1 and in which Roy and I played for an hour. Mick later revealed that he hadn't thought the defeat was such a bad thing – he felt that the result lowered outside expectation and helped us to not get too carried away after some excellent results in other recent friendlies. We enjoyed a stirring send-off at Lansdowne Road and Paddy Reilly, then a member of the Dubliners, came on to the pitch to give a rendition of 'Fields Of Athenry'. Both sides ended the occasion with a lap of honour.

Mick McCarthy wanted a relaxed build-up to the tournament and decided that Saipan, a large tropical island in the Pacific, should be our base. It is one of the most humid places in the region and was deliberately chosen by Mick as he believed that if we could acclimatise to the stifling conditions there we would be able to cope anywhere.

There was pandemonium at Dublin airport where we were due to embark on the seventeen-hour KLM flight to Saipan via Amsterdam and Tokyo. Hundreds of well-wishing fans, wanting autographs and photographs, crowded out the check-in area. In the VIP lounge Bertie Ahern, Taoiseach and huge Manchester United supporter, added his presence to the crowds and two guys dressed as leprechauns promoting the *Sun* newspaper were hassling Roy Keane. For me all this was just part of the pleasure of playing for Ireland – we were unlike any other footballing country and I loved every moment of it.

Our base in the South Pacific hideaway of Garapan, Saipan, was the Hyatt Regency hotel, which was situated right on the beach. It was a fantastic, luxurious place in which to recharge our batteries after a long, exhausting season. The island of Saipan was a fascinating place and on 2 June 1944 had been the scene of a notable battle between Japanese and American forces during the Second World War. While there, I experienced an incredibly poignant trip to 'Suicide Cliff'. The tour guide informed us that, in the last days of the battle, more than a thousand Japanese civilians living on the island committed suicide. Emperor Hirohito was concerned that the residents might be used by the Americans for propaganda purposes and so promised that the civilians would be assured an equal spiritual status in the afterlife with those of soldiers who had died in combat. Tragically, entire families leapt from 'Suicide Cliff' in age order – the youngest first. The father would then jump backwards, facing the enemy and thus in defiance of the Americans.

The Regency Hyatt was very comfortable with all the facilities you could ask for, but we soon realised that other arrangements were not as they should have been. The training pitches were definitely sub-standard. In fact, they were rock-hard, full of potholes and positively dangerous. They were as dry as dust and when they were finally watered after our arrival, the pitches flooded. We also quickly discovered that the skips containing our training kit and equipment hadn't arrived and were stuck in an airport somewhere. We had to practise in our own clothes. Initially there were also no footballs and only two goals had been provided. The hydration drinks, which we had been told were so important, were also missing. There was a shouting match between Alan Kelly and Roy at the end of one training session when it was decided that the goalkeepers were too tired to be involved in a practice match. Packie Bonner had worked them extremely hard in shooting and fitness sessions earlier and the humidity had really taken it out of them.

Naturally, we all thought that these things were extremely unfortunate, but that we didn't have any choice other than just to get on with it and make the best of a bad situation. Roy felt differently. He had experienced an extremely competitive season for Manchester United and wanted to keep up the momentum and the work ethic going. He was despairing of the preparations, which at best he perceived as much too laid back and at worst chaotic. He felt that by failing to prepare, we had to be prepared to fail.

Of course Roy's criticism of the FAI had some history – he had previously been horrified that the 'blazers' of the Irish FA were sitting in the first class section of the aeroplane when flying to Cyprus while the players were stuck in 'cattle class' with the journalists. His experience at Manchester United was that the players were treated with the utmost respect and given the best treatment. In addition, his relationship with Mick McCarthy had been uneasy ever since Mick's uncertain beginnings as manager and then the two of them had fallen out at the end of a US Cup competition in Boston in 1992 when a heated argument nearly led to blows.

A few days after our arrival in Saipan, Mick arranged a beach barbecue at the hotel. Although some members of the press had been invited, Mick had told them that the event was to be strictly social – there would be no interviews and notebooks and cameras were banned. The sight of the backroom staff sporting garish Hawaiian shirts that Taff had purchased at the market earlier in the day added to the informality and raised a laugh and some comments from the lads. Mick trusted us and allowed us a few beers, but no one overdid it and it was a very relaxed atmosphere. Unfortunately, Roy, who had hardly spoken to

Right: St. Gregory's Primary School team with teacher Keith Aspinall, who was also in charge of the ball boys at Preston North End. *Courtesy of Ian Rigby*

Left: Farrell, Geraldine and myself at home with Dad. *Courtesy of Teresa Kilbane*

Right: My heroes have always been Irish. *Courtesy of Teresa Kilbane*

Left: My proud mum looks on as I sign on the dotted line for PNE aged 14. And I wore my best jacket for the occasion. *Courtesy of Teresa Kilbane*

Below: The teenage years: Farrell myself and Geraldine with mum. *Courtesy of Teresa Kilbane*

Bottom: PNE under 18 youth team, including at the end of the front row Chris 'Boz' Borwick and standing next to me, goalkeeper David Lucas who has enjoyed a successful professional career.

Above: My initial big move was from PNE to WBA. *Courtesy of Laurie Rampling*

Below: Nervously awaiting my 1997 international debut against Iceland in Reykjavik. Roy Keane was inspirational both on and off the field to me at the time. *www.sportsfile.com*

Above: A Mackem welcome. Journalists, myself and Quinny with his Sunderland player of the year trophy. Foreground: Michael Walker and George Caulkin. Back from left to right: Bob Cross, the author, Niall and Colin Young.
Courtesy of Colin Young

Left: In action for the Black Cats with Tottenham's Gary Doherty appealing for something or other.
Owen Humphreys/Press Association Images

Above: Elsie, Isla and adoring dad.

Below: Devastation in Suwon – after the penalty miss against Spain in the 2002 World Cup. *Getty Images*

Left: Scoring for Everton against Manchester United. I have nothing but fond memories of my time at Goodison. *Getty Images*

Right: Me and Bainsey at Wigan Athletic. A lovely club.
Barry Coombs/EMPICS Sport/Press Association Images

Left: Scoring for Hull against Burnley. A club full of characters. *Getty Images*

Right: Town's celebrations after penalty shoot out victory against Bournemouth.
Adam Davy/EMPICS Sport/Press Association Images

Left: Sadly my career at Derby County was cut short due to injury. *Getty Images*

Left: A slight suspicion of handball? The ref got the decision 100% wrong.
Philippe Lecoeur/EPA

Below: Our reaction to Thierry Henry's hand in France's play off winning goal.
Gamma-Rapho via Getty Images

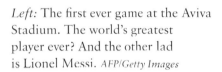

Left: The first ever game at the Aviva Stadium. The world's greatest player ever? And the other lad is Lionel Messi. *AFP/Getty Images*

Below: June 2011. With the lads before my last international – a European Championship qualifier against Macedonia in Skopje. *www.sportsfile.com*

Left: A Paddy Power driven milk float: fundraising for Down's syndrome charities.

Courtesy of Paddy Power

Above: Presenting a medal to a fellow Hull City player at the DSActive tournament.

Photo by James Jordan, courtesy of DSActive

Left: Celebrating with John Fleck, shortly before my retirement. Time for some 'Sky Blue' thinking.

Dave Howarth/EMPICS Sport/ Press Association Images

reporters for some years, was now in the company of some of the very journalists who had been critical of him in the past. He wasn't best pleased about that either.

We knew that Roy was disgruntled but had no idea quite what was going on behind the scenes. Roy was, in fact, extremely unhappy and had actually told Mick that for personal reasons he wanted to leave the camp. He had been temporarily persuaded by Mick Byrne to stay but had then insisted that he wanted to return home.

We knew that Roy had done an interview with the *Irish Times* during this period but we didn't know what he had said. We were living in a bubble in Saipan and, as it was in the days before global internet access, we were unaware of all the media interest. The day after its publication Mick received a fax of the interview from the FAI. Roy had been highly critical of the setup and had not only been scathing about the preparations but also criticised some of the players' abilities and questioned their attitude in being prepared to put up with such lax arrangements.

I was initially unaware of what was going on that afternoon as Carso, Clinton Morrison, Jason McAteer and I were at the cinema, watching *Spiderman*. We came back to the hotel for dinner, which was due to be served at 7 p.m., and had been told that Mick wanted a meeting afterwards.

I was rooming with Niall, who was always late for everything – usually catching up on his sleep – and so by the time we came down the two main tables were filled by the lads and staff. We sat on a smaller table and were joined by Steve Finnan. Soon after Roy joined us and sat down next to me. His first words were, 'It's going to go off tonight.' Although by now I knew about the interview I had no idea what he meant or of the ramifications.

Towards the end of the meal, Gary Kelly invited Mario, the chief entertainer and his resident band, who were performing in the adjoining lounge, to play for us. The troupe agreed and the lads all really enjoyed singing along to their medley of South Pacific songs before we all launched into a version of my old favourite, 'Stand By Me'. There was lots of clapping and cheering and the mood was pretty upbeat. However, the atmosphere changed immediately when Mick entered the dining room and asked the band to leave. The place immediately went silent.

Mick addressed Roy directly – I think he was looking for an apology – but when Mick started reading the fax from the FAI, Roy simply exploded and launched into a verbal attack which lasted about five minutes. Mick hardly got a word in. I've witnessed lots of arguments on and off the field in my time, but I had never heard such a tirade – sometimes it reached screaming pitch. I was sure it would come to blows. Roy called Mick all sorts of names, but, contrary to popular belief, didn't call him, 'an English cunt'. We just sat and listened open-mouthed and although I would have liked to have made myself scarce I was wedged in and couldn't move! There are various versions of the exact words and terminology but I remember that at the end of the diatribe Mick eventually asked Roy, 'Where do we go from here? It's either me leaving or you leaving and I'm not going anywhere!'

Roy simply got up, muttered, 'Good luck lads', and left. That was the last we saw of him. No one had tried to interrupt – we were too shocked. There was a stunned silence and in an attempt to break the atmosphere goalie Dean Kiely called out, 'If you're looking for a midfielder, I can do a job.' That brought a few laughs. Mick told us that he needed our support more than ever, following which Gary Kelly initiated a round of applause for the manager.

There were rumours later that this had been a premeditated attempt by Mick to put Roy in his place in front of the squad but this was untrue. The exchange had been spontaneous and left Mick shaking and ashen-faced. But one thing was certain. Roy was off and that was that. No one had even tried to stop him or reason with him.

The following morning hundreds of reporters, journalists and other interested parties arrived in Saipan trying to get a story. But that day we were on our way to spend a week at the training base in Izumo, a small city south-west of Tokyo, and were accompanied on the ninety-minute flight by the city's mayor, who had arranged a series of welcoming ceremonies on our arrival. There were some songs from local children and a rendition of the Irish national anthem, which was touching, but the speech by the mayor at the specially built dome seemed interminable and we all got the giggles as it went on and on. The residents of Izumo were brilliant and made huge efforts to make us feel at home. Not only were there Irish flags all over the place, but they organised Irish exhibitions and even offered draught Guinness in one of the shopping centres!

The organisation at Izumo was great and we settled in really well. I felt brilliant when we got to Japan – the temperature seemed bearable after Saipan and I felt that Mick's planning had been successful. The only disadvantage was the accommodation at the Royal hotel, situated in a quiet suburb of the city. The bedrooms were really small and Niall and I could barely fit into the cramped room together!

Soon after our arrival we played Hiroshima in a warm-up match in front of 11,000 fans at the excellent new Hamayama Stadium. Although we won 2-1, I think we were distracted by all the backstage dramas. I limped off with a bruised foot, but Jason McAteer was the victim of a really wild tackle from Cameroonian player Romarin Billong that injured his knee and put him in doubt for the group stages. After the game Billong came to apologise, but received short thrift from some of the lads.

Although we were unaware of it, the fuss back home was extraordinary. There was still a lot of talk about whether Roy was coming back to the camp and the rumour mill was working overtime. It transpired that Niall was negotiating behind the scenes with Michael Kennedy, a solicitor employed by both

Quinny and Roy, and it was said that one telephone call with an apology from Roy could pave the way for his return. Mick would apparently welcome him back into the fold for the good of the nation. Bertie Ahern had also become involved and there were apparently three separate offers by owners of private jets to fly Roy back to the Far East. Meanwhile, a few of the lads, Alan Kelly, Steve Staunton and Quinny, were working on a statement backing Mick which was written on the bus by Kenny Cunningham and released to the press; it included the line, 'the interests of the squad were best served without Roy's presence'.

Roy was scheduled to do a half-hour prime-time interview on RTÉ and was supposedly going to apologise and, if so, the FAI were likely to back his return to the squad. I never thought that was likely and was proved right when the interview went out and we were told that Roy showed no sign of remorse.

The saga finally came to an end on 29 May when Roy issued a statement in which he said that he 'didn't consider that the best interests of Irish football will be served by my returning to the World Cup'. That was it. Once and for all. On the team coach to the airport, one wag had placed an 'RIP' sticker on Roy's usual seat. We had been party to the biggest ever Irish World Cup story – and the tournament hadn't even begun.

Colin Healy, who had been alerted to join the squad, was denied permission by FIFA and so we had one less player than the other countries. Some of the younger players were bemused by events, but it made us more determined than ever to make Ireland proud.

Most of the lads couldn't understand Roy's behaviour but felt that such disorganisation was nothing new for us. The Irish players put up with more hassle at international level and muddled through because of their pride in playing for their country. Roy was one of us but he was idolised like no one else – everywhere we went there were pictures of Roy and people wanted a piece of him.

The Irish camp in every tournament was pretty much open house. Many of the fans stayed in the same hotel as the players and so we would mingle with them after the games and were expected to pose for photographs and sign autographs. In fact, when we played in Dublin it was often the only opportunity for the Irish-born lads to see their families. As far I was concerned it was not an issue, but at Manchester United Roy was protected from the press and public and he found the difference between the professional setup at United and what he perceived as the amateurishness of the FAI more and more difficult to accept. Roy had been instrumental in getting us to the finals and, although we had a strong squad and players who would give their all, Roy was one of the best players in the world. There was no doubt he would be missed.

vs Cameroon 1-1, 1/06/02 Niigata

The first Group E match against Cameroon took place on 1 June at Niigata's Big Swan Stadium. We got to the ground two hours before kick-off and thousands of our fans were already there. Even things like the size of the dressing room and the number of FIFA officials indicated something different from the norm. Mick was worried about how the fans would react to him following the Keane saga but this was soon put to bed by their response: when we came out on to the pitch an hour later to warm up, the place erupted. The atmosphere was electric.

Thoughts also turned to everyone back home who would be getting up early to watch. This was an incredibly emotional experience for many of us. After all, it had taken a lot of hard work to get here. I don't think I'd ever been so nervous before a game and even some of the quieter lads were excited and more vocal than usual. The singing of the national anthem was also quite something, so deafening. The pride of the Irish there for the whole world to see.

Given that it was an afternoon kick-off, the humidity in Niigata was a concern. The importance of rehydrating had been drummed into us since we'd arrived in South East Asia. Thankfully, I thought we all coped well with it, mainly because of our time spent in Saipan. The first half went by in a flash for me; I wasn't at my best, but the team was doing fine. However, not for the first time during the tournament, we would find ourselves in a losing position at the interval. Five minutes before half-time, Samuel Eto'o got to the by-line and cut the ball back to the recent Sunderland loanee Patrick M'Boma, who slid it home from the edge of the six-yard box. It didn't feel deserved.

The words 'No regrets' had been written on the clipboard by the time we got to our dressing room. This became the theme of the tournament. Mick's 'golden rule' was always to make sure we gave our all at every moment. If the results went against us then so be it, but we should always leave the field with no regrets about the commitment and endeavour for the Irish cause.

And it certainly felt as if we were capable of getting back into it. I found out later that Mick had apparently considered taking me off but believed I could improve in the second half. The team talk urged us to push up a bit, and, sure enough, we equalised not long into the second half. I was told to venture further forward and to whip more balls in. The goal game from one such cross. The ball was headed straight out to Matt Holland, who hit it first time on the half-volley and into the bottom corner of the net. This was an ironic postscript to all that had gone on as Matty, alongside Mark Kinsella, had been a dominant presence in the centre of midfield. Late in the game Robbie hit the post. We really finished the game on the front foot.

Cameroon were fast and strong, but we played them off the park and should have won. We felt brilliant and there was plenty of singing in the dressing room afterwards – led by Mick Byrne, of course. We heard that Eamon Dunphy had appeared on RTÉ wearing a green shirt with a red tie (Cameroon colours), which he later said was a joke. Hilarious.

vs Germany 1-1, 5/06/02 Ibaraki

After the Cameroon game we moved to our next base, the amazing five-star New Otani hotel in Chiba City, and we stayed there for the rest of our time in Japan. Spirits were running high before the big game in Ibaraki. We realised that we needed to get something out of the match against Germany and the fact that it would take place at night provided some personal comfort – the sun would not beat down on the left side as it had done for the first forty-five minutes in Niigata!

Having played in all Ireland's World Cup matches up to this point, the game against Germany was to be Steve Staunton's hundredth cap, making him the first Irishman to achieve this, and to mark the occasion he would also captain the side. Steven Reid, as the youngest member of the squad, made a speech and presented Stan with a Cartier watch, the result of a team whip-round.

Unlike the preparations before the Cameroon game, we were driven down to the stadium on the day of the Germany match itself. This was Steve's Staunton's idea, given that the training conditions in Chiba City suited us and an early run-out on the pitch in Ibaraki seemed unnecessary. Along with Damien and Robbie, I was again encouraged to run at the German defence whenever the opportunity arose.

To prevent the possibility of us showing our opponents too much respect, Mick emphasised that we were facing the *current* German side, not the ones that had won three World Cups. Having said that, this crop were no pushovers and proved the point when they took the lead twenty minutes into the game. Miroslav Klose, who'd just scored a hat-trick of headers against Saudi Arabia, ran on to a diagonal chip by Michael Ballack and nodded in to put Germany one up.

At half-time, Mick instilled the belief in us that one goal would change the whole complexion of the group and give us a massive opportunity to progress. We desperately needed an equaliser. Early on, I put Duffer through for a one-on-one with Oliver Kahn, but the German keeper denied him with an athletic save. With twenty minutes to go, Mick eventually switched to his plan B of 3-4-3 and so I played in more of a wing-back role. Shay did not have a great deal to do all game and we never gave up. Quinny's introduction made a difference and we pushed and pushed, but time was running out. On their way to the second round, Germany slowed the game down with late subs, and the prospect of sweating on their result in the last game looked likely as the match approached stoppage time.

With ninety seconds remaining, the ball went out for a throw-in in our own half and, in sheer desperation to get the ball, Gary Breen all but knocked over the German substitutes in their dugout. Steve Finnan quickly launched it forward, and Quinn flicked the ball on. It landed at Robbie's feet. Hemmed in by two defenders, he took one touch and then smashed it into the net off Kahn and the inside of the post. There was a deafening response to the equaliser from our fans. The scenes of jubilation were incredible and Robbie had to be torn away from the adoring supporters. It was magical: Quinny reckoned it was Ireland's best ever World Cup moment. It's hard to disagree.

Unfortunately, because of a compulsory drugs test, Robbie and I were denied the immediate post-match celebrations. Of course, when you've just played ninety minutes you get really dehydrated and peeing can take quite a while. Robbie was especially furious, having been chosen for the ordeal at random for the second game in succession. The team coach left without us and so the FAI arranged a car to take us back to the hotel.

We missed dinner at the hotel, at which the whole squad was applauded by the hotel staff...and the lads followed suit by clapping Mick. The bar was opened at the FAI's expense and the six-pint 'sensible' limit was lifted, as was the curfew. Wives, girlfriends and children were included in the celebrations and joined in the inevitable singsong in which Damien's brother, Jayo, played guitar. This was the first opportunity for us to meet up with them since we had been away. Officially they were booked into a different hotel but actually stayed in ours. The plan to spend the following day on roller coasters at Tokyo Disneyland wasn't the best choice for some proud Irishmen with sore heads and unstable stomachs.

vs Saudi Arabia 3-0, 11/6/02 Yokohama

We had to beat Saudi Arabia by two clear goals, without needing to worry about other results. It was great to be in charge of our own destiny and there was a real chance of progressing as the Saudis were already out of the competition and had nothing to play for. Mick had watched them against Cameroon and reminded us that we'd beaten Iran to get to the finals and, from what he'd seen, the Saudis were no better than the Iranians. We should be confident, but we needed to dictate the game. It felt like a long gap between our second and third games and, just three days before the match, I went over on my ankle in training. I sat out the rest of the session, but was fit enough to be included in the squad. On the day of the game, we travelled to the Sheraton hotel, across the particularly grey concrete landscape between Tokyo and Yokohama Bay, where the World Cup final was to be played. There was a lot of banter about coming back there later to play in the final!

We led early on after Robbie grabbed a goal, but couldn't press home the advantage and went in with a slender lead at half-time. Mick was livid that our performance had dropped off as the half progressed. Hartey had picked up a knock and so was taken off at the interval and I was put at left-back. It took us until the sixty-second minute to double our lead when I was tripped, and from Stan's free kick Gary Breen hit it with the outside of his right foot beyond the keeper. Being without a club at the time, Gary made the most of the post-match interviews and he had a great story about his grandma telling him to put his dole money on scoring in the match.

Damien, deservedly for all his efforts, grabbed the third, as his shot at the near post slipped through Mohammed Al-Daeyea's hands. Carso was thrown on for his first World Cup appearance – Mick was big on the harmony of the squad as a whole, and this was Carso's reward for his loyalty and dedication to the team. The lap of honour could have gone on for hours! Another night of celebration took place.

vs Spain 1-1, 16/06/02 Suwon

Our initial aim had been to get to the second-round stage, but this was no bonus game. We now felt we could beat Spain and make the quarter-finals and then who knows? The stakes were getting higher. On our way to South Korea to prepare for the second round, the reality of our achievement hit us by way of the World Cup organising committee sending the wrong-sized plane. It turned out that they'd expected Cameroon – with their smaller delegation – to qualify! Journalists had to leave all their luggage behind and the flight to Seoul was delayed by two hours. Once there, our base was in the middle of the city and we arrived on the day of South Korea's group stage victory over Portugal. Thousands and thousands of Korean fans had taken to the streets, and it was wonderful to experience the World Cup celebrations in the capital city of one of the host nations.

In South Korea we trained at a military base but began to get a little bored of being cooped up in the hotel when not training. Some of the lads managed a couple of trips to a karaoke bar where, at one point, Gary Kelly nearly knocked himself out with the microphone. On the eve of the game there was a great buzz. Confidence was high. We had an 'old players' versus 'young players' match with Mick joining in. Everyone was so fired up that, fearing a spate of injuries, Mick ended it early. The 'oldies' ended up losing on penalties.

Our fans waved us off from the hotel on match day with their customary fervour and we embarked on our hour-long coach journey southwards from Seoul to the city of Suwon, the centre of cutting-edge technology companies and the home of Samsung. The old part of the town is entirely surrounded by fortress walls, dating back two hundred years.

Before the game, Taff wound up some of the squad members by putting the starting eleven in one dressing room and the substitutes and staff in another. It was Dean Kiely who took the bait and complained, to which Taff innocently replied that all he was trying to do was give everyone a bit of space.

Spain began with a solid back four and it was clear from the first whistle that the full-backs had no intention of crossing the halfway line. The defence was going to be as hard to breach as the fortified defences around the city. And, to make matters worse, for the third time in four matches we found ourselves behind. The Spanish scored in a flash in the eighth minute. From a throw-in on our eighteen-yard line, a one-two led to a Puyol cross from the right, which Fernando Morientes nodded in. It seemed much too easy.

Spain controlled the first half but Mick wasn't too disheart- ened at half-time. I had a shot cleared off the line by Fernando Hierro when Iker Casillas misjudged a high ball. Another great chance to get back into the game came in the sixty-second minute when Duffer, fantastic all game, ran at defender Juanfran down their left and was tripped in the area. When Hartey missed the penalty, the rebound fell at my feet but ricocheted off my shin and went past the post.

John Beck, my old Preston manager, had always said to be on the move, in tandem with the penalty taker, albeit a few yards behind, so that if there's a rebound you're already in a good position to strike the ball. I did this okay but when the ball did come to me I tried to put my boot through it when I should have side-footed it.

The clock was against us as we chased the equaliser that would keep us in the competition. To our disbelief, with just a minute left on the clock, referee Anders Frisk pointed to the spot for the second time. Hierro, the World Cup veteran, had pulled Quinny's shirt. The Spaniards protested vehemently, but it was the right decision. Hartey had already been substituted and so Robbie placed the ball on the spot this time. He showed no sign of nerves as he sent Casillas the wrong way and us into extra-time.

David Albelda, a substitute who'd just come on, picked up a groin injury, which meant Spain would play with ten men in extra-time. We were on top for the first fifteen minutes and we looked likely winners. Belief ran through the team that we could find the golden goal, which would decide the game, but it was hard to break them down. Spain put us under more pressure in the second half and the action was end to end – Ruben Baraja had a shot parried away seconds before David Connolly sent the ball just wide.

Perhaps our last game in training had been prophetic, because the final whistle went and we were in a penalty shootout. Potential takers Ian Harte, Gary Kelly and Steve Staunton had all been taken off. On the back of yet another last-minute success, Robbie volunteered to take one straightaway. I wanted one too, along with Matty, David Connolly and Steve Finnan. Quinny would take the sixth if required. Spain won the toss, and so the shootout would take place at the opposite end to where Hartey and Robbie had taken penalties in normal time.

Robbie took the first, and once again slotted it home, this time with more elevation. Hierro then equalised, and proceeded to shake hands with the ref in a relieved gesture of goodwill. Matty, David Connolly, Juanfran and Valeron all missed theirs. Finnan scored but then so did Mendieta, in a manner that has since been compared to the time Cascarino stubbed the ground in Genoa. Spain won the shootout 3-2. I should probably mention that I also missed the seventh.

We'd been practising virtually every day in training and I had been scoring easily. Although I was confident, it was a nerve-racking walk from the halfway line to the penalty spot. I tried to be focused and not think about what it meant to the team, the fans or the millions of people watching. But I just didn't hit it as I had been doing in training; it was a very tame shot and Casillas didn't have to work hard to save it. I still don't know why, as I ran up, I decided to try and place it. Maybe the pressure of the situation just got to me.

I couldn't believe what I had done. I was close to tears as I started the even longer walk back to the lads whose faces were etched with disappointment. They tried to gee me up but I was devastated. Afterwards Mick spent a lot of time trying to console me, Matty and David by praising our courage, but there was nothing he could say to make me feel better. We were out of the competition and going home. The dressing room afterwards was unlike anything I'd experienced; everyone was so disheartened. Nevertheless, Mick told us to be proud and to celebrate in Seoul.

Although we practised penalties, it's impossible to get any-where close to replicating the taking of a penalty kick in front of tens of thousands of spectators in the ground and even more at home. I could score against Shay Given, Alan Kelly or Dean Kiely, or any keeper in world football in training, but that was nothing like facing Iker Casillas in the last sixteen of the World Cup. In training, and in the six penalties I scored in games or shootouts since the 2002 finals, I went for power and accuracy. The agony of the miss will never go. No regrets? I'm not so sure.

The World Cup was the greatest experience I've ever had in football. Everything about it was exciting – the buzz, the fans and the hype all made it so memorable, but losing on penalties and missing out on a place in the quarter-finals was heartbreaking.

On our return I didn't want to go to the official 'welcome home' party at Phoenix Park in Dublin, where we were treated like heroes by 50,000 fans; the players addressed the crowd, but I refused to take the microphone – I was too wound up. I didn't want to go drinking afterwards. I just wanted to go home.

My next international involvement was a few months later in a European Championship qualifier against Russia. My confidence, following the incident in Genk with Sunderland fans, had really taken a blow and I had arguably my worst ever game in Moscow in September when we lost 4-2. (The only positive part of that trip was when we arrived at back at Dublin airport and I met Richard Ashcroft, lead singer of The Verve, one of my favourite bands. I asked him for his autograph. He signed my Irish passport, 'Love and Peace, Richard Ashcroft'. I still have the passport.)

Another defeat a month later, this time in Dublin against Switzerland, saw the onset of a great deal of negative press aimed at Mick. He rang me after the game and asked how I was. 'Terrible,' I replied. 'It's bad enough losing at home but the atmosphere was horrible.' In fact, Mick rang every squad member for their thoughts about where we should go next and what they felt about the general situation, which I thought was very respectful. Mick told the players that he didn't feel he could take the team any further and that it was time to step aside.

I felt very sad when Mick resigned. It was unfortunate that both Niall Quinn and Steve Staunton retired after the World Cup; I know they could have made a difference in the game against Switzerland. I would have loved Mick to have stayed, as would the majority of the squad, although the fallout from the Roy Keane drama had split the nation. People were either with Mick or with Roy – it really was as simple as that. And I think Mick knew, especially after we lost heavily to Switzerland, that with all the hype still surrounding the team at the time his position was untenable. I sincerely hope he does return to manage Ireland again one day and I believe that we would have qualified for more tournaments if he had stayed in charge. Mick is a great manager and coach and had everyone's respect.

On 26 January 2003, Brian Kerr became the new full-time manager, an appointment welcomed by fans and most sections of the media. Brian had managed Republic of Ireland youth teams and had done really well and he had mentored some of the players such as Damien Duff, Robbie Keane and John O'Shea, all of whom went on to win full international caps.

Brian Kerr's first game in charge was against Scotland in Glasgow just a couple of weeks after his appointment. We were all desperate to draw a line under the Roy Keane and Mick McCarthy saga, which had dominated the camp for so long, and we wanted a fresh start. Of course most players have some concerns when a new manager takes charge – there's always the fear that he might not want you to be part of his plans and adopt the 'new broom' approach – so I was delighted to be chosen for the team and even more delighted to grab the first goal of the new regime. It was amazing to play at Hampden Park and I performed well. It was great, too, for Brian to experience a victory in his first game – especially at Hampden of all places – but now we had to return to competitive matches. It was now going to be tough to qualify for the Euro finals. Brian had been left a huge challenge to achieve qualification.

On 29 March we were pitched against Georgia in Tbilisi and won 2-1. Damien opened the scoring and the late winner came from 'Ginger Pele' himself, Gary Doherty, five minutes from time. However, the game was marred by ugly crowd scenes. Glass bottles and ball bearings were thrown at us throughout the game and both Gary Breen and Carso were struck by missiles. I had a lucky escape when I was hit on the arm by a six-inch-long open flick knife that one of the Georgia supporters threw at me. I didn't realise what it was until I picked it up. Shocked, I then handed the weapon to the referee. Iran and Turkey were both intimidating places to play but Georgia was because there was a really dangerous element to it. It could have turned out really nasty. I'd never known anything like it before.

There were two further qualifying matches against Albania – we drew 0-0 in Tirana and then beat them in the return match in June. I played poorly in the second game. I hadn't been at all consistent in the Euro qualifiers and lot of the press were calling for me to be dropped. I thought this was inevitable and wasn't expecting to play against Georgia a few days later, but Damien Duff pulled a hamstring in training and so fortunately I kept my place. Brian was brilliant. Despite my misgivings and the pressure I felt under, he gave me great support, which helped my confidence. I played much better against Georgia in Dublin and we won 2-0. That game was a particular turning point for me and was the start of a good run of form for both club and country.

The campaign continued in autumn 2003 with the penultimate group game against Russia in Dublin. Although we were without Robbie, we started well and Duffer scored on the half-hour. Russia equalised just before half-time and were probably unlucky not to score a winner. We were still in contention, but it meant that we needed to win in Basel against Switzerland in the last match and that Georgia would have to get a result against Russia.

The Swiss game marked my fiftieth cap. Although I didn't want to make a big deal of it, I was incredibly proud. Unfortunately, it wasn't an occasion to celebrate. We went behind as early as the sixth minute and never really recovered. On the hour, Switzerland doubled their lead and we needed three goals in the final thirty minutes. We pressed but just couldn't get anything out of the game and we learned that Russia had secured a place in the play-offs by beating Georgia 3-1.

As the Swiss team and fans celebrated their automatic

qualification for Portugal 2004, we finished third in the group and failed to qualify for the finals. The three thousand Irish fans tried a rendition of 'You'll Never Walk Alone' but, like our performance on the pitch, it soon fizzled out. It was a tame end to a campaign that had promised so much.

Chapter Seven

A Box of Chocolates?

'All I can be is me – whoever that is.'

BOB DYLAN

Back in England I had been 'rescued' from Sunderland by my old ally, David Moyes, who I'd remained in touch with since our Preston days. We'd occasionally swapped football stories and if he was thinking about a signing he would sometimes ask for my opinion if I had played with the lad or I knew anything about him. Now I would have to stop referring to him as Moyesy, which is how I had known him since the age of sixteen. From now on he was 'the gaffer'!

David had taken over as manager at Deepdale following my move to West Brom and had subsequently been appointed Everton's boss in March 2002. He had made an immediate impact at Goodison by declaring Everton 'the people's club' and had guided them to a safe fifteenth place in the Premiership in the last few games of the season when relegation had seemed a distinct possibility. In his first full season (2002–3), the team had finished seventh, their highest position in the top league since 1996, and had just missed out on a UEFA Cup place.

Everton were founding members of the Football League and were formed in 1878, just under a hundred years before I was born. It was an honour to join such a famous club. David realised that I had had a rough time at Sunderland and luckily at the time he wanted a left-sided player. He also knew that I would work hard and do a job for him and could be employed in various positions across midfield and even at left-back. I was happy to play anywhere he wanted.

I made my debut against Newcastle at Goodison on 13 September 2003. Francis Jeffers returned on loan from Arsenal and Nigel Martyn and James McFadden had also joined the club. Morale was pretty low as Everton had lost 3-0 to Liverpool the previous week, but we managed a 2-2 draw with Tomasz Radzinski grabbing a goal and Duncan Ferguson levelling from the penalty spot two minutes from the end. It was quite an introduction; a very physical game in which Wayne Rooney was stamped on by Olivier Bernard and was sent off and, by the time Rob Styles blew the final whistle, there had been three penalties, ten bookings and two dismissals. There should have been another penalty when Andy O'Brien brought me down in the area!

We lost at Middlesbrough in the next game and after fifteen games had only recorded three victories. It was a tough start to my Everton career and we were just not getting the results. Fortunately, the fans were brilliant. They knew that we needed support rather than abuse and got behind us, something I found they were particularly good at when things were going wrong. And the atmosphere at Goodison was electric. At Sunderland, the lads would talk about how, if they didn't score early, there was pressure from fans. But at Everton the supporters recognised that they could help rather than hinder their own team.

Brian Kerr welcomed my move to Everton and told the press, 'It's a good move for Kevin and I think he will do well there. The Everton fans will appreciate him because he's an honest worker and does a good job. From our point of view it means Kevin will be playing at a higher level and the more players we have at the top level of the game, the better.'

Following my transfer to Everton, Laura and I moved from Durham and rented a house in Wilmslow. Laura's sister, Sally, was at Manchester University and so would be nearby. Also quite a few of the Everton players lived in the area so we were able to share the driving to the Bellefield training ground, which was just forty-five minutes away.

Although Laura was still suffering from severe sickness, her pregnancy seemed healthy enough. She had had an initial consultation in Durham and had asked about tests for the baby but had been told by one of the medical staff, 'Don't be silly, you're young and healthy. There's no need to worry – there's absolutely no chance of anything going wrong.' At the same time, Laura had also been asked, 'In any case what would you do if something was wrong?' Laura had another scan when she was five months pregnant and all seemed fine.

In my first Christmas at Everton I was told that it was a club tradition for new players to sing a song – James McFadden sang '500 Miles' by the Proclaimers and I performed my own version of the tune I had heard sung by Dean Martin, 'Let It Snow'. We performed in the canteen at Bellefield following a festive meal with the full works. All the staff, including apprentices, attended and so we had quite a full house. There was inevitably lots of heckling and the meal ended with Brussels sprouts and roast potatoes being hurled at the unfortunate performer. Most clubs have some sort of similar seasonal festivity: at Preston the lads improvised unrepeatable lyrics to the 'Twelve Days of Christmas'...

By the beginning of 2004, the team was working hard, confidence was returning and I was playing well and had been enjoying my football much more since I had come to Merseyside. Our form at Goodison was really good and we'd been playing some great stuff which we needed to take into our away games, where we had been inconsistent. I was pleased by an interview with the club's then vice-chairman, theatrical producer Bill

Kenwright, who stated, 'It's fair to say Kevin is doing a great job for us. He was our man of the match in those wins last month against Portsmouth and Leicester, which meant that everyone here could enjoy Christmas. Since then, he has scored a couple of goals against Norwich and Fulham and we are all very happy with him. The spotlight is invariably on Wayne Rooney but Kevin has been an unsung hero.'

Bill Kenwright was pretty well respected for his energetic involvement and affection for the club, which he had supported as a boy. He never interfered with the footballing side of things and only once gave us a talk, in a London hotel on an away trip, when the team were struggling. He told us how much the club was behind the lads and the gaffer and that he was sure every-thing would be fine. We all listened without any smart remarks or mickey-taking.

It was, of course, true that Wayne was always front-page news since he had exploded on to the scene at the age of sixteen the previous season and became, after the legendary Joe Royle, the second youngest ever Everton first-team player. And there was, of course, his spectacular last-minute winner against Arsenal five days before his seventeenth birthday, which ended the Gunners' thirty-match unbeaten run and made him, at the time, the youngest goalscorer in Premier League history.

I'd seen him play on television before we became team-mates, but was amazed by his incredible physique. He was so strong and physical for his age. He was always early for training and loved to play. He liked a laugh in the dressing room, but was polite and well-mannered – not at all brash. Sometimes, however, in training the red mist would come down and he'd clear someone out. He was capable of what we at Preston called 'the Scouser' tackle' – they always seemed to be tough to play against and their tackling could be characteristically aggressive.

Wayne had been talked about at Everton since he was eight years old, made his debut for the youth team at the age of fourteen and was now a first-team regular. There is no doubt that he is one of the best footballers I've played with, although I've always believed there was little to choose between him and Robbie Keane.

In February 2004, I played in central midfield in a 0-0 friendly against Brazil in Dublin. It was a great game and the Brazilian team included Cafu, Roberto Carlos, Ronaldo and Ronaldinho. Afterwards we all wanted to swap shirts but the World Cup champions weren't keen – their kit man offered me a training shirt but that wasn't exactly what I wanted!

There was talk around then of the possibility of Brian Kerr bringing Roy Keane back into the squad. This was a pretty dramatic story at the time because of that falling out in Saipan nearly two years before. Generally, we didn't feel that it was a slight against Mick and recognised that having Roy back could only strengthen the team. I told the press that I would 'happily sacrifice my place in central midfield if Roy Keane decided to return. It's up to Roy. It's his decision ultimately. He is a wonderful player and would benefit any team.' That was as long as I featured somewhere in the side! There was also a chance that I might have to miss Ireland's friendly against the Czech Republic the following month because Laura was due to give birth around then. I had spoken to Brian Kerr and made him aware of the circumstances.

In fact, Laura went into labour on 14 March, a couple of weeks before the Czech game. As I have written, Laura had been unwell for most of her pregnancy so it wasn't just a feeling of excite-ment as the birth approached – there was also a palpable sense of relief as she had been so ill. When her waters broke, we went to Macclesfield General Hospital but nothing much happened and we were sent home. I rang David Moyes to explain what was going on and he agreed that I could miss training the following morning, and wished us luck. The next day, things started to move. Laura was getting regular and painful contractions and we returned to the labour ward accompanied by my mother-in-law. It was too late for Laura to have an epidural and when they tried to give her gas and oxygen she fainted.

Laura was incredibly brave throughout and refused any pain-relieving drugs, although she regretted it afterwards. Although it seemed a lot longer watching poor Laura suffer, we'd only been at hospital for about two hours when Elsie, our beautiful daughter, was born. She weighed 5lb 7oz. I wouldn't normally remember details like this but the dramatic aftermath of her birth has meant that this statistic is forever etched on my mind.

Elsie was taken into an incubator for a little while before she was returned to Laura and was very limp – even for a newborn baby. I remember Laura saying, 'I can't seem to hold her properly, she's so floppy.' Laura had worked with babies at the nursery and couldn't understand why she suddenly seemed to have lost the knack of cradling a baby. She also noticed Elsie's particularly flexible fingers. What was more worrying a little later was that Laura wasn't able to breastfeed Elsie. Despite Laura's concerns, which I thought were perfectly natural for a new mum, I was completely made up. I was so proud of my wife and my newborn daughter. I left Laura in hospital and sent a group text to all my mates that all was well and I was 'over the moon' at being a dad. I realised that I had used a terrible football cliché, and might have been describing an away win at Man Utd, but it was how I felt.

After I had gone Laura was moved to a private room, which happened to be available. A little later one of the other new mothers came in and said to Laura, 'Can I see your baby?' The woman took one look at Elsie and gasped. She then rushed out of the room. Laura thought that the woman's reaction was because she thought Elsie was so beautiful.

That evening when it was time for Laura to sleep, one of the nurses took Elsie away for the night to give Laura a bit of a rest. At about three in the morning Laura heard a baby crying and, slightly disoriented, she wandered out of her room and found the child she thought was hers. She was about to pick the baby up when a midwife appeared and snapped, 'That's not yours. Go back to bed.'

The following morning the same midwife popped in to see Laura and told her that the hospital paediatrician, Dr Mimosa, wanted to see both of us together. Laura was pleased that the doctor wanted to include me in anything involving Elsie and had no inclination that anything was amiss. I was a bit late as I went to buy some flowers first. I had no idea of what was going to happen next. When I arrived at the hospital, the midwife was holding Elsie, which I thought was a bit strange, but then handed her to Laura. The doctor came in and immediately asked us, 'Do you think the baby has any characteristics from you or your husband?'

We couldn't really understand what he was getting at.

I said that Elsie looked a bit like Laura when she was a baby. Dr Mimosa replied, 'That's interesting because we think she's showing signs of Down's syndrome.'

Now we knew what he was getting at...

We both looked down at our tiny daughter. Before we could reply, he continued, 'In fact, I'm ninety-five per cent certain that she has Down's syndrome.' He then coldly informed us that Elsie might not walk, talk or be able to do very much for herself. 'The blood test will confirm the diagnosis.' All so impersonal – no feeling – no emotion. Just the facts.

We looked at Elsie again – this time with a feeling of dread and fear – and we sat in silence for what seemed an age. Our heads were spinning. We were completely shocked. We knew very little about Down's syndrome, but at the time having a disabled child seemed to be the end of the world. Laura started to cry and I asked for the midwife and doctor for some privacy: 'Can you leave us, please? We need some time.' Laura's mum, Christine, who was waiting outside, joined us. Through our tears, we told her what the doctor had said. We were both distraught and sobbing. I'll never forget my mother-in-law's first words: 'It doesn't matter. She's your daughter. And she's my granddaughter.'

For the first hour Laura somehow thought Elsie had tricked her – she'd lost the baby she wanted and she had somehow been replaced by another one – a stranger and interloper in our family. Elsie wasn't the baby she was expecting. The three of us went to the hospital chapel and prayed that everything would turn out all right. Within a very short time, however, Laura's attitude changed completely. She was incredible and I remember her saying, 'We should be thankful I'm so lucky. A lot of women can't have children and I've got a beautiful girl.'

These feelings manifested themselves in a fierce protectiveness towards her new baby. The medical staff wanted to put Elsie on a drip but Laura, like a mother bear shielding her cub, couldn't bear the thought of Elsie being hurt. The midwives were amazed that Laura had bonded so quickly with Elsie. (In the months that followed, when other mothers gave birth to babies with Down's syndrome, the midwives cited Laura as an example of how it is possible to have a strong maternal bond from early on.)

Laura stayed in hospital that night but couldn't wait to come home the following day. Unfortunately, Elsie was underweight and jaundiced and had to remain in hospital for three endless days. Laura was so desperate to leave she even dressed Elsie in a yellow babygro in the hope that it would make her skin look less affected by the jaundice!

Laura and Elsie had already been allocated a private room, which gave Laura some seclusion. It was a real blessing and we were lucky in that respect. Laura couldn't bear the thought of having to face all the mothers with their 'perfect' newborn babies. She needn't have worried about having to talk to other mothers as none of them tried to communicate with her. It was as if the Down's syndrome would rub off on their children but I suppose it was just that they didn't know what to say to Laura. As helpless as we felt, other mothers had absolutely no idea how to react.

I cried for virtually the whole day we were told that Elsie had Down's syndrome. I rang Carso as soon as I left the hospital and told him about Elsie. We had been friends since we both broke into the Irish squad and we were now team-mates at Everton. We shared a lot: like me, he had chosen to play for Ireland (his grandmother was from County Cork); on the same day I was asked to join the Irish Under 21 squad he, too, was offered the chance to join the England Under 21 squad, but opted for the Republic. We also became room-mates (Carso reckons he's been tidying up after me ever since).

The other – and at this time the most – important thing about Carso was that he had a five-year-old son, Connor, who had Down's syndrome. Of all the people I knew, Carso would be able to empathise because he had gone through this experience some years before; he had been in exactly the same position as I was now in. I had met Connor a few times and was very fond of him, but even then didn't know too much about Down's syndrome or the different effects that the condition can have. In fact, Carso later told me that my initial call had brought back all his feelings at Connor's birth and the subsequent diagnosis.

That night, Carso came up to Macclesfield Hospital. I met him in the car park. We sat on a bench outside A and E. I managed to stop the tears for the time we talked. I didn't want to break down in front of Carso because a negative reaction would also be saying something about Connor, and this was the last thing I wanted to do. It would feel as if I was being disrespectful to Connor. Everything had become so complicated since Elsie's birth.

But, of course, Carso knew exactly what I was going through and I realise I should just have been myself. He felt that the two of us now had yet another bond to cement our friendship. After he had left I started blubbing again! Carso had a reserve match the day after Elsie was born and was so affected that he couldn't concentrate on the game. Ten minutes after kick-off, he asked David Moyes if he could come off. The manager was his true, sympathetic self and agreed to the substitution.

Meanwhile, Steve Harrison had telephoned David Moyes to tell him about Elsie. David had been very excited for us; not only did he know and like Laura, but Harry was also a friend of his. David couldn't believe the news and later said, 'As managers we can deal with all sorts of problems that footballers and their families can experience, but on this occasion I really didn't know what to say. I hadn't been taught to deal with such things. I wondered why it had happened to such a lovely couple but then I thought, if anyone could deal with this situation it would be Kevin and Laura.' David Moyes rang Carso and asked him, 'What should I be asking? What's expected of me?' Carso told him, 'Just treat Elsie the same as any baby. Just get on with it as normal.'

When I spoke to David he said he wanted me back in the team as soon as I felt ready. He was incredibly supportive and told me, 'You need time to come to terms with this. Take as long as you want off.' Carso also felt I should take as much time as I needed. I was still numb and didn't know what to do for the best. Maybe it would be better for me to get back to work and some kind of normality. I just didn't know.

Carso was just as inspirational as a friend as he was for the team: before I came back, he arranged an informal meeting with some of the lads and gave them a rough insight into what it all meant. Of course they already knew Connor as Carso had brought him to the club, but he told them about a few basics about Down's syndrome. It was a very close-knit group and they didn't want to feel uncomfortable when I returned to the fold. My mate Alan Stubbs later remarked, 'We were conscious of not referring to children with Down's as all being the same. Carso stressed the importance of not generalising or stereotyping and treating people with Down's as individuals. We wanted to be sympathetic but it was important not to be pitying.' Stubbsy also told me that one of his best friends, player and now coach Mark Seagraves (later my coach at Wigan), had a daughter, Megan, who had Down's syndrome. It was another connection that somehow seemed to help.

I reported for training on the Friday, five days after Elsie's birth. But I didn't want to face my team-mates. It was just too soon. As I drove into Bellefield, Norman, the training ground 'gatekeeper', approached and greeted me with a firm handshake. 'I'm sorry to hear about your daughter.' 'Yes,' I replied, somewhat nervously, 'she has Down's syndrome.' Norman smiled and gripped my arm. 'Well, I'll tell you this. If that's the case, you'll have a lovely girl. They're loving children. You have a daughter that you'll grow proud of.' It was a lovely gesture and something I'll never forget, although in years to come I was to hear children with Down's syndrome being described, stereotypically, as 'loving affectionate children' on many occasions.

On the verge of tears, I sat in the car park for twenty minutes. If any of the lads came up to me or tried to offer sympathy or make references to Elsie, I knew I was likely to start crying. Perhaps I should have just driven away and tried to get the weekend over with. Should I have been with Laura and Elsie? What could I have done to make them feel better? What could I have done to make myself feel better?

Anyway, I realised I had to face the music and wandered into the changing rooms. The first team-mate I came across was Kevin Campbell, who gave me a bear hug and simply said: 'Congratulations!' I mumbled, 'Thanks', while still suppressing the waterworks. Gradually, all the lads came to see me. Most of them congratulated me. It was incredibly touching. I can never thank them enough for the way they handled the situation.

David Moyes decided that I shouldn't be in the squad for the following day's game against Leicester, which made total sense. I really wasn't up to it and my omission was explained to the press as being for 'family reasons'. Everton's press officer, Darren Griffiths, did a fantastic job in keeping it quiet and protecting me. Everyone, including all the medical and backroom staff, was brilliant. I couldn't have been at a better place or with better people.

It was agreed that I would train that day with the reserves while the first team prepared for the match. I shouldn't have bothered. I was useless. It was as if I had never kicked a ball in my life. I couldn't control it, I had no coordination. I couldn't do anything right. My mind was with Elsie. At that time I didn't want anything to do with football. It just didn't feel right.

But I did return to training the following Monday and in time I'd drive into Bellefield with David Weir. David, recently appointed manager of Sheffield United, Gary Naismith and Steve Watson were all incredibly supportive; they wanted to know all they could about how Elsie was doing and, in the nicest possible way, were inquisitive about Down's syndrome.

Kevin Campbell was fantastic when Elsie was born, quickly realising how I was feeling, and he always did his best to support me. I remember that he spoke to his mum, who was deeply religious. She told him that children with Down's syndrome were very special people: 'It's a blessing. He and his wife are lucky to have a child with Down's syndrome.' When Kevin repeated that to me, I was pretty confused as I just couldn't think of Elsie in those terms. But Laura and I certainly did feel blessed in those early months.

Footballers are seldom out of the public eye and we receive a great deal of criticism – sometimes rightly for irresponsible behaviour. But we live in a very macho world where any sign of softness can be construed as weakness. I have to say that my team-mates and colleagues at Everton weren't afraid to show their feelings and emotions and to support me in a sensitive way.

I missed that match against Leicester then went back into training, and on the Thursday or Friday before the Middlesbrough game Moyesy called me into his office, told me I had been training well and said he wanted me to be involved: 'If you want to play you're in. We need you.' I told him I was ready and I played against Boro', my first game since Elsie's birth. It felt good to be back on the pitch at Goodison and we forced a 1-1 draw, a point we badly needed to help stave off the developing threat of relegation.

A week after Elsie was born, Laura's mum rang the Down's Syndrome Association and we were put in touch with an education officer, Eric Nicholas, who was based in Liverpool. Eric visited the following day with his then seventeen-year-old son, Michael. I think Eric felt that, by introducing us to his teenage son, this would help us see how normal things might be in the future. I know he meant well, but, looking back, we probably weren't quite ready to face a young man with Down's syndrome while Elsie was still a tiny baby.

Eric stressed the importance of treating Elsie like any other baby, who needed just the same love and affection. Eric held Elsie and told us what a beautiful baby she was and that we should face the future one day at a time. He encouraged us to attend a local support group in Macclesfield, which we did. He also suggested getting the PFA involved and that I could help the Down's Syndrome Association with fundraising!

Christine, Laura's mum, had stayed with us for about a month, but then, understandably, had to return home. Although Laura continued to receive a great deal of support from her mother, she did struggle a bit. It was much harder for her having to cope with all the day-to-day things with Elsie while I could get out nearly every day, exchange banter with the lads at training and play in matches. Laura was isolated – she found that for some reason she wasn't invited to her antenatal group's outings. She took Elsie out to the park every day, but felt that everyone was staring at her and Elsie and pitying them both. She admitted that it was probably all in her imagination but that's the way it affected her at the time.

After six weeks, Laura and Elsie attended a nursery and family centre called Charnwood. This was a great breakthrough as Laura felt at home with the other mothers in her situation, who also had children with special needs. She didn't feel she had to explain herself or how she was feeling all the time.

After the Boro' game, I went away with the Irish squad to play in a friendly against the Czech Republic in Dublin. Before I joined up with the squad – a day after the other lads – Brian Kerr also enlisted Carso to brief my international team-mates, as he had done at Everton. Once again, they were all incredibly supportive and Brian was fantastic with me. He asked how I was feeling and whether I wanted to pull out of the squad, but I told him I was ready and willing to play for my country.

I roomed with Carso on the trip. We talked into the early hours about what the future held for Elsie and what I should expect. Carso was great – but, of course, none of us has all the answers...

I remember a conversation with kit man Johnny Fallon around about that time. He admitted that he didn't know much about Down's syndrome – 'I didn't really know what to say, you don't learn them things at school' – but he always managed to say the right thing and, as usual, helped me with his sensitive and wise words.

Back at Everton, our form was patchy and we continued to flirt with relegation, but then we enjoyed a five-game unbeaten run and beat Spurs 3-1 on a Friday night at Goodison to ensure our safety. A couple of weeks later, I tweaked my hamstring against Blackburn and was substituted with ten minutes to go. It was the first time I'd had such an injury and I also missed the last three games of the season. I remember Baz Rathbone informing me that maybe my body was telling me I needed a rest.

We finished my first season a very disappointing seventeenth. I'd been playing for a while with a dodgy ankle. It was hoped that, with rest, it would settle down, but in June I had to have surgery to remove a small piece of bone from the back of the joint.

It was around this time that I had my only run-in, albeit a slight one, with Moyesy. At the end of the season I was negotiating a new option on my contract. I wanted a long-term contract, which I believed Everton also desired. I was still being represented by Wayne Rooney's agent, Paul Stretford, who, for obvious reasons, wasn't the most popular figure at Everton at the time. Negotiations were taking longer than expected and one day, while we were in the referees' room at Bellefield, David remarked, 'Everyone I spoke to about signing you said not to touch you with a barge pole. Don't you think you should show me some loyalty?' I ignored him and left to join the other lads in training. Later that day, Moyesy came to apologise for snapping at me, but I accepted that I owed him a debt of gratitude: a lot of managers wouldn't have taken me from Sunderland.

In July 2004, the club embarked on a ten-day pre-season tour to the USA and I was seated next to Kevin Campbell on our flight to Houston. Kevin had just seen the movie *Radio* and had brought a copy with him. He insisted that I watch it on my portable DVD player. Based on a true story, Cuba Gooding Jr plays the character of Radio, a man with a learning disability who strikes up a friendship with small-town football coach Harold Jones (Ed Harris). Because of his mental disability, Radio is ridiculed by the townspeople and lives a lonely, sad existence, regularly the victim of bullying and teasing. Jones, however, takes Radio under his wing, encouraging the young man to become the team's unofficial mascot and cheerleader. Together they inspire the football team to become champions, resulting in the locals learning to appreciate Radio's innate goodness and ultimately opening their hearts to him.

Of course I was very moved by this heart-warming and

hopeful tale, especially when I found it was based on a true story. I am also a fan of the film *Forrest Gump*. I know the movie has been criticised for being overly sentimental, but I thought its handling of a man with learning difficulties was both moving and brilliant. There are some marvellous quotes in the film. Apart from the well-known 'Life is like a box of chocolates – you get what you're gonna get', 'Stupid is as stupid does' is a simple statement that has always resonated with me because the principal character, Forrest Gump, possesses an intelligence and sensitivity beyond his IQ, which is how a lot of people with learning difficulties are unjustly judged. Before Elsie was born, I never used to cry, but now any sentimental story, film or television programme – even *The X Factor* – can get me going!

Anyway, at the time of the Houston tour, Moyesy was in trouble. We had been beaten in a pre-season friendly by Crewe and lost at Burnley the night before we left. It was a poor performance and we got a lot of stick from the crowd. There was much negativity around the place. Rumours abounded about the future of Wayne Rooney and there was talk of a possible takeover, which might have led to the sacking of the gaffer. Fortunately, Bill Kenwright managed to keep control of the club.

To be fair to him, Moyesy was brilliant and it was the best I'd seen him. He appreciated that we were away and needed some fun. He agreed to us having a couple of nights out and this bit of freedom actually helped us bond and gave us a lift. No one behaved stupidly and we all enjoyed ourselves. Most of the lads still remember those times and describe it as their best ever pre-season tour. We came together and respected Moyesy for his attitude – he quite rightly always expected the maximum from us – but we had a great group of characters and he appreciated it and recognised that the lads needed to relax.

We spent a lot of time together in the luxurious surroundings of the Westin Galleria hotel in Houston. Even Moyesy relaxed, which was most unlike him. We arranged a game of golf at the

Woodlands Country Club and I played with Jimmy Lumsden against Nigel Martyn and Chris Woods, the goalkeeping coach. We even took some money off them, never easy with Chris Woods.

One night we all went out for a meal and I got roped into singing 'Ice Ice Baby', a hip-hop song written by American rapper Vanilla Ice. I was to reprise this performance later at Euro 2012 when I was covering the Republic's matches in Poland…but that's for later.

The downside of the tour – maybe the result of *too* much relaxation and bonding – was that we got battered in two games by two Mexican sides, Pachuca and Club America, in the Copa de Tejas tournament that was staged in the 60,000-capacity Reliant Stadium, home of the NFL's Houston Texans American football team.

The 2006 World Cup qualifying campaign began in autumn 2004, when we played three matches, which included a 3-0 win over Cyprus in Dublin, a 1-1 draw in Basel against Switzerland and arguably my best ever match for the Republic in a 0-0 draw against the French in Paris. I was chosen to play in central midfield, partnered with Roy Keane, who had now been recalled by Brian Kerr. In front of a crowd of 75,000 in the Stade de France, we played them off the park. I'd been in good form for Everton and felt confident. I loved every minute of it. The Irish fans sang the 'Marseillaise' and were applauded by the French supporters. It was a great occasion.

It was after this performance that a range of T-shirts became available on Merseyside with a picture of me and the name 'Zinedine Kilbane' emblazoned across the chest. I was hoping that a similar T-shirt with 'Kevin Zidane' was also on sale in Madrid…

I received the award for senior international player of the year for 2004 at the City West hotel in Dublin. I was absolutely delighted and almost lost for words at the ceremony. It was a great time for me.

A few days after the France game we played host to the Faroe Islands and won 2-0. I can't remember much about the game, but I do recall that Brian Kerr had told us that we weren't allowed out at night. We thought differently and planned to sneak out to the local pub for a couple of drinks. As we were about to leave, Alan Lee emerged from his hotel room, all suited and booted for a night out...just as Brian Kerr was passing. Alan, who is a lovely, funny lad, told the gaffer he'd just come back from seeing a friend and went back into his bedroom, wishing Brian a cheery goodnight.

Gary Doherty bumped into Brian Kerr as well and was also dressed up for a night out. *His* excuse was that he was just testing out his gear for the night on the town, planned after the Faroes game – though in fact we were due to fly out straight after the match and we weren't even going out that night! Gary returned to his bedroom where his room-mate, Kenny Cunningham, was skulking under the bedclothes, also fully dressed!

The Group 4 World Cup campaign continued with a game in Ramat Gan at the end of March 2005, in which we drew 1-1. Israel equalised a minute into injury time and in the home leg in June we surrendered a 2-0 lead at Lansdowne Road to let Israel salvage another draw. In Torshavn, a few days later, we endured a frustrating first half against the Faroe Islands, but after the break Hartey scored from the penalty spot and I added a second. We were now top of the group.

Unfortunately, the performance against France in Dublin didn't match our display in Paris and we lost 1-0. I remember Shay making a fantastic save from Zinedine Zidane early on. Richard Dunne was superb and Thierry Henry only got one chance in the entire game – from twenty-five yards out; the trouble was, that was all the Frenchman needed. It was very tight and a draw would have been a fair result. Despite the defeat, victories in our last two games against Cyprus and Switzerland would leave us with a good chance of making the play-offs.

Although not very convincing, we managed to do the job in Lefkosia with a narrow 1-0 win over Cyprus, thanks to an early goal from Stephen Elliott. Shay was fantastic again, saving a penalty and making three other world-class saves.

The final group match took place in Dublin on 12 October 2005 against Switzerland. If we won, we'd be in the play-offs unless Cyprus sprung a ridiculous surprise and toppled France in Paris, in which case we would go straight through to Germany. Our task was made more difficult by being without the injured Roy Keane and Damien Duff. Andy Reid and I occupied the wings and John O'Shea started in central midfield with Matt Holland. Brian Kerr vowed to the press that we would come out 'with all guns blazing' and in all he made four changes from the side that disappointed against Cyprus. Niall Quinn was on Sky before the match and delivered a battling call to arms: 'The Swiss, let's be honest, they've been cocky all week. I hope the lads go out there and put in a truly *rambunctious* performance. Like in the good old days!'

We started lively enough. Hartey's headed chance early on was the closest we came, and although we pressed for most of the game we couldn't break the Swiss down. As the game wore on, the Lansdowne Road crowd began to get as frustrated and anxious as us, but we just didn't create any clear-cut chances. The guns had been blazing but sadly we were firing blanks. Although we finished just three points behind group winners France and were only beaten once, we ended fourth in a very tight group. This was the second time we had failed to qualify for the finals of an international competition and Brian Kerr came in for criticism from the media, who felt that his tactics were overly negative.

In turn, Brian himself felt that the press hadn't been helpful to him and became less approachable. As a result, many journalists withdrew their support and gradually became more critical of him. This was particularly ironic as, at the time of Brian's appointment, the Irish journalists had been delighted. They knew Kerr was always available, sociable and was someone who was willing to share an informal drink. However, this all changed once he had got the job and became a target for the press.

The 2004–5 domestic season was one of the most successful in Everton's history. After struggling the previous season, and now without Wayne Rooney, who had been sold to Manchester United for a club record fee of £27 million at the end of August, we had a squad of great players with incredible spirit and camaraderie. Without a shadow of a doubt, it was the best club side I have ever been involved with and those of us who were a part of it still talk on a regular basis.

We had a brilliantly consistent spine with Nigel Martyn in goal and the fantastic David Weir and Alan Stubbs, who were great communicators and superbly organised. Carso was outstanding in midfield and, with Marcus Bent up front, we were quite a force. The dressing room was a great place to be. Although we had some big characters, there was no one with airs and graces or big egos to upset the balance.

Carso was a big player for us – he performed his defensive duties with great skill and discipline and allowed Thomas Gravesen's creativity to flourish and for Tim Cahill to bomb on and score goals. Tommy Gravesen was quite a character and something of an enigma. Technically one of the best players I've ever worked with, despite his strength and reputation he was actually wary of being on the end of a tough tackle.

Jimmy Comer, the club's renowned masseur, never liked to tell Tommy who he might be up against in the next match because, if it was a real hard man, believe it or not Tommy could freeze. He could also be something of a bully. In training he'd test out new players by telling them in his gruff Scouse/Danish accent just how crap they were. He was an expert in taekwondo and one of the strongest men I'd ever seen. In the changing rooms at Bellefield, he'd sometimes grab Les, the training ground's caretaker, from behind, hold him in a vice-like grip…and pretend to shag poor old Les. Tommy once blew up one of Nick Chadwick's brand new boots and launched a giant rocket firework through the gym, leaving scorch marks throughout the building.

Tommy was definitely a big loss for us when he signed for Real Madrid in January 2005, although David Moyes promptly broke the club transfer record when he signed James Beattie for £6 million in the same transfer window. It was an amazing season in which we played some great football. We ended up fourth in the table, ahead of Liverpool and in the club's highest position since 1988. Incredibly, we'd qualified for the Champions League!

As much as we loved Elsie, Laura and I were still coming to terms with having a disabled daughter and this impacted upon our lives in different ways. Elsie's birth had affected my faith and I questioned why God would do this to us. I had been raised a staunch Catholic and my great-uncle, Father Bill, was a priest, based in Boston. I used to go to Mass regularly and only missed it if I was playing. After Elsie was born, I stopped going completely. Normally we would have had Elsie baptised straightaway but we put it off and even contemplated not going through with the ceremony at all. However, when Elsie was about a year old, we were feeling stronger and finally able to come out of our shells.

I had naturally asked Carso to be Elsie's godfather and Laura's sister, Sally, and best friend, Lizzie, who happened to be a speech therapist, working with children who had Down's syndrome, agreed to be godmothers. We were delighted that the three of them would be involved with Elsie now and in the future. The christening finally felt like a celebration of Elsie's life and the love of her family and friends made us feel that we had come through the worst. We had accepted that Elsie was who she was and wouldn't be Elsie without the Down's.

At about the same time I was in touch with fellow footballer Eddie Lewis, whose wife had just given birth to a baby boy,

James, who had Down's. Hailing originally from California, Eddie was now at my old club, Preston North End, and was a regular US international.

Eddie and his wife, Marisol, had gone through the 'normal' reactions of shock and grief when James was born. Eddie had spoken with several family members and close friends and they had all tried to support him as best they could. As much comfort as people close to him had tried to provide, he admitted: 'It did not give me any peace of mind.'

I think the fact that we both came from footballing backgrounds and had actually played against each other in international matches, and that I had a child with Down's, helped Eddie accept some of the things I had to say, although I wasn't saying anything very different from his family and friends. It was a bit of an eye-opener for Eddie when I told him that I had gone through exactly the same feelings he was now experiencing, and what to expect in the future. I told him: 'Eddie, everything is going to be okay. I know it's hard now, I know what you are thinking, but you have to believe me. Everything will turn out fine, and you are going to feel great about yourself.'

Eddie later wrote to me saying that these words, which he had heard on a number of occasions, 'took on a meaningful sense when it came from you. You had been in my shoes, you were walking the path I was now destined to take. To listen to your kind, calming, and positive voice was very helpful to me. In my hours of lonely sadness, this gift of hope was priceless. You truly helped me in a time of need.' I suppose it was indicative of how I was feeling that, just a year after Elsie was born, I was able to offer some positive thoughts and support, something I never thought I would be able to do.

The Lewis family have now moved back to California. Eddie and Marisol continue to work for local charities and he takes pride in being a spokesman for the Down's Syndrome Community.

In July 2005, Everton participated in the FA Premier League Asia Cup, a four-team tournament held every two years with matches played at the Rajamangala Stadium in Bangkok. The other teams were the Thai national side, Bolton Wanderers and Manchester City. We had a squad of twenty-one players for the trip, including Mikel Arteta, who had just signed a permanent deal with the club. I think this tour was about the only time that Joseph Yobo was ever warm enough – he was always cold and wore layers and layers of clothing. He got away with it in the winter and it was at about this time that lads started wearing snoods and gloves. In my days at Preston and Sunderland, we certainly weren't allowed such luxuries – it was T-shirt and shorts in training, whatever the weather!

We lost both our matches against Thailand and Man City on penalties, but in fact the football was the least important part of the tour. In conjunction with our partnership sponsors, Chang Beer, it was arranged that some of us should visit Ban Nam Khem, a village near the beach resort of Phuket. Ban Naan Khem had been renamed the Everton-Chang village, which was being built with money raised from the Asian Disaster Fund. The charity had been established after the previous year's tsunami, which claimed thousands of lives in Thailand and resulted in nearly a quarter of a million deaths in other countries either in or bordering the Indian Ocean.

David Moyes' assistant manager, Alan Irvine, accompanied me, Carso, James Beattie, Tim Cahill, Duncan Ferguson and Stubbsy in a flight from Bangkok to Phuket and from there by military helicopter to the village. We were incredibly touched by the warmth of the greeting from hundreds of villagers and smiling schoolchildren and we were taken on a tour of the devastated surrounding area where more than 1,300 people out of a local population of 4,500 had lost their lives seven months earlier. The club had raised over £135,000 to fund about fifty new homes built by the Thai army and some of the houses were actually named after Everton players. I also recall seeing two huge fishing boats that had been dragged nearly a mile inland by the tidal waves and had ended up in the middle of the village. The boats had been cleaned up but were left exactly where they had been washed ashore as memorials to the victims. They remain there to this day. The whole visit was an altogether unbelievably humbling experience and one I'll never forget.

More parochially, the 2005–6 Premier League season was, I'm afraid, hugely disappointing. Despite the excitement of the previous season and the Champions League qualification, our European adventure ended prematurely with a defeat by Villarreal in the qualifying stages.

We threw it away at Goodison, losing 2-1, and in the away leg in Spain we lost by the same margin. We were robbed of a late equaliser when referee Pierluigi Collina ruled out a Duncan Ferguson header that might have taken us into extra-time. Villarreal broke away and Diego Forlán scored the winner in the last minute. Considering how well we'd played, and how hard we'd worked in the previous season to qualify for the Champions League, it was a bitter blow, especially for the loyal Everton fans. I remember the thousands of our supporters completely filling the Villarreal stadium on that very warm night, even though we had only been allocated a few thousand tickets. And then, to add insult to injury, after being demoted to the UEFA Cup we were immediately knocked out of that competition by Dinamo Bucharest.

We were actually in the relegation zone in October 2005, but the draw against Chelsea ended their nine-match-winning run. We put a few good results together with a run of five straight Premiership wins and a draw, which constituted the club's best run of results since the inception of the Premier League. A top-half finish was a possibility team, but we were frustratingly inconsistent and a lack of goals resulted in an eleventh-place finish, well out of the European qualifying places.

At the end of the season, the gaffer called me in for the usual end-of-campaign review. He told me I wasn't playing well. I remember his exact words very clearly: 'You're smiling too much. You need to get the eye of the tiger back!' I had always given my best, but it was probably fair to say that I hadn't been playing as well as previously and Moyesy was right in some ways.

The most important event of that season, however, had nothing to do with football.

Laura had wanted another child as soon as possible. This seems to be a common reaction with women who have had a child with Down's syndrome. She felt she had been robbed of the joy that a birth normally brings. It wasn't a question of replacing Elsie so much as rediscovering the positive experience of giving birth and the ensuing joy. It was all a bit daunting and I was nervous about another baby as the chances of having another child with Down's syndrome were much greater.

Anyway, within a year of Elsie's birth Laura was pregnant. She was once again really sick during the entire pregnancy and in and out of hospital. The Everton doctor recommended a particular specialist and Laura had more scans than usual. However, we decided against an *amniocentesis*, a pre-natal test that can provide a diagnosis of chromosomal abnormalities. We thought about this because, if the new baby did have Down's, we would have time to prepare ourselves, but we decided against it as the test carries a greater chance of miscarriage and in any case Laura wouldn't have undergone a termination. And, after all, what would that have said about Elsie?

In any case, I was on my way back from Goodison after the game against Chelsea at the end of October when Laura rang to say she was having contractions. We raced to Macclesfield General and, within fifteen minutes of our arrival, Isla was born. The first thing Laura said when Isla was born was, 'Does she look like Elsie?' She did look like Elsie, but she didn't have Down's syndrome. It was a great relief that all was well, although we felt a bit guilty even thinking that. We were thrilled that Elsie was to have a sister.

In the same month, Brian Kerr was sacked for our failure to reach the 2006 World Cup finals, in what had, in truth, been a tough qualifying group. Brian had always been brilliant with me, especially after Elsie's birth and Laura's pregnancy with Isla. I played my best football in the Irish shirt while he was manager and really enjoyed working with him.

FAI official John Delaney was charged with appointing a successor to Kerr and, several months later, Steve Staunton was released from his role as assistant manager at Walsall and was officially named on 13 January 2006 as Kerr's replacement. Sir Bobby Robson was to support him in the role of international consultant.

I felt sorry for Steve because Delaney had been talking about a 'world-class management team' appointment to oversee Ireland's qualification campaign for the 2008 European Championship. Stan's was something of a shock appointment in light of some of the names that had been bandied about in the press. Fortunately, his first game in charge was a 3-0 victory over Sweden in Dublin on 1 March 2006.

Apart from Stan's managerial debut, in which he gave the captaincy to Robbie, the game was memorable mainly for the appearance of Mick Byrne, whom Stan recalled at the age of sixty-five to resume the role of physio he had lost under Brian Kerr. The players were delighted with Mick's recall. There was a good vibe around the camp, which Mick only added to, and he reminded us of the time he once said, 'I am everything the players need – mentally and physically.'

Sadly, the happy mood didn't last long and the victory over Sweden was followed a month later by a disappointing 1-0 defeat to Chile. The day before Stan's third game, another friendly against the Netherlands at Lansdowne Road in August, he was threatened at gunpoint by a man outside our hotel in Portmarnock. We watched from the window as Martin Byrne, one of our security men, brought down the perpetrator on Malahide beach with a flying rugby tackle. The Garda subsequently arrested the man for firearms offences. His weapon turned out to be an imitation Uzi machine gun and, although Stan was unhurt, he was understandably shocked. We all thought it was a bit of a laugh. The FAI pledged to review security around the team following the incident as it was the same hotel in which we were staying in three years earlier where an armed robbery took place and shots were fired from *real* guns while we were dining in the restaurant, oblivious to all the goings-on!

The match that followed was just as disastrous, a demoralising 4-0 thrashing, our worst home defeat in forty years.

It transpired that I wasn't going to feature much during Everton's 2006–7 campaign. We started well, beating Watford at home and then drawing at Blackburn before gaining our first league win at White Hart Lane in twenty years, despite the fact that I was sent off for two bookable offences. (Maybe that helped the lads!) Sadly, this game turned out to be my last for Everton. I then went off to join the international squad for the European Championship qualifier against Germany, due to take place in Stuttgart.

We were still in Dublin when I received a call from David Moyes telling me that Wigan had tabled a bid for me, which had been accepted by Everton. He told me that he hadn't even really wanted to tell me about the bid as he didn't want to let me go. I also didn't want to leave – I was very happy at the club and my time at Everton had been my best – but I knew that once a club accepts a bid it means you're not wanted and a move usually ensues.

I went to see Steve Staunton and warned him that something might be happening. Stan was getting anxious because a couple of other players were in discussions about moving to other clubs and these negotiations were obviously unsettling them. Transfer deadline day was ruining Stan's preparations. Often on international duty, players approach international colleagues and advise of interest, which can disrupt the squad and the manager's plans.

Although I wasn't under contract to Paul Stretford, Wigan had been in touch with him as he was involved with other deals. Paul contacted me and we talked about the contract offer. I was offered an incredible deal. It had also become clear that Everton were happy to move me on. It was another big decision to make and so I flew back to Manchester to sort it out.

The news broke on Sky Sports when Stan told the media that I had left the squad. Despite the money involved, I was still in two minds about leaving Everton. I loved the club and the camaraderie of this special team the gaffer had created. I wondered whether I would be able to recapture my best form and the spirit of the team elsewhere. I spoke to Carso, who told me to take my time to think about it.

Moving to Wigan would certainly be a challenge. Although they had risen rapidly through the leagues, they were now trying to establish themselves in the Premiership. It meant I could stay in the North West and I had no idea what was likely to happen in the years to come. If I hadn't agreed to a move then, it was more than likely that I would have moved later on down the line, and who knows where I might have ended up?

Anyhow, I decided to move and the fee was undisclosed. I didn't even know what it was myself, but believed it to be in the region of £2 million. I signed the forms and then flew direct from Manchester to Stuttgart to join the Irish squad.

This Euro qualifying game was Stan's first competitive match in charge and we were desperately unlucky to lose to Germany 1-0. We played so much better than in the last game against Holland and for the first hour easily matched the Germans. Steve Staunton watched the last fifteen minutes from a seat in the stands, banished there for kicking a water bottle on to the pitch during the second half.

I returned home to a new club, but with mixed feelings. My time at Everton had been my best so far. I realised I was leaving a great club and knew that I would never have it so good again. I've played under quite a few managers during my career and I have to say that David Moyes has been the most meticulous in his planning, obsessively studying countless videos and DVDs of the opposition. His knowledge of the game is incredible. Nothing is left to chance and his commitment and energy are unparalleled.

In his acclaimed book *The Smell of Football*, Baz Rathbone sums up David pretty well: 'He is like the bloody Rain Man. David's almost supernatural ability to read, understand, analyse and recount every single passage of play while he is in the dugout is truly amazing...he could remember everything you said – and yes, everything you had said the previous week as well. If there was an inconsistency, God help you. He would have made a fantastic barrister.'

David now has an even greater challenge, one might argue, than that of any legal eagle: in May 2013 he was appointed Manchester United's new manager, following in the footsteps of the incomparable Sir Alex Ferguson. I wish him luck!

Chapter Eight

To Craggy Island Via Wigan Pier

FATHER TED: What was that sermon about?
FATHER DOUGAL: Sorry, I was concentrating too hard on looking holy.
ARTHUR MATHEWS AND GRAHAM LINEHAN, *FATHER TED*

On 31 August 2006 I signed a three-year deal in a transfer fee estimated to be around £2 million. The manager, Paul Jewell, had done pretty well at Wigan considering that the town was better known for its rugby league exploits. In his second season (2002–3) the club won the Second Division championship and on the final day of the 2004–5 Championship season the Latics clinched promotion to the Premiership, bringing top-flight football to the club for the first time.

I didn't know Paul Jewell before joining the club, but I took to him immediately. He had first seen me play when I was at Preston and had followed my career. He told me he had always liked me as a player and the fact that I could play in a number of positions and was also good in the air were attributes that, he felt, would add depth to the squad. I was also pretty experienced by then and he thought I could help bring on some of the youngsters – as well as being an influence in the dressing room with some of the more established players. He wanted someone who would take responsibility and wouldn't hide – although there were probably times when he wished I would have!

Paul was straight-talking and, although he could at times be harsh with players, he was usually very fair in his criticism. I preferred it that way and have always responded better to an honest manager. It seems to me that nowadays there is much less straight-talking between manager and players, who often seem to have more power. Coaches and managers also have to be more sophisticated to get the best out of players and although we are used to an unforgiving environment from an early age a head coach whose only weapon in his psychological armoury is to shout and scream isn't going to achieve anything. David Moyes could be tough, but he knew when to lay it on and also when 'an arm around the shoulders' was going to help. Some players are galvanised by an embarrassing rant in front of their team-mates, but others needed a more sophisticated approach.

There were some good characters and players when I was at Wigan; for example, we were never the same if Emile Heskey wasn't playing. Despite not being a prolific goalscorer, he worked tirelessly and won everything in the air. Leighton Baines had come up through the ranks and was beginning to show the beginnings of the player he is today. There was brilliant goal-keeper Chris Kirkland, Ryan Taylor, Matt Jackson, the latter a fantastic pro who had won the FA Cup with Everton; Antonio Valencia had signed on loan from Villarreal and Emerson Boyce is still a first-team regular. The skipper, Dutchman Arjan de Zeeuw, was a great lad, who was voted the best Wigan player of all time. He was an interesting character and, following his retirement in 2009, began working as an investigative detective, specialising in forensics.

Perhaps Arjan could have expended some of his skills work-ing out the mindset of goalie Mike Pollitt, still between the sticks at Wigan and also mad as a hatter. Mike is a larger-than-life character and my fondest memory of him was at a Down's syndrome charity event when he told me, in all seriousness, 'I'm off the drink'. He then proceeded to guzzle seven bottles of wine and ended the night dancing completely starkers on one of the tables.

Because of the red card I received at White Hart Lane, I was suspended for what should have been my first game and so my debut was – guess where? Yes, against Everton at Goodison of all places! I remember in the tunnel, waiting to go on the pitch, all my mates and team-mates of just a week or so earlier were now lining up alongside. Carso, Stubbsy, Leon Osman and the rest slaughtered me in the tunnel with a torrent of derogatory remarks designed to wind me up. I was trying to get in game mode, to be focused and to concentrate on the game ahead – and also trying desperately not to laugh at the lads' attempts to put me off.

I got a brilliant reception from the Everton fans, one I'll never forget. The game ended in a 2-2 draw and I set up a goal for Paul Scharner. I discovered later that the Austrian-born utility player was also quite a character. He spoke excellent English, was very intelligent and self-possessed – he liked to go hiking on his own and described himself as a deep thinker. I played against him for Everton in a game in which Big Dunc gave Scharner a bit of 'a rib tickler' and was sent off for violent conduct. That gave Paul something to think about.

Every time a Wigan match was due to be broadcast on television, Paul would have an outrageous new haircut or wear brightly coloured boots in order to get noticed. He was always being quoted in the Austrian press about where we were going wrong and suggested the team's tactics were not helping. Inevitably, he would then deny this, suggesting that he had been misquoted or something had been lost in the translation into English! He retired from international football because he felt the Austrian FA was going in the wrong direction, although he later retracted this and made a comeback for his country.

Wigan owed much to their chairman, Dave Whelan; the club made continual losses but was always rescued by Mr Whelan, who would turn up at training once or twice a month. He was a big personality with a huge presence and, an ex-player himself (with Blackburn Rovers), he acquired further kudos with the lads. Despite all this, he never interfered with Paul Jewell's work and had a great relationship with the manager.

I have to admit that the first season was a bit of a struggle. I'd had regrets about leaving Everton, a huge club with a great history and tradition. Wigan, essentially a rugby town still finding its feet in the Premiership, was quite a different proposition. Many of the lads at Goodison were good friends and the backroom staff had been long established by David Moyes who kept everyone on side. I missed kit men Jimmy and Tony.

Laura and I had moved into a comfortable new house in a suburb of Stockport two months after I signed for the Latics. Elsie was doing well. She had started walking at eighteen months, which was earlier than we had been led to believe, she had started nursery and we had received a great deal of support in the statementing process – the legally binding method by which the local authority can provide extra educational support for children with special needs. Laura and I were quick to realise that a lot of families in our position were unaware of the assistance available or what they were entitled to, and the help available very much depended on where they lived. There is no question that some local authorities were much more progressive than others and that there existed, and still exists now, 'a postcode lottery'. Laura worked very hard on Elsie's behalf and we were beginning to see how Elsie was benefiting.

A month after the Republic's loss to Germany in Stuttgart, I was back with the international squad. The second 2008 European Championship qualifying group match pitched us against Cyprus in the country's capital, Nicosia. We were crushed 5-2. Although we were missing a number of key players, it was an embarrassing result. Next to the 4-0 home defeat by the Netherlands, this was my worst ever result in an international and certainly the worst I'd ever felt after a game. This defeat by Cyprus heaped additional pressure on Stan ahead of Ireland's next game, at home to the Czech Republic on 11 October.

It was a shit week and we got so much stick on our return to Dublin. Cyprus were, according to the newspapers, a team of part-timers who should have been despatched with ease. The press were merciless, accusing the players of either not caring about playing for the national side or of simply not being good enough. They levelled the idea that Steve Staunton was out of his depth as a manager in the international arena. A few of the lads didn't fancy the qualifier against the Czechs and returned to their clubs suffering from sudden unexplained injuries, although some did turn out for their clubs that weekend. The *Sun* sent over someone in a Miss Piggy costume to the training ground at Malahide. 'Miss Piggy' was supposed to get as close to Stan as possible for the press to take photos and embarrass him. Fortunately, security prevented the photo opportunity taking place.

A 1-1 draw against the Czechs eased the pressure on Stan a little. Although I scored, the joy was short-lived because, in the celebrations, I was poked in the face by substitute Clinton Morrison – his nail scratched my eyeball and I had to come off! It was a great relief to get something out of the game, to recover a little pride after the Cyprus performance and a testament to the spirit in the squad. There was a much better feeling in the camp.

In mid-November, in our next European Championship qualifier, we were pitched against San Marino in the last match to be played at the old Lansdowne Road ground. We won 5-0. The return fixture took place a couple of months later (February 2007) at Serravalle, the national stadium of the 'Most Serene Republic of San Marino', which claims to be the oldest surviving sovereign state and constitutional republic in the world, with an estimated population of just over 30,000. The idea of playing against such a small footballing nation in southern central Europe conjures up colourful images of Ruritania-type castles, beautiful princesses and dashing swordsmen, but I have to say I have travelled all over the world representing Ireland and we get to see very little of the various countries and their cultures. Sad to say but the most important things on these travels are a comfortable bed and decent food in a reasonable hotel. Not much else matters when you're playing and there's little time to see the sights.

Despite the setting, there was very little romantic about the game. We struggled throughout and after I had headed us into the lead, we conceded a late equaliser and needed a goal five minutes into injury time from Stephen Ireland to secure a 2-1 win and the three points. Coming so close to dropping points against a team ranked 195th in the world at the time of the match sparked further calls for Stan's resignation.

Fortunately, we returned to form with two successive 1–0 home victories over Wales and Slovakia (28 March 2007) at Croke Park, Dublin. The venue was extraordinarily significant as this was the first time a football match was played at Croke Park. The stadium was the scene of 'Bloody Sunday', a massacre by the Royal Irish Constabulary on 21 November 1920.

On that dreadful day the Dublin Gaelic football team were due to play Tipperary, with the proceeds of this 'great challenge match' to be donated to the Irish Republican Prisoners Fund. On the night of 20 November, Michael Collins sent a squad to assassinate the 'Cairo Gang', a team of undercover British agents working and living in Dublin. A series of shootings took place throughout the night that left fourteen members of the British forces dead.

In order to revenge the killings, the Crown Forces had mobilised in Dublin on the morning of the match with orders to go to Croke Park and search the crowd for known gunmen and weapons. Five minutes after the throw-in to start the match, the police, supported by the British Auxiliary Division and the 'Black and Tans', began to shoot indiscriminately into the crowd and fourteen people lost their lives, among them Michael Hogan, a player on the Tipperary team (after whom the Hogan Stand is named). It was therefore a huge decision to hold an international football match at Croke Park and I was proud to be part of this landmark occasion.

The actual result brought us into contention for second place in Group D of the qualifying groups, something the media had not expected, and drew a comment from RTÉ presenter Bill O'Herlihy at the end of the match expressing his disbelief that we were now in contention for qualification for Euro 2008.

Before I joined them, Wigan had successfully survived their first year in the Premiership and reached the League Cup final. Although I was new to the setup, the team suffered what has now become known as 'second season syndrome' whereby a newly promoted side can do well in their first season in the top flight, but struggles the following year. Perhaps it can be put down to a false sense of security or simply to a lack of confidence that always comes with a losing run. But it certainly had nothing to do with lack of effort. Paul Jewell wasn't the man to allow any sort of complacency. He wouldn't let that happen. He was always well prepared and training was pretty intense every day.

I remember there seemed to be an awful lot of forfeits during and after training – the losing team had to do extra running over heavy terrain around the training ground, which wasn't the best in the business and reminded me of my Preston days. Paul really worked us hard. He wanted to give us an edge, a winning mentality in training matches, and so the lads on the losing side, threatened with having to do an extra lap of the pitch or more press-ups, worked that much harder and did that little bit extra. Training was high-tempo and competitive and as a result we had a very fit and tough team.

In any case we struggled and we were defeated in a lot of games by the odd goal; and although it sounds like an excuse, we didn't get the rub of the green in a number of matches. We were in a very dangerous position and in a relegation dogfight. By the end of April, we hadn't won in six games and then we got beaten 3-0 at home by fellow strugglers West Ham. I had a bad game and was dropped for the following match, the last game of the season at the JJB Stadium.

The visitors were Middlesbrough and before the match, Bill Green, the very experienced chief scout, decided to call in a sports psychologist who he thought might motivate us and turn the tide of results. Paul Jewell wasn't overkeen on the idea but went along with the suggestion. We all met in the canteen at the training ground and the tables were moved so that we could all sit in a circle. The motivator, whose name I can't remember, so I'll call him 'Fred' (as good a name as any), produced small pieces of balsa wood and handed one to each of the players. On it he asked us to write what we were most afraid of.

Fred began by writing his own personal fear and then asked Bill to grip the wood with both hands and hold it at arm's length. Fred then tried to smash it with his hand. Unfortunately, the balsa wood slipped from Bill's grasp, flew into the air and knocked his glasses off. We all fell about and Fred was a bit annoyed that the presentation had started so comically. Anyway, we all wrote down what was worrying us (most wrote 'relegation') on the pieces of wood and then Fred would hold them and in turn we would smash the wood, thereby symbolically destroying our fear at the same time. I say all – in fact, Paul Jewell and Leighton Baines refused point-blank to have anything to do with this rubbish.

Fred also produced a blanket covered in broken glass and walked over it to show us that, with huge amount of self-belief, we could even conquer pain. He obviously saw himself as a sort of Lancashire fakir and considered that all we had to do was adopt the philosophy of mind over matter. Well, despite all the mumbo jumbo we lost 1-0 to a Mark Viduka goal, a result that cemented Boro's place in the Premiership. We never saw Fred again.

Our final game was against Sheffield United at Bramall Lane. It was an all-or-nothing game. We had to win, although there various permutations affecting the other games. The Blades were dependent on West Ham's game at Old Trafford. Assuming that West Ham lost to Man Utd on the same day, the Blades would stay up too, on superior goal difference. But if the Hammers were to get a point then Sheffield United also had to win. If we lost, the Blades stayed up. It really was a fight to the finish. No one gave us a chance. Neil Warnock's team had home advantage and nobody expected West Ham to get anything at Old Trafford.

I went to have a chat with Paul Jewell. I told him that I understood why he'd dropped me but that I was keen to do all I could in the final game. Before the conversation ended, Paul told me that he had decided to pick me for the game. Quite calmly and confidently he also told me that he had no doubt we would win. I was amazed by his cool demeanour.

Our form going into that match had been poor. We'd lost the last three games and failed to score in any of them. I don't know what it was but training that week was brilliant. The lads all looked sharp and surprisingly confident. Everyone outside the club had written us off – we were destined for the Championship and perhaps that spurred us on. We had nothing to lose. The boss was incredibly calm and repeated that he was absolutely certain we would win the last game. These were not hollow words to keep up our spirits – we could tell he genuinely meant what he said and his faith certainly rubbed off on us.

We travelled to Sheffield on 12 May, the day before the match, and stayed in a comfortable hotel with extensive grounds. On a walk around the gardens, Paul Jewell stopped us and told us how happy and proud of us he was. He was absolutely sure we would be safe and reiterated his positive feelings about the match. I don't think I've ever, now or since, felt as confident in a manager as I did in Paul that week.

The gaffer's belief continued into the dressing room before the game and we all felt surprisingly relaxed. He didn't actually give a team talk, but just before we took to the field he played us a tape of Al Pacino's 'Inch by Inch' speech from *Any Given Sunday*. I have to say that I have heard this speech played or delivered by a number of managers and it began to wear a bit thin by the end of my career, but that day it certainly had the desired effect.

We started at a furious pace and should have had a penalty in the opening minutes, but the referee, Mike Dean, turned down our appeals. But we continued to press and were rewarded with a goal. During training and in matches, Paul Scharner liked to attack from midfield and often asked me to find him between the penalty spot and the eighteen-yard line. And that's exactly what I did. I received the ball on the left and pulled it back for Paul, who scored with a brilliant finish. We were a goal up and the three thousand travelling fans went crazy. The Sheffield United supporters were stunned. The score from Old Trafford was all square. As things stood, we were staying up and the home side was going down.

Conditions were terrible – the already sodden pitch was becoming more difficult to play on as the rain lashed down. And with so much at stake, the challenges were flying in from every angle. In the thirty-eighth minute the Blades equalised. Bramall Lane erupted. Ryan Taylor was injured and had to be replaced by David Unsworth. We'd lost two of our defenders and it wasn't even half-time. Emerson Boyce moved to right-back.

Then news filtered through from Manchester that Carlos Tévez had scored for West Ham. Although this goal had no direct bearing on us – we still had to win – it certainly motivated the home team and their fans roared them on. A minute before the break, Emile was fouled and I fired the free kick into the area. Phil Jagielka rose to head but instead punched the ball away. Penalty! David Unsworth stepped up to take the spot kick. When the season started Unsy had been a Blades player and had actually missed from the spot in a goalless draw with Blackburn at Bramall Lane in September. Not this time. Thankfully, Unsy converted and Mike Dean blew for half-time. We were 2-1 up and playing really well.

The entire second half was unbearable. The longest second period of my life. Wave after wave of United attacks: Danny Webber was one-on-one with Mike Pollitt – his chip beat 'Polly' but the ball hit the foot of the post and rolled along the goal line, almost in slow motion, before being cleared by Bainsey. When Lee McCulloch was sent off in the seventy-fourth minute for a second bookable offence, however, it just got worse. Sheffield threw everything at us and we were defending for our lives.

They pushed centre-half Chris Morgan up front and pumped lots of balls towards him. Emile ended up dropping back and marking him, playing an immense centre-half role. With no change in the score from Old Trafford, Sheffield United had to score to stay up.

We hung on until the end of full-time but there was still five minutes' stoppage time to survive. Paul Jewell finally lost his cool and skirmished on the touchline with United's assistant manager, Stuart McCall, and the fourth official when the ball was returned just a little too quickly for his liking. After what seemed like an eternity, the final whistle went. We were safe! There was chaos.

Dave Whelan came on to the pitch and directed the fans' cheers and applause to Paul Jewell standing next to him. In a post-match interview for Sky, Paul admitted that he was emotionally and physically drained, but that he had always maintained his faith in us. He also generously wanted everyone to acknowledge the work of the unsung backroom staff.

I really felt for the Sheffield United players. I tried to go around all of them. What could I say other than to wish them luck? Most of them didn't say a word. They shook hands but some were too distraught to look at me. Then we went to celebrate with the triumphant Wigan fans before returning to our dressing room for post-match champagne, celebrations and general mayhem. Those moments remain something of a blur, but I do recall Chris Morgan coming into our dressing room to congratulate those of us still there. I also remember his bone-crushing handshake. He is a United legend and it must have taken a lot for him to show such sportsmanship. We had a cup of tea together and chatted. Funnily enough, some years later, we ended up doing coaching badges together in Belfast.

The day after that extraordinary match, we went to the training ground. There was no actual training involved, but it is usual at most clubs for players to be given schedules for pre-season before everyone goes their separate ways and to say their goodbyes before the break. Some of the lads were still pissed from partying the previous night and the smell of alcohol in the room was rank. We were expecting a triumphant speech from Paul Jewell and a call to arms for next season, but what he said stunned us. Paul announced very briefly that he was resigning. Everyone was gobsmacked and those still under the influence sobered up very quickly. He quickly became very emotional and just told us, 'I need to take a break.' There was no other explanation. This should have been Paul's finest hour and now he was going.

Dave Whelan came in and said that the assistant manager, Chris Hutchings, would be taking over first-team affairs and we were left to take in what had happened. Paul had achieved real success and had been responsible for signing nearly all the current players on the books. There was real concern how the team would now function.

We later discovered that Dave Whelan had tried to change Paul's mind and, thinking he just needed a short break, had offered him a two-week holiday at his home in Barbados. But Paul wouldn't think about it and was determined to take a proper break.

The implications of the relegation struggle and the game at Old Trafford have been well documented. Dave Whelan was absolutely convinced that West Ham should have been relegated because Argentinian international Carlos Tévez had scored crucial goals in the last few months and had kept them in the league. Premier League rules state that no player can be owned by a third party and when Tévez signed for the Hammers he was owned by a group led by Kia Joorabchian. The Premier League had fined West Ham £5.5 million but had not deducted any points.

A ruling at the Court of Arbitration later found in Sheffield United's favour and recommended that West Ham should compensate Sheffield United to reflect loss of earnings from relegation – estimated at between £20 and £30 million. United's players took wage cuts as a result of relegation and Neil Warnock resigned.

Initially, I wasn't going to be needed for an international tour of the USA taking place at the end of the domestic season as Steve Staunton wanted to blood some younger players. Unfortunately, a number of players subsequently dropped out and, as Stan needed some experience in the squad, he rang to say I was needed after all. He also wanted me to skipper the team. I agreed immediately. I never needed to be asked twice to play for my country but it was a little unnerving to discover that the other lads were so inexperienced that the number of caps in the whole squad didn't match those that I had acquired over the years.

In fact, one of these lads, Joe Lapira, who was playing in the States, joined up with the squad when we got over there. Stan explained that Joe had previously done okay at Aberdeen, was being watched by Glasgow Rangers and had had a spell in Norway. I'd certainly never heard of him, and neither had anyone else. As captain, I felt it right to welcome him into the fold. I asked him who he played for and I think he replied, 'Baton Rouge Capitals'. I'd never heard of them – the reason being that they were a USL Premier Development League team, pretty much a Sunday pub team for young lads. I have trained with hundreds, if not thousands, of players over the years, and Joe Lapira was no worse than many I've seen. He was young, enthusiastic and did his best.

We stayed in Hoboken, Frank Sinatra's birthplace, a small suburb overlooking the Hudson River with great views of New York City. Stan gave us one day off to explore New York and a few of us headed down to Ground Zero, which at that stage was still a hole in the ground. It was a place a few of us wanted to see in order to pay our respects and it had a sobering effect on some of the lads ahead of the game against Ecuador at the Giants Stadium in New Jersey.

The second friendly in Boston, against Bolivia, was played at the Foxboro Stadium, home of the NFL's New England Patriots. The ground was also shared by the New England Revolution, then managed by Stan's former Liverpool team-mate Steve Nicol, who popped into our hotel to say hello.

Our next international match was another friendly in Denmark in August and an eight-match unbeaten sequence since the Cyprus result was cemented with a convincing 4-0 win. We headed into the next set of Euro qualifiers placed third in the group. Against Slovakia in Bratislava, we bossed the game but conceded in injury time and the game ended in a disappointing 2-2 draw.

As Carso and I were coming off the pitch we were approached by FIFA officials, who told us that we had been selected for drugs testing and would have to give urine samples. Although we realised that the procedure had to be carried out, it was always a bit of a drag. We weren't allowed to go to the dressing room and had to be kept away from the other lads. Carso and I had to sit in the medical room and chat to a couple of the Slovakian lads who had also been picked out. We were sitting there drinking lots of water and waiting for nature to take its course when Alan Byrne, the Irish doctor, came in. He had just come from the dressing room and gave us some sad news. Just before the game, Stephen Ireland had received a telephone call to say that his grandmother had died. The lads were consoling him and, by all accounts, physio Mick Byrne had been great in trying to counsel Stephen, who was naturally really upset. By the time we had fulfilled the requirements of the drugs test, the team bus had departed and Carso and I had to join them back at the hotel later.

At the hotel, Stan explained that Stephen was going to be allowed to leave the squad and a private plane had been arranged to fly him home to be with his family. Stan gave a press conference telling journalists what had happened.

The following day at training, word had begun to spread that Stephen's maternal granny, Patricia Tallon, was still very much in the land of the living and when the story got out she made it known that the rumours of her death were very much exaggerated. Back in Manchester, Stephen claimed that it was actually his paternal grandmother who had passed away. The press checked up on this version and discovered that Brenda Kitchener was also alive and well and living in London.

Of course by the time we realised it was all a load of rubbish and that Stephen was concocting these stories because he didn't want to play in the next game, we all thought it was hilarious. The lads had a field day: 'How many more grannies has Stephen got?' 'They're dropping like flies.' 'When's the next relative going to go?' 'I wouldn't like to be one of his family.' 'They're all doomed.' Etc etc.

But it was all quite sad. We knew that Stephen had some personal issues and he later told the press that his young girlfriend had suffered a miscarriage and he needed to be with her, but he had panicked and come up with the dead grand-mother stories – known from then on as 'Grannygate'. It was even more unreasonable as Stan is a very sympathetic man and would have understood that some things, contrary to Bill Shankly's famous saying, are more important than football and would have released Stephen from the squad.

'Grannygate' offered a bit of a diversion from the fact that our next game in Prague was just a few days away and anything less than a win would see our qualifying campaign effectively come to an end. Despite a battling display with ten men, after Stephen Hunt was harshly dismissed, we lost 1-0.

The following month we drew 0-0 with Germany at Croke Park, a result that meant that we were all but mathematically out of the competition. I particularly remember this game because I suffered an accidental clash of heads with Sebastian Schweinsteiger and cut my eye. He had to be substituted but my wound was glued for the remainder of the game and I had to have half a dozen stitches after the match. My mum always said I was hard-headed...but the pain of going out of the Euros was far worse than anything physical.

We desperately wanted revenge on Cyprus for the 5-2 defeat in Nicosia, but we were outplayed and lucky to grab a draw thanks to an injury-time volley from Steve Finnan. There were 15,000 empty seats in the stadium and those spectators who were there greeted the final whistle with boos. It was a bitterly disappointing end to our campaign in which qualification was secured by Germany and the Czech Republic.

It wasn't just the players and the fans who were saddened and upset. The RTÉ post-match discussion included a panel comprising Liam Brady, John Giles and Eamon Dunphy, all of whom expressed their dissatisfaction. Their ire was directed at the manager, Steve Staunton, who they felt wasn't up to the job, lacked coaching nous and whose judgement they questioned.

Despite admitting that he had been a great servant to his country and was a very nice man, Johnny Giles said he felt it was time for Stan to go. Eamon Dunphy wanted him to be replaced by what the FAI had promised before: a world-class management team.

The FAI duly announced that an emergency meeting was to be called to discuss Steve Staunton's position. Chief Executive John Delaney refused publicly to back Stan and seemed to want to distance himself from any involvement in Stan's appointment. Stan responded by stating that he intended to see out the remainder of his four-year contract.

Soon after, the FAI confirmed that Stan's twenty-one-month reign as international manager had come to an end and he was to be replaced by Don Givens on a temporary basis. I was sad to see Stan go, but could understand that the results weren't satisfactory. There had been negative feelings at the time of Stan's appointment and he never really had a chance to prove himself. I felt that we had let him down but, as ever, it's the manager that takes responsibility and ultimately pays the price. Stan's a great guy and he never really recovered from the sacking. Apart from a brief spell at Darlington, he hasn't managed since. He was a great player to have in your team.

In November we were scheduled to play against Wales in what was now a meaningless game for both teams. Before the match, we stayed at Celtic Manor Resort in Newport – the venue for the Ryder Cup a few years later. Some of the senior players, including myself, Robbie Keane, Shay Given, Carso and Steve Finnan, had been asked by John Delaney to attend a meeting to discuss the next managerial appointment. We weren't very keen on the idea and I didn't think the players should have been involved in the decision. We all had our favourite bosses, and had heard rumours about others. During the meeting a lot of notable names were mentioned, including those of Kenny Dalglish, Paul Jewell, Terry Venables and Gérard Houllier. There was rumour and gossip and objectivity was the least of it.

Anyway, we agreed to attend but made it clear that we wanted the meeting to be kept secret. John Delaney assured us that it would be and that what was discussed in the room would remain in the room.

However, the first FAI official I bumped into before the game asked me, 'How did the meeting go?' and before long it was reported in the press.

During this time I had been asked to participate in an eccentric fundraising event for the Down's Syndrome Association, of which I was now a patron, and Down's Syndrome Ireland. The plan was to push a milk float around the Republic for forty days and nights early the following year, covering a distance of 787 miles!

The idea was based on a scene from the cult comedy series *Father Ted*, in which the 'Craggy Island Creamery' milk float had been featured. Forty teams were due to participate in the event, supported by bookmakers Paddy Power, to raise cash and also to publicise Down's syndrome. I was only involved in the launch in Dublin but was delighted to be part of such a fun and useful occasion.

Wigan also wanted to publicise the event and arranged for a photo shoot. Matt McCann, the club's madcap and much liked press officer, arranged for a milk float from a local dairy to be driven to the training ground, but became quite angry when he discovered that there wasn't a single bottle of milk on the cart. I remember him saying, 'Where's the fucking milk? We need some milk!'

The 2007–8 season had begun well for Wigan and, after victories over Everton, Middlesbrough and Sunderland, we were actually at the top of the league – for the first time in the club's history. During the close season, Leighton Baines moved to Everton and, as we didn't have a recognised left-back, Chris Hutchings moved me into that position and I played for most of the season. However, after the bright start our results were mixed. Emile Heskey, who was playing brilliantly, was recalled to the England squad for the first time since 2005. Unfortunately, he broke his foot and was out for six weeks and we struggled to score.

From the end of September we went on a disastrous run, losing eight league games in a row while conceding twenty goals and Dave Whelan, fearing yet another relegation scrap, decided to cancel Chris Hutchings' contract. Dave Whelan described Chris as 'a brilliant coach with a super attitude but not tough enough with the players – he doesn't have a killer instinct'. Whelan also stated that Chris knew everything about the game but 'couldn't put fire into the players' bellies.'

The man the Wigan owner thought could fire up the players was Steve Bruce, then managing Birmingham City. Dave Whelan negotiated, at great cost, the release of the Blues manager and in November Steve took the reins. He tightened the defence straightaway – the full-backs weren't encouraged to attack and we had more shape. Emile also returned to the team. We were unbeaten in April and our Premiership status was secured at the beginning of May with a game to spare. We finally ended up fourteenth with forty points – three places higher than the previous season and two points better off. It was an amazing turnaround considering where we had been in November.

On May 1st, 2008, Giovanni Trapattoni was appointed Ireland's manager. Born, prophetically, in Milan on St Patrick's Day 1939, Trapattoni had achieved legendary status as a player and coach. He had played for Italy in the 1962 World Cup and had enjoyed a coaching career spanning three decades in which he had won ten Serie A titles, a European Cup, a Cup Winners' Cup and three UEFA Cups. He had managed Italy at the 2002 World Cup, but had been criticised for defensive tactics. Up until his appointment, he was sporting director of the Austrian club Red Bull Salzburg.

Marco Tardelli was confirmed as Trapattoni's assistant manager but, more pertinently, Dublin-born Liam Brady, who had been capped by the Republic seventy-two times and had won two Serie A titles under Trapattoni at Juventus, joined the back-room staff. Liam was a great appointment – not only did he have a fundamental understanding of Irish football, he commanded a huge amount of respect and, as a bonus, he was also fluent in Italian. Trapattoni could speak very little English and, although he had interpreters, Liam's role would be crucial. Liam had been working with Arsenal's academy and was also doing some television work for RTÉ. At the beginning he was a little nervous that his former media role, in which he had occasionally been critical of the national side, might affect his relationship with the lads, but this never happened. Liam's presence gave us all a lift.

The appointment of Trapattoni had come out of the blue – Terry Venables, Martin O'Neill, Gérard Houllier and Graeme Souness had all been mentioned and there was even talk of Mick McCarthy coming back. We knew of his reputation, which was synonymous with world football. His contract at Red Bull had been coming to an end, he was in much demand and had received a number of offers, but decided that he would come to the Republic when he was approached by the FAI.

There is no doubt that Giovanni Trapattoni has incredible charisma. There is an aura about him. He lived in Milan and made it quite clear that he wasn't going to move permanently. As far as I know, he rarely, if ever, attended a Premiership match and only spent time in Ireland before games and at the training camps. He did recognise, however, the influence and strength of the Irish media. In his first meeting with the players, he told us that today's newspaper was tomorrow's toilet paper and mimed wiping his bottom! Liam Brady didn't need to translate that gesture!

'Trap' swiftly asserted his authority by hinting that Ireland was capable of becoming the 'new Greece' (Greece has unexpectedly won the European Championship in 2004). He had an ability to command respect and said all the right things from the outset: 'It's dangerous to change too much – I don't want to make drastic changes too quickly. I'm just going to focus on little details and show the players DVDs of the things they can alter. Players are delicate – so I'm also going to have to work on their psychology.'

A back injury kept me out of the squad for two friendlies against Serbia and Colombia in May 2008. The first ended in a 1-1 draw and the second saw the Republic run out 1-0 winners. There were reports that I had decided to quit international football. At that time I had played eighty-seven times for Ireland and it was claimed that I wanted to spend more time with my family. In fact, I've often been asked about retiring from international football – the first time I was just twenty-seven...and then after every campaign. Perhaps the journalists were just trying to get rid of me! It was never in my mind to pull the plug on my international career.

My third season at Wigan began with two defeats, but we then went on a six-match unbeaten run. In the third league match, at the KC Stadium at the end of August, I fractured my cheekbone in an aerial challenge with defender Sam Ricketts in a 5-0 win over Hull. I knew it had gone immediately because I had a big V-shaped dent in my face. I didn't want to go off but our head physio, Dave Galley, persuaded me that I had to and I underwent surgery the following day.

My first thought was that I would miss the Republic's opening 2010 World Cup qualifiers with Georgia and Montenegro. The first match of the group stage against Georgia was due to be played a few days later. Initially, I was told that I would be unable to play for six weeks but the surgeon cleared me to play on if I wore a special mask to protect the bone. The club doctor was a just a little bit wary about me playing with a broken bone so soon after the injury, but Steve Bruce, who must have broken plenty of bones during his career, just told me to be careful and said he wouldn't have a problem with me playing in the game as long as everything was done correctly.

When I got to Dublin they made a mould of my face and gave me the mask, which was reasonably comfortable and didn't hinder my vision. I took a bit of stick about it but it was better than not being able to play. I couldn't train for the first couple of days but I was desperate to play.

Trapattoni was very flattering in his response when I told him that I wanted to be included, despite the injury, and was quoted as saying, 'But what is important is his mentality. With that mentality, I am confident we will go forward. He will have another check but I am not worried – I am sure he can play. He is a big example to all the Ireland players.'

The game against Georgia took place at Bruchweg Stadium in Mainz, Germany, because of the political upheavals in Georgia and the fallout with Russia over the support of breakaway states. This was Trapattoni's first competitive match in charge. I played the full ninety minutes and we ran out 2-1 winners with a performance more convincing than the scoreline suggests. There was no doubt that we benefited from playing on a neutral ground.

The match against Montenegro four days later marked my ninetieth cap and also brought up a half-century of consecutive starts in competitive matches. I didn't think too much about this milestone – I just wanted to play in the games. Not being fit and available to play would have been a massive disappointment to me. Playing for my country was always a huge honour, which, if anything, became even greater every game I played.

In fact, the game itself was a scrappy 0-0 draw, but we were happy with a point and were now unbeaten in two tricky ties. The final game of the World Cup campaign that year took place a month later at Croke Park – Trapattoni's first home match in charge. We got off to a perfect start with yet another important goal from Robbie. We defended well and Shay managed to keep the ball out late on for us to hang on at 1-0. It was a vital win for us in the end and kept us ticking over nicely in the group.

Back at Wigan our fortunes were mixed – the club was still getting stick for the state of the pitch at the JJB, which we shared with Wigan Warriors, the rugby league club. During my time there, the pitch was always in a terrible condition, but I have to say that it did work to our advantage against the opposition as it stopped some of the real footballing sides from playing a passing game. I remember many Premiership managers complaining about the pitch at post-match press conferences.

The January transfer window turned out to be pretty busy for the club. Emile went to Aston Villa, we took Mido on loan, signed Colombian international Hugo Rodallega from Mexican club Necaxa and swapped Ryan Taylor for Charles N'Zogbia. We also sold Wilson Palacios for £12 million to Spurs...and I was soon to be shipped out as well.

I had switched from midfield to left-back to cover some injuries but when Steve Bruce made a permanent signing of Honduran international Maynor Figueroa, who played in the same position, I knew my time at Wigan was limited. I was, however, still keen to stay at the club. My contract was up in the summer and I went to see Steve Bruce about an extension. He seemed a bit ill at ease during our discussions and said that my age counted against me.

'You're thirty-four after all.'

'No, I'm not,' I replied. 'I'm thirty-two.'

Steve looked surprised. 'Oh, I thought you were thirty-four – nearly thirty-five.'

'No, I'm still thirty-two.'

The gaffer looked relieved. 'Well, you're over thirty.'

I couldn't argue with that. I nodded and helpfully added, 'True.'

'Well, in any case,' Steve concluded, 'I've agreed to let you go to Hull.'

It was clear that I didn't figure in his future plans and there was to be no contract extension. Steve told me that the two clubs were talking but no deal had yet been struck. Hull were in the Premiership and, if there was a chance of moving to Yorkshire, it was a no brainer.

It was clear I was on my way again.

Chapter Nine

Milestones, Tricksters and Conspiracies

'They were on the side of the angels, even if the angels weren't entirely sure that this was a good thing.'

JOHN CONNOLLY, *THE REAPERS*

I joined Hull on 15 January 2009 on a permanent deal for an undisclosed fee, but which was probably about £500,000, on a two and a half year contract with the Yorkshire club.

In a statement to the media Steve Bruce stated that I was out of contract in the summer and for financial reasons it made sense for me to be sold. He made all the right noises in terms of our relationship and was quoted as saying: 'On a football level, I'm very disappointed to lose a very experienced squad member in Kevin and a true professional in every sense. But I feel we are well stocked on the left-hand side and we left it up to Kevin to make the final decision. Kevin has been a really valued member of the team, never given less than 100 per cent and sets a terrific example in the dressing room. However, at his age I can understand he wants to be playing regularly, something which we have not been able to offer him of late. He goes with all our best wishes.'

In all I had made eighty-four appearances for the Latics and really enjoyed myself there. I always had an excellent relationship with the supporters, who were always great to me. I still have a very soft spot for Wigan. It's a small, friendly club with a great atmosphere and I think I joined at a very good time. When I look back, I think we overachieved; if so, this was very much down to the team's work ethic and the ministrations of Dave Whelan.

I didn't know that much about the man who signed me, but City's manager, Phil Brown, was flattering when I joined Hull: 'He is thirty-two years old; he has got ninety-odd internationals. He has been a credit to the game at the highest level. That kind of experience is priceless to us at the moment.' I was delighted to complete the move and wanted to stay in the Premier League because I wanted to play as many games in the top flight as I could. I was allocated the No. 17 shirt, previously worn by Irish compatriot Paul McShane before he was recalled from his loan spell by Sunderland. I'd never been superstitious about shirt numbers. Some players want to know what number they will be wearing before they sign for a new club or at the beginning of the season insist on a lucky number. I've always taken whatever number I was allocated.

I made my debut for Hull on 17 January at the KC Stadium against Arsenal. The team hadn't won since the beginning of December and morale was pretty low. At the pre-match meal, Phil announced the line-up. Striker Marlon King, on loan from Wigan, who had been excluded from the team, muttered something under his breath. The next thing we knew was that Marlon was back at Wigan. It was a pretty interesting start to my Hull career.

Although we lost the match 3-1, I thought we showed promise. The fans were terrific and it was quite an atmosphere. In fact, Phil Brown had done a great job at Hull. He'd been appointed as the permanent manager in January 2007, having taken them out of the Championship relegation zone in his role as caretaker manager. The following season Hull City won promotion to the Premiership for the first time in the Championship play-off final on 24 May 2008.

On the day I arrived at Hull, there was still talk of the controversial incident that had taken place a few weeks earlier on Boxing Day at Manchester City. Following a poor first-half performance after which Hull were losing 4-0, Phil Brown conducted his half-time team talk on the pitch, in the penalty area right in front of the Hull supporters. I was on the bench at Wigan that day and at half-time goalkeeping coach Nigel Spink told us that Phil Brown was giving the Hull players a bollocking. News travelled fast that day! The lads couldn't believe it and couldn't wait to see it all on *Match of the Day* that night.

You could see that the Hull lads were mortified; they went on to lose 5-1. It seemed that the damage this ill-judged and dramatic behaviour caused had still to be repaired.

Phil made another signing just a few days after I arrived. This was a more expensive acquisition. Flamboyant midfielder Jimmy Bullard joined from Fulham at a cost of around £5 million. Jimmy had left Wigan a few months before I signed for them, but apart from his undoubted footballing talent Jimmy had a reputation for being pretty wacky and more than a little wayward.

There was the famous story about the time the floodlights failed during a League Cup semi-final tie against Arsenal and the JJB Stadium was plunged into darkness. It was said that he first inspected Freddie Ljungberg's shorts to see whether the Swedish part-time model was wearing the Armani underwear he advertised and then ran the length of the pitch, and when the lights came back on Jimmy was standing on Arsenal's goal line with the ball at his feet and a huge grin on his face.

A night out with Jimmy was frightening, You couldn't rule anything out and some of the things he used to get up to in the dressing room had very little to do with football. Unfortunately, he had a very dodgy knee and our worst fears were confirmed when, on his debut against West Ham, he injured his knee and was out for the rest of the season.

Jimmy didn't return until October 2009 and when he scored against Manchester City from the penalty spot the celebration was pure theatre. We all sat down on the pitch and Jimmy waved his finger at us in a piss take of Phil Brown's half-time admonishment from the same fixture the previous season. Of course there was nothing spontaneous about the celebration – we had planned beforehand that whoever scored would impersonate the boss. It seemed only right that Jimmy took centre stage, or, should I say, centre circle. And Phil took it well.

We struggled for most of the second half of the season and found ourselves in the drop zone. Before the last but one game of the season, away at Bolton, the squad was taken to the Lake District in a bid to boost morale. Phil advised us at the start that there was to be no sense of seniority while we were there and told us, 'Call me Phil!' We spent three days in various team-building exercises, including clay-pigeon shooting and archery, but the most interesting drill was driving a four-by-four blindfolded and relying on a co-driver/passenger to give us directions. Just to make it a little more difficult, the steering had been reversed so that when your co-driver told you to turn left, you had to steer the wheel to the right. It certainly built up trust and, amazingly, no one was killed.

Anyway, it was a great distraction and whether or not it was down to our time in the Lakes, we played really well and came back from 1-0 down to take a valuable point against Bolton, which gave us a chance to stay up. I played at centre-half in this and the last match of the season, against Manchester United. Before the Man Utd game, we 'celebrated' the Player of the Year do.

Michael Turner won the award for the second year running and then Phil Brown gave a speech, thanking the players and addressing the supporters. He then started to give his own rendition of the Beach Boys song, 'Sloop John B'. The lads looked at each other in embarrassment and were even more mortified when, after the cheering and applause had died down, he announced, 'And if we stay up I'll sing again.'

I'd been in the same position of Premiership survival and dependent on the last day of the season two years earlier with Wigan. This time we were relying on Newcastle's result against Aston Villa. Nervous tension was in abundance at the KC Stadium that day and the anxious fans were distracted by the game going on at Villa Park. A win would have made us safe but we just froze. Although we were up against a weakened Manchester United team, we lost 1-0; but somehow we got away with it as Newcastle were defeated by Aston Villa by the same margin. We finished in seventeenth place, a point above the Geordies. I couldn't believe we'd stayed up.

And, of course, Phil carried out his threat. At the end of the game, he went on to the pitch with a microphone and started singing 'Sloop John B' triumphantly to the delirious crowd.

The Republic's World Cup qualifying campaign continued in February with a 2-1 victory over Georgia at Croke Park. It was quite a bizarre game in that we were handed two goals...well, shouldered would be more accurate. We were trailing to the Georgians and unable to force an equaliser when we were awarded an unbelievable penalty after the ball brushed the shoulder of one of their defenders. Robbie converted and then added a second when an attempted header also came off his shoulder and slowly crossed the goal line. The crowd went crazy and so did we! There had been talk that Giovanni Trapattoni was a lucky manager; that night he lived up to his reputation.

At the end of March we drew 1-1 with Bulgaria in Dublin. It looked as if we might have the edge on them after Richard Dunne's header opened the scoring. We missed some chances and they rarely threatened, but, with full-time approaching, Stilian Petrov drove a cross shot from inside the penalty area. It hit me on the leg and went into the net. There was nothing I could do. It was the first own goal of my career and I was gutted. Of course, it had to happen in such a vital match, didn't it?

A few days later we were in Bari to face the Azzurri and, thanks to a very late goal from Robbie, kept up our unbeaten run in the qualifiers. The Italians were reduced to ten men early on and we drew 1-1. There was no doubt that our results and the atmosphere in the squad were boosted by Giovanni Trapattoni. He certainly brought more steel to the team and we had stopped conceding silly goals...well...until our next match.

By the beginning of June it was clear to me that Bulgaria would never be my favourite nation. In the match in Sofia we were 1-0 up when there was a disastrous misunderstanding between myself and Sean St Ledger in which we allowed the ball to run between us, leading to a Bulgarian equaliser. It was a huge disappointment to have conceded in such a fashion. I felt terrible after the game and didn't want to talk too much about it. I just wanted to get home to the family. I was looking forward to a holiday with them and a bit of a summer break, but sometimes after a mistake like that it's helpful to have another game soon so that you can take your mind off it.

A word here about Richard Dunne. We had managed to withstand huge pressure in that game – thanks mainly to Dunney, who was immense and had also scored our opener. Richard is a brilliant lad – he has absolutely no airs and graces and is a solid and dependable character – not at all flashy, much like he plays. He's happy sitting in the corner of a pub, nursing a pint and enjoying a singsong although he'd never join in. In fact, I've never heard him sing. You always felt you had a chance when Dunney was in the team. He played some of the best forwards in the world off the park with his strength and surprising pace. He's also great in the air and grabbed the odd goal. An Irish legend, at the time of writing he has returned to the Republic's fold after being out for the best part of the year through injury.

In the summer of 2009, Phil Brown strengthened the Hull

squad with the signings of Seyi Olofinjana, Jozy Altidore (on loan from Villarreal), Ibrahima Sonko, and a couple of compatriots, Stephen Hunt and Paul McShane. Free agent Jan Vennegoor of Hesselink also joined the club at the beginning of September 2009. Unfortuately, Michael Turner left to join Sunderland, after Hull received a large bid they felt they had to accept.

I was delighted about Stephen joining us and helped him make his decision. I felt he needed to be back playing in the Premiership, although I realised he might play in my position and take my place! I recommended him to Phil – Stephen had played in front of me on a number of occasions for the Republic – he has an incredible work rate and always worked his socks off, defending and attacking in equal measure. The distance he covered during a game often shattered the Prozone records. I know that Hunty can come across as a bit brash, but I think this is because he says what he thinks. He is very honest and genuine and always expects the best for himself and from his team-mates. That's also true of Paul McShane: he has an unparalleled attitude to training and conducts himself brilliantly off the pitch.

Despite the additions to the squad, we lost six of our first seven games, including a 6-1 defeat at Anfield. It was a bad day and there were repercussions. Phil Brown felt that we were too pampered and after the Liverpool defeat he supposedly told some of the canteen staff not to come in for a week, so there was no food before or after training. Phil even had his assistant Brian Horton place an 'Out of Order' sign on the coffee machine. I asked Paula who worked in the canteen why it wasn't working. She said, 'It just isn't.' Then one of the team inspected the appliance and discovered that the plug had deliberately been pulled out at the back and reconnected it before gleefully shouting, 'It's all right, lads, I've fixed it!'

Paula's only response was a frustrated, 'You can't do that!'

Phil was actually an excellent coach although his personality and eccentric ways sometimes detracted from his talent. I got loads of texts from players at other clubs wanting to know about Phil: 'Is Phil Brown bonkers?' 'What's with the headset and microphone?' And the most popular, 'Why is your manager wearing that pink sweater around his neck on *Goals on Sunday*?' Whenever we had an international get-together, Phil Brown was often the first subject to be discussed.

We had resumed our World Cup campaign in September with a 2-1 win over Cyprus, which left us buzzing and on target for South Africa, but we had all got together before the Premiership season began with a friendly against Australia in a new stadium in Limerick. The day before the match we spent the afternoon at the Coolmore Stud Farm and trainer Aidan O'Brien's Ballydoyle stables. Aidan himself drove us around the gallops in a minibus and we were given tours of the multi-million-pound racing empire. I had a photograph taken with the amazing Galileo, best known for winning the Epsom Derby, Irish Derby Stakes and King George VI and Queen Elizabeth Stakes. He was then retired and had been put out to stud, having been insured for €100 million. He actually got a bit frisky with me, but I won't elaborate – I'm not going to go all *Equus* on you. And as for the match – we lost 3-0 and were booed off. I suppose we performed more like carthorses than Thoroughbreds that evening. I have always had an interest in the 'sport of kings' and now co-own a couple of horses – St Devote and Honest Strike – in a syndicate with some of my fellow internationals. The Cheltenham Festival is one of my favourite sporting events – for obvious reasons!

Anyway, we followed up the Cyprus result with a draw the following month against Italy in Dublin. Italy got the point they needed to secure their place in South Africa and it ensured us a play-off place. I'm not surprised the strains of Hot Chocolate's 'Everyone's A Winner' boomed from the PA system. It was a great achievement to remain undefeated throughout the group and we came close to victory over Italy in both games, pushing them in both matches. Trapattoni had created a competitive team which was hard to beat and growing in confidence.

Our attention was drawn to the play-off games, scheduled for November, but first we had to host Montenegro. It was a meaningless game in terms of the qualifying group, but had special significance for me as I was due to earn my hundredth Irish cap.

On the morning of the match, I woke up at 8.30, the normal time for an evening kick-off. A match day can sometimes feel as if it lasts forever but that day seemed even worse. I stayed longer than usual at breakfast with a few of the lads. Kevin Doyle was one of those who was normally up early and we stayed chatting about all sorts with a few of the staff members, including Alan Byrne (doctor), Ciaran Murray (physio) and Martin Byrne (security).

Martin always raised the topics for discussion, anything from politics to sport or music. Martin is the expert on all issues – at least that's what he tells us until we really look into what he has said and discover it's either made up because he doesn't really know what he's talking about or the content has been exaggerated to make the story sound more impressive. Martin and Bobby Ward, also security, are a great team and I have loved spending hours in the corridors of team hotels in their company over the years sharing their tales and forceful opinions.

Today, I just wanted to kill as much time as possible before we had our usual 11.30 walk along Malahide beach. It was like clockwork on match days and the timetable was always very predictable. We then had a team meeting to discuss the Montenegro team and to run through video clips of their danger men and watch all their set plays. Following a light lunch, Shay, who was coincidentally also winning his hundredth cap, and I were presented with a framed signed shirt by the entire squad and an engraved watch by our captain, Robbie Keane. Shay said a few words of thanks after but I was so emotional I could hardly speak. I just said that I concurred with what Shay had said! I'm usually quite good at speaking up in public but this time I just couldn't muster anything.

Most of the lads would normally have an afternoon sleep before a night game but I just sat and watched television for a while and decided to spend a bit more time in the corridor with Tony Hickey, the head of security, and Martin. I just needed more chat to distract me as the butterflies in my stomach were becoming more active!

After our pre-match meal there was another short meeting to finish our preparation and a reminder of our set plays and how we could punish Montenegro. At the end of our meeting, our video analyst Brian McCarthy played a DVD looking back through both my and Shay's international careers. The DVD had some great music playing over the clips of a few of my goals and some of Shay's memorable saves over the years. I was in tears.

On the coach to the game I had managed to regain my composure, but the wait after arriving at Croke Park prior to the game seemed to drag on for hours. I was glad that the result didn't really affect our chances of qualification; I don't know what I would have been like if it had.

Shay had the number '100' sewn into his gloves to mark the occasion. I was so pleased for him and it was brilliant to be sharing this honour. At that time, I felt that Shay was the best keeper in the world. He was very commanding, and his shot-stopping and bravery were second to none. Umbro, the kit manufacturers, had sent me a special pair of boots with the number '100' imprinted on the tongue, but I didn't wear them. I felt more comfortable in my own boots.

I recalled what our former kit man Johnny Fallon had said to me when I made my inauspicious debut against Iceland. He was no longer part of the backroom staff, but I wanted him to be there. The FAI had provided a box for our families and I invited Johnny and his wife, Margaret, to be my guests. Johnny now works for Macron kits and I am still in touch with him every week. I am grateful for all he has done for me.

I didn't really enjoy the actual match, which ended in a disappointing goalless draw. I was so nervous and I was just glad I came through it without cramping up as I felt very tense throughout. I remember that the supporters were great and, despite the boredom of the game, tried desperately hard to lift us and sang some celebratory songs directed at Shay and me.

After the game I brought Elsie and Isla down to the dressing room when everybody had left. I just let them run wild around the showers and warm-up room. I then took them on to the pitch under the floodlights for a run on the hallowed turf. Elsie made a dash for goal from the halfway line, neatly sidestepped me and ran straight into the net. They just ran all over the pitch and probably covered more ground than I had on the night – and maybe through my whole career. Their laughter and squeals of joy echoed around the old stadium. It was the perfect end to an amazing occasion.

The play-offs were due to take place in November, but we had been dealt a cruel blow after getting to that stage by an outrageous and unfair decision by FIFA who announced in late September that the play-off draw would be seeded. There had been no hint until then that that was how the competition was going to proceed. It was clear that FIFA wanted the more glamorous teams of France and Portugal to play in the World Cup finals. It would have been okay if this had been decided before the tournament so that we knew where we stood, but to introduce a seeding system in the middle of the competition was at best unjust and at worst corrupt. To add insult to injury, the top four seeds were to get home advantage in the second leg.

In the end we were drawn against France and the first leg was held at Croke Park on 14 November 2009. Although neither team played particularly well, we lost to Nicolas Anelka's deflected shot, which went in off the post. We were unlucky and hoped that the luck would be with us for the second leg in Paris. How wrong we were.

Looking back on the Dublin leg, we felt that the French were there for the taking and we shouldn't have allowed them to play. I think a lot of the lads were nervous and we didn't perform as well as we were capable of doing. We should have taken the game to them and not played so deep. Overall, Trapattoni had got us much tighter and more organised. We were much more disciplined and harder to beat and got results playing in this way – although we did rely a bit too much on Robbie to score in tight games. It was true that Trapattoni had been criticised for being too defensive but generally I felt it was the right thing at the time. The spirit and commitment had never been in question, no matter who the manager was.

Trapattoni had been asked about playing more adventurously in France, but seemed to dismiss this notion and he was quoted as saying, 'Maybe we take risks in the last minutes. This is a warm game for cold heads.' The trouble is we thought that this was exactly the occasion for taking the game to France – not to abandon the game plan exactly and risk all, but we thought that we could go there and try to win.

So, before the match the players got together and decided that we would do just that and try to take the game to the French. We hadn't done that in the first game and played our usual rigid formation and system. The French had won the first game without playing particularly well and we thought that if we got at them, pressed them higher up the pitch – and stopped them playing – we would have a chance. If we were going to get beaten and knocked out of the competition, we would at least go out fighting. We didn't see it as undermining the manager, but did decide to adopt slightly different tactics.

The return game took place at the Stade de France, Saint-Denis, on 18 November and, taking the initiative, we grew in confidence and fully deserved the opening goal in the thirty-third minute. I played a one-two down the left with Duffer, who pulled it back for Robbie to smash a low drive past the French keeper, Hugo Lloris, into the bottom right-hand corner. We had several other chances to increase the lead and when the half-time whistle went, France were given the bird by their supporters after what they considered a dismal opening forty-five minutes.

We were convinced we could finish the job and, although France had a few chances, we continued to dominate in the second half: Damien was clean through but was blocked by Lloris and in another attack Robbie rounded the keeper but couldn't keep the ball in play. At the final whistle the score was 1-1 on aggregate. Now we were into extra-time.

And then, of course, what followed was the biggest travesty in the history of Irish football. Three minutes before the end of the first period of extra-time, a free-kick was lofted into our penalty area from the French half; it broke for Thierry Henry who controlled it with his hand and then flicked it across the face of goal for Gallas, who was virtually on the goal line, to nod home. There were two players offside when the ball was played in – never mind the blatant handball. And it wasn't just a reactive handball by Henry: he stopped it first and then brought it under control again with his hand.

Shay rushed out of his goal to remonstrate with the referee and a number of us raced to confront the various officials, all of us pointing at our hands to demonstrate what we'd seen. Of course they seldom change their minds but we were furious and couldn't believe what had happened. We reluctantly kicked off, knowing that we just had to get on with things. We plugged away at France and sent a few high balls into their area and Dunney was booked for a frustrated barge on Lloris, which brought an angry reaction from some of the French lads. But to be honest we were just so deflated by what had happened that we didn't create another clear-cut chance. The final whistle went. We were out. Cheated of an appearance in the World Cup finals.

Immediately after the game I approached Thierry Henry, who admitted handling the ball but maintained it was accidental. I then went to the referee, Martin Hansson, and asked if he'd seen the handball. He told me, 'I can one hundred per cent say it wasn't handball.' I knew full well that he was just lying when he said that to me, because he hadn't even seen it. That was the worst thing about it – the total arrogance. It's clear from replays of the incident that the Swedish official was 100 per cent wrong!

The mood in the dressing room was desperate, a mixture of anger, sadness, bitterness and great disappointment. Boots and shirts and drinks were being chucked around. Hunty was really agitated, Robbie and Shay were furious and Damien was in tears. Some of the younger lads who had never played in the final stages of a World Cup had been robbed of their dream and might never have another opportunity. Most of us senior players, who at least knew what it was like to play in the finals, would definitely never have another chance. I'd never felt so angry. Sean St Ledger was absolutely devastated and summed up the mood: 'We feel cheated – we were the better team over the two legs, every football fan in the stadium will say we were the better team tonight. It's cost a lot of us our dreams – as a boy I used to dream of playing in the World Cup, and now I'm not.'

It had been a performance to be proud of, but we were left with nothing but pain, which the nation would also have to also bear. There was some criticism of Thierry Henry that he didn't admit to the handball at the time, but he was never going to do that. And, to be fair, none of our lads would have come clean either. These sorts of things happen on the pitch. I didn't blame him – the decision was the responsibility of the officials. The referee succumbed to the pressure, which was very disappointing as he had done well up until then.

In fact, the referee agreed to be the subject of a documentary the following year. The former firefighter lived alone on a farm in a quiet village and had been criticised in the media over the years for a number of other controversial decisions. One of his neighbours said, 'He's one of the village – we protect and take care of him.'

Hansson admitted that he believed his own World Cup dreams had been shattered after his performance in Paris. After the game the officials hugged each other in the dressing room but he knew 'It didn't feel right. So many Irish players reacted – we knew something had gone wrong.' The FIFA observer didn't come to the dressing room until fifteen minutes after the match and told Hansson that it *was* a handball. He said that he broke down – clearly not out of guilt, but because he feared he might not be selected for the World Cup finals in South Africa that summer. He briefly considered giving up refereeing, telling the interviewer, 'My name will always be connected with the Thierry Henry handball.' Then, in March 2010, he received a list from FIFA of those chosen to officiate at South Africa's World Cup. His name was on the list. His response? 'I drank champagne.' Well, we weren't celebrating.

Giovanni Trapattoni refused to label Thierry Henry a cheat but did admit that FIFA's fair play campaign had been damaged. He did say, however, 'It's murder. Even a blind man would have seen the double handball by Henry. The linesman was on line as the images show and he had perfect vision. I think the time has come to have TV replays for these extreme cases. In thirty seconds you avoid colossal errors.'

The silence from Sepp Blatter, head of FIFA, was deafening.

The decision to seed the play-offs still rankled with us and conspiracy theories raged afterwards. There was a feeling that the tournament is run by people who want to decide who gets there and to ensure that the big teams get the big decisions. There was talk in the press about the match being replayed but I really didn't think there was a hope in hell of that happening. I knew I would feel terrible in a couple of weeks' time when the draw was to be made and we weren't in it. We played so well and we should have won the game.

John Delaney, FAI chief executive, insisted there was a precedent for such action. In 1999, Arsenal successfully persuaded the authorities to sanction a rematch of an FA Cup fifth round tie with Sheffield United when Marc Overmars' goal was scored after the visitors had expected the ball to be returned to them from a throw-in after an injury. Delaney stated that the whole world had been watching our match, and if FIFA believed in fair play and integrity this was their opportunity to step forward.

The Irish justice minister, Dermot Ahern, also called for a rematch and for FIFA to be called to account in the interests of fair play. He said, 'They probably won't grant it as we are minnows in world football but let's put them on the spot...it's the least we owe the thousands of devastated young fans around the country. Otherwise, if that result remains, it reinforces the view that if you cheat you will win.'

The Irish Taoiseach, Brian Cowen, praised the team's performance. 'The team's efforts kept the nation enthralled for a hundred and twenty minutes of football,' he said. 'To a man, they did Ireland proud.' Liam Brady also backed calls for a replay. 'Sepp Blatter goes on about fair play – let him reflect on what happened last night. Where is football going if a team is cheated out of fair play? Where are we going if this decision stands?'

In response, FIFA called an extraordinary meeting at the beginning of December to discuss events. We thought at the very least there was the possibility that they would finally agree to introduce video technology – long overdue.

Even Thierry Henry stated that a replay would be the fairest solution and I believe that he was probably sincere. His old manager and fellow countryman Arsène Wenger insisted that a rematch was the only way of restoring French credibility: 'French football and France as a country have a duty not to leave Thierry out there alone against the whole world. France has to say: "Yes, it was a handball and we offer a replay."'

One person who wasn't clamouring for a replay was Roy Keane, who felt we should 'get over it' and that he was more upset with our defending and the inability to clear the ball in the six-yard box than the handball: 'France were there for the taking and Ireland didn't do it. Same old story…it's the usual FAI reaction – "we've been robbed, the honesty of the game…" It's rubbish.'

Although I was vociferous in demanding a rematch, I knew in my heart that it was unlikely. Roy, not for the first time, had upset many with his opinions and was proved correct in his prediction. FIFA rejected the call for a rematch, despite the best efforts of everyone, and a spokesman referred to Law 5 of the official rules, which stated that the referee had 'full authority to enforce the Laws of the Game in connection with the match to which he has been appointed' and that 'the decisions of the referee regarding facts connected with play are final'. The French Football Federation conceded that it was a 'bitter qualification' but it had 'to abide by what FIFA say'.

And, of course, another major disappointment was that, in South Africa, France simply didn't turn up and contributed nothing to the finals. The way they conducted themselves and the negativity surrounding the French team just added to our belief that we should have been there and with our fantastic fans would have brought so much to the occasion. My favourite moment was actually after the tournament, while watching the Spanish team's triumphant coach ride through the streets of Madrid. Manager Vicente del Bosque handed the FIFA World Cup trophy to his son Alvaro, who has Down's syndrome, and all the Spanish players cheered and applauded!

Quite by chance a few months ago I bumped into Thierry at the Landmark London hotel, opposite Marylebone Station. It was the first time we had met since the handball. We had a brief, polite chat, talking about future plans. Thierry, playing for the New York Red Bulls, was then hoping for a loan spell at Arsenal. We avoided any mention of the incident, much to the disappointment of the mate I was with, who was hoping for a punch-up or at least a public confrontation. Incidentally, if you're ever in London I suggest you avoid the Landmark hotel – not only might you bump into your nemesis, but they also serve the most expensive coffee in the capital.

A day after my return from Paris, I was back training with Hull, feeling pretty miserable and dejected. But it was good to be back with the lads and to have another match within a few days to concentrate on. There wasn't time to dwell on the play-off result. And, in fact, the mood in the Hull camp became a little brighter in November – we were unbeaten during that month. The team had climbed the table and there was a newfound belief and optimism in the squad. The results had also eased some of the strain on Phil Brown, although inevitably he had recently embroiled himself in another incident that had nothing to do with the team's performance.

To break the day-to-day training routine, we'd gone for a walk and a jog across the Humber Bridge. Nothing much happened. The boss then announced to the media that he had 'talked down' a suicidal woman from jumping off the bridge while we were jogging across it. We had come across a few other joggers and walkers, but there had been no sign of this person with a death wish about to leap into the water. The lads were howling with laughter the following day when we heard about Phil assuming the role of Samaritan. There was no one to corroborate his story and no report of any such incident from the company that monitors the suspension bridge; no one was remotely aware of such an incident. A reporter from the *Observer* put it to Brown that the apparently suicidal female was a figment of his imagination. According to the newspaper, Phil looked rather sheepish, hung his head and eventually said, 'No comment.'

When the team was struggling, Phil Brown enlisted the

services of a motivational psychologist, who was a jeweller by trade.

The team's previous psychologist had been sacked and in our first meeting we all had to hug each other. We weren't used to doing that unless someone scored! He told us to 'feel the love', which didn't go down too well with a crowd of hard-bitten professional footballers. He then proceeded to give a Powerpoint slide show. There was a picture of him with Arsène Wenger and the Premier League trophy and he then produced quotes from various managers and players whom he had helped, among them Wenger, Houllier and for some reason John Terry's brother. There was a glowing reference from Emile Heskey, who, I later discovered, barely knew the man.

He also informed us that he had been asked to work with Bangor City who were involved in a European tie and had lost the first leg 8-0. 'We had a great week together and thanks to my involvement Bangor only lost the second leg 2-1.' No doubt Bangor's opponents had either played reserves or weren't bothered. I would guess it had absolutely nothing to do with his psychological motivation.

(He left the club when Phil was sacked and Iain Dowie took over. His last sighting was supposedly in Monte Carlo…)

At the beginning of the year there was some unrest among the squad and some of the lads who were out of favour found themselves training with the Under 21s. I believe Caleb Folan, Bryan Hughes, Nathan Doyle and-loan defender Ibrahima Sonko were told to find new clubs. Hungarian international Péter Halmosi was also told that he was no longer required – a real turnaround for him as he was the club's record £2.5 million signing. I felt sorry for my team-mates, but all this was done in an attempt to reduce the wage bill as the club's financial situation was becoming perilous.

During the January transfer window there had been some talk of moving me on and there was reputedly interest from

Sheffield United and Ipswich. I was also linked with Celtic in the press, but this wasn't true. I would have loved to have played for Celtic at some stage in my career but the opportunity only arose when I had just signed a new contract at Everton, which I wanted to fulfil.

Phil maintained in media interviews that I was still an important member of the squad and that my versatility was an attribute, even though I wasn't getting many games. I'd captained the team at Fulham earlier in the season, but I'd only been given six starts and was having trouble fighting my way back into first-team contention. I was desperate to play in every possible game. I did go and see the manager about my position, not to demand a starting place but to ask what I could do, how I could improve and what I had to do to in order to be considered. In fairness to Phil, he was always willing to take on board what I had to say and tried to give me some answers. I'd played in a number of positions, including left and centre midfield, central defence and left-back, since I'd signed for Hull and it seemed that my versatility had made me a useful substitute!

The Humber Bridge featured again in another piece of adverse publicity the following month, when Phil had to apologise for the public bust-up between Jimmy Bullard and Nick Barmby after an altercation between the two of them when training near the bridge. As far as I and the other lads were concerned, it was a run-of-the-mill incident, the sort of thing that happens on training grounds regularly, and was blown out of all proportion by the local press. Unluckily, on this occasion it was witnessed by a very large group of nearly a hundred women from the local Women's Institute, who were apparently walking across the bridge at the time. Phil had to make a public apology for the 'unsavoury incident'. He went on to say, 'These things do happen. I'm not condoning that kind of behaviour but it's an emotive game, it's a passionate game. Emotions do run high and certainly then the pressure is cranked up – which it is, we are coming to the business end of the season.'

Unfortunately, Phil wasn't in charge at the business end of the season as, within a few days and after four successive Premiership defeats, he was relieved of his duties. He wasn't sacked but placed on 'gardening leave'. His replacement, Iain Dowie, was greeted with disappointment by some fans who were optimistically hoping for someone with a more impressive CV. We were nineteenth in the league and very much in the relegation zone. I suppose it was on the cards that Phil wasn't going to get any more time. There was a lot of tension in the squad and morale was low. He gave a farewell speech to the team and told us he would have liked the opportunity to keep us up and thought we could still avoid the drop. He spoke very well and with great dignity and I wish some of his critics could have had a chance to witness this particular talk – an occasion that belied his egocentric reputation and eccentric behaviour.

We lost against fellow strugglers Portsmouth in Iain's first game in charge, a disastrous 3-2 defeat after being 2-1 up with two minutes to go. We were now three points from safety with eight games remaining. To lose a game like that in the manner in which we did was heartbreaking; a win at Pompey would have given us a huge lift. But I did feel that Iain Dowie was well equipped to guide us to safety. He wanted to concentrate on the team shape and demanded a great deal of hard work. He was always really enthusiastic on the training ground and felt that the lads would respond to his ideas. We had to become much harder to beat and couldn't afford to give away too many goals as we definitely suffered from a lack of firepower.

We won our next game against Fulham but then lost the next two matches, only scoring once, before gaining a point at Birmingham in a goalless draw. Then we gave away two bad goals in a home defeat to Aston Villa, having outplayed them for most of the match.

Our bid to stay in the Premiership all but mathematically

ended at the end of April when we lost at home 1-0 to Sunderland and West Ham won their game 3–2 against Wigan. I was on the bench for an eventful game in which Jimmy Bullard missed a penalty and Jozy Altidore was sent off for head-butting Alan Hutton, who was also dismissed. We played with plenty of spirit but created very few chances. Despite a number of them being in tears, the fans were amazing and applauded the players off the pitch. Because of our poor goal difference, we now needed a huge margin of victory in the next game, and for West Ham to be thrashed, to secure an unlikely survival.

I was back in the team for the match at Wigan. We had actually led 2-1 but conceded an equaliser when Steve Gohouri scored with an overhead kick. There was chaos a minute before the end of the match when fans invaded the pitch, but at the final whistle our fate had been officially sealed. We were down and would be playing in the Championship the following season.

It was a terrible time and was the second occasion in my professional career that I had been relegated. It brought back all the awful memories of the Sunderland demotion. Although I was more mature and could view the situation more philosophically, it was also symbolic that my own career was on the wane. But, of course, I couldn't just look at this selfishly. Relegation is without a doubt the worst experience a player can have but it is more than just a personal thing because it can affect an entire city or town and hurts so many people. At Sunderland I had witnessed the results of relegation for all club employees; I had seen office staff being sacked, leaving the club in tears and facing an uncertain future. No doubt this was also in store for some of the staff at Hull.

We were still shocked, however, when we discovered quite how bad the financial situation was at the club. Debts were estimated to be around £35 million and before the final match of the season, Liverpool's visit to the KC Stadium, there were rumours that the club had gone into administration.

Twenty-four hours after the game, we were called to a meeting at Cottingham, the club's training ground, where Adam Pearson, now reinstalled as the club's head of operations, and PFA officials greeted us. Adam confirmed that the club's very existence was at risk. It was a stark message and, even if we survived, the threat of administration and therefore points deduction next season was very real.

Adam Pearson asked us to do our bit by taking a pay cut or deferral. I certainly didn't expect this and my first reaction was one of shock. But I realised that other club employees were going through much worse. We were well paid for our work and it somehow seemed only right. Although the players weren't responsible for the club's finances, we certainly weren't blameless for the club's current predicament. I agreed to halve my salary for an extra year's contract. I had one year remaining on my current deal and was now committing myself to the club for a further two. Don't get me wrong, I'm no Mother Teresa – I didn't see this as a huge sacrifice, but I felt Hull were a good club and I was happy to stay with them and help return them to the top flight. I just wanted to carry on playing and this also gave me the security of an extra year. I had also taken a pay deferral at Sunderland, so this wasn't a new experience for me.

A number of the other lads also agreed to cut their wages and according to Adam Pearson this gesture eased the financial pressures on the club. Adam was also extremely critical of the previous administration for incurring debts that had spiralled out of control: 'We're stood here at Cottingham on a piece of land that I bought for £200,000 eight years ago and the pitches are okay, but it's not the best...this and the centre of excellence definitely need some money spending on them. It's a shame when we've had £140 million come into the club over the last two years that not one penny has been spent here. There's definitely still work to do.'

Phil Brown's managerial contract was permanently terminated

in June 2010 and at the same time the club confirmed that Iain Dowie would not be retained in a managerial capacity. By the end of the month, the Leicester boss, Nigel Pearson, was confirmed as the new manager. I felt it was a shame that Iain wasn't retained. I would have liked him to become full-time manager. I had a good relationship with him and, although we had only collected four points under his stewardship, he had come in at a very difficult time and I thought he had done pretty well. It wasn't down to him that we were relegated.

But there was a new regime now. We had done what we could off the pitch to secure our future and it was up to us to show what we could do on the pitch in our quest to return to the Premiership.

Chapter Ten

To Hull and Back

'Being Irish, he had an abiding sense of tragedy, which sustained
him through temporary periods of joy.'

ATTRIBUTED TO W. B. YEATS

'No one hands you cups on a plate.'

TERRY McDERMOTT

The Championship season had barely begun before I was involved in international matches. And there had been a major change in backroom personnel. In April 2010, Liam Brady left his role as the Republic's assistant manager at the expiration of his contract. Liam still held the post of director of youth development at Arsenal and he felt that he could no longer combine the two roles. It was sad to see Liam go – he was one of the best players Ireland has ever produced and was an incredibly dedicated and committed member of Giovanni's staff. Liam was an important figure in any success we had and, because of Trapattoni's poor communication skills, he was vital on the training field and in the dressing room. Trapattoni barely said a word at half-time and it was often left to Liam to give us instructions. After Liam left, Trap was, I'd say, a little lost without him.

The last game that Liam was involved in was a match against Brazil at the Emirates Stadium. The attendance was about 40,000 thanks to a lot of London-based Irish fans and a surprising number of Brazilian expats. We lost 0-2 but it was a great occasion and I remember being very impressed with Kaká, who starred that night.

Back in Dublin, the first ever game at the brand new £350 million Aviva Stadium took place in August against the other South American giants, Argentina. The stadium was built on the site of the former Lansdowne Road ground, which had been demolished in 2007. It seats nearly 52,000 spectators.

The friendly marked Robbie's hundredth international appearance (his son Robbie Jr was a mascot) and Marco Tardelli took charge as Giovanni Trapattoni was in hospital, having just undergone abdominal surgery. I played for an hour, but unfortunately the team's performance didn't match the occasion and we were beaten by a goal from Angel Di Maria.

The qualifiers for the 2012 European Championships, to be held in Poland and Ukraine, began in early September in Yerevan where we were playing Armenia. It was hot and humid with a hostile atmosphere and I played in my sixtieth consecutive competitive match against the backdrop of Mount Ararat, where, it is said, Noah's Ark came to rest. Well, if the floodgates didn't exactly open, we played decently enough and got the campaign off to a winning start thanks to a Keith Fahey strike.

We were back in Dublin for the game against Andorra. As I said earlier, I do like playing Andorra and the chant 'Can we play you every week?' springs to mind as, in our second qualifier, we went top of Group B with a 3-1 win. I scored the first ever Irish goal at the Aviva with a header from a Liam Lawrence corner after I'd given my marker the slip. Kevin Doyle and Robbie each scored to give us a comfortable win, although we would have wanted the margin to have been greater.

The next pair of games in the competition took place in October and in the first we were outplayed by Russia in Dublin. The 3-2 scoreline flattered us and it was clear that Russia's technical ability, system and quick passing was the difference between the two sides. We were 3-0 down to Dick Advocaat's side before getting two goals back in the last twenty minutes. There was a response from the lads with a hard-fought one-all draw against Slovakia in Zilina.

I played in quite a few games for Hull during the first half of the season, but life in the Championship under new boss Nigel Pearson was something of a struggle and the team was very inconsistent. One defeat in particular said a lot about the young team. In only our second game we were stuffed at Millwall but it was clear that we had lost the game as soon as we got off the team coach. There was a hostile reaction from opposing fans and the lads were intimidated to the extent that most of them wouldn't even go on the pitch before the warm-up and stayed in the dressing room. There was no way we were going to perform when, in our heads, we were already threatened by the atmosphere in the ground and consequently we lost 4-0. Confidence is such a huge part of a footballer's psyche and if you go into a game feeling anxious and full of self-doubt, you are in trouble.

There wasn't a lack of quality in the Championship – the existence of parachute payments for relegated clubs and the numbers of players endeavouring to prolong careers beyond the Premiership have resulted in an extremely competitive league. I'd played at most levels and knew that there were a lot of lads in the lower leagues who could make their mark at the top level given the opportunity. There were some good teams in the second tier. The proof of this was that we were inconsistent at home and, until a win against Norwich at Carrow Road in September, we had endured a run without an away win stretching back eighteen months.

By the end of the following month we were one point off the bottom three and any thoughts of promotion were long gone. In the middle of November, I returned to Deepdale for the away fixture at Preston and we managed a 2-0 win. But what was great about that night was that my dad, who I hadn't seen for years, came to the game and afterwards we spent a couple of hours together.

In the middle of December, Hull were in London for the match at Crystal Palace and we had come down the night before. I was having breakfast on the morning of the match and at the table was a lad then eighteen, and on loan. Out of the blue he started telling the lads about his faith in Jesus. There were about ten of us listening and he started really to lay it on: that if we didn't have Jesus in our hearts then we were all sinners, but we could have redemption if we fully accepted Jesus into our world.

I thought it was bit odd as this wasn't exactly the place or time to be 'spreading the word', but it was just the usual 'Holy Roller' stuff that I had heard before. Then he announced that the diseases and unhappiness in the world were caused by our sinning. We suffered because we had brought everything on ourselves by our ungodliness. 'The reason for children being born with disabilities,' he continued, 'is because we are all sinners and because we have all sinned.'

Now this pressed a raw nerve and I wasn't going to let him get away with this crap. Calmly, I told him that I had a disabled daughter and asked him: 'So does Elsie have Down's syndrome because I have sinned?' I had heard that certain people who believed in reincarnation and bad karma had the extraordinary notion that the disabled were being punished for their transgressions in a previous life. 'Or perhaps it was Elsie who had sinned before she had even been born?' Naturally, he hadn't expected this response and was taken aback when I started to press him. He tried to explain what he meant, but maintained his belief that *all* illnesses and *all* disabilities are caused by sinners.

I was furious and the other lads were embarrassed. I couldn't believe that such a young man not only possessed such controversial views but that he had the confidence to hold forth. But then anger turned to disbelief when I discovered that he had requested – and been given permission by Nigel Pearson – to address the lads in a more formal meeting later that day. (The match was live on Sky Sports and so kick-off was at 5.20 p.m.)

The pretext was to preach to the lads for an hour about the real meaning of Christmas. I wondered about not going but then decided to attend and arrived about twenty minutes after the talk had started. The subject of Christmas had long since been abandoned but then he proceeded to repeat to the lads and the management team what he had been saying at breakfast. Paul McShane, himself a religious man, questioned him and knew enough to quote the scriptures back at him. Later I went to see Nigel Pearson to complain that the lad had been afforded the time and opportunity to voice such objectionable opinions in a totally inappropriate situation. I think Nigel was embarrassed himself and was wondering the same thing.

Towards the end of 2010 I was in and out of the Hull team and, although willing to stay and fight for my place, I was getting a little frustrated. With the January transfer window approaching, I was interested to hear that several clubs had made contact about a loan move for me.

On Christmas Eve Nigel Pearson advised me that a deal had been agreed with my old club Preston North End. I spoke to Darren Ferguson before his departure and then to my old team-mate David Unsworth, who took over as caretaker when Ferguson left. Although tempted, I've never thought it a good idea to go back and, to be honest, PNE were in a state of flux, struggling in the Championship, and I'd had my fill of relegation scraps.

There was no training on Christmas Day but I played against Sheffield United on Boxing Day and was kicked in the head – there was some concern that my retina was damaged and I spent a few hours in hospital – but all was okay.

On 1 January 2011, as the transfer window reopened, Huddersfield came in for me and agreed a loan deal with Hull.

Although Huddersfield were in League One and it would mean me dropping down a division, they were riding high. The history of this famous club also appealed, as did the relative proximity to our home in Stockport. I spoke to manager Lee Clark, who impressed me with his ambitious plans, and I was convinced that 'the Town' were going places. Lee wanted to add some experience to the squad, which contained some good young players, and another bonus was that Gary Naismith, a good mate from Everton, was also at the club. Old Evertonian Steve Watson, ex-Newcastle and Millwall midfielder Paul Stephenson and the legendary Terry McDermott comprised the senior coaching staff and I soon felt at home.

I also texted Giovanni Trapattoni. I wanted to make sure I would still be in his reckoning if I was playing in League One and I was advised that there would be no problem. It was better for me to be playing regularly than sitting on the bench.

I made my debut on the day the deal was agreed in the 2-2 draw against Carlisle United at Brunton Park and my first game at the Galpharm was in the Yorkshire derby against Sheffield Wednesday. It was a big occasion and a fabulous one on which to make my home league debut. We won 1-0, thanks to a brilliant Anthony Pilkington goal.

I'd only been at the club for a couple of weeks when I was faced with the possibility of playing at Wembley in the Johnstone's Paint Trophy. I'd never played on the hallowed turf and remember thinking about the chance of getting to the final of this competition in my Preston days. While winning promotion was paramount, this was another target and we were now within two matches of Wembley. We were up against Carlisle in two legs of the Northern final – the first leg was at Brunton Park. Despite the fact that we were well ahead of Carlisle in League One, we got beaten 4-0. We came agonisingly close to pulling off a miraculous aggregate victory in the home leg three weeks later, which we won 3-0, but were unable to make up the deficit from the first leg. I had to forget the dream of playing at Wembley.

I was omitted from the final twenty-two of the Republic's squad for the Carling Nations Cup, but these games were really intended to give some of the younger players some international experience; the qualifiers were all that mattered. I had seriously considered retiring after losing to France in the World Cup play-offs. I spoke to a few people and the general advice was that you're a long time retired – basically, if the manager doesn't pick you, then he's retired you himself! Mick McCarthy asked me, 'Would you feel gutted if you weren't picked?' I told him I would. So Mick continued, 'If you don't get picked then you don't get picked – there's no decision to make. Just carry on.' He also felt that it was very self-indulgent to make such a decision, an attempt to put yourself in the limelight: 'Look at me! This is what I'm doing in the best interests of the nation!' Liam Brady told me to carry on as long as I could.

When footballing people of the pedigree of Mick and Liam are of the same opinion, it carries a lot of weight. To be picked for my country was the pinnacle for me and I wanted to play in every international. That's the way I had always viewed it and this feeling didn't change with age. You have to do what is right for you. Paul Scholes regretted his decision not to go to the World Cup and once you have been involved in the international scene, you always want to be part of it.

I found Huddersfield to be a fantastic old club: the chairman and lifelong fan Dean Hoyle had made his money from 'The Card Factory', a chain of greetings card and gift shops that had been sold the previous year for an estimated £350 million. The Galpharm Stadium is an impressive modern stadium in a retail park surrounded by imposing scenery, and a plaque on the side of the Direct Golf UK stand typifies the local loyal support: 'Harry Donkersley 1922–2004 an unswerving fan through good times and bad.'

Brand new training facilities were being built at the time but then training occasionally took place at the undeveloped Canalside sports complex, which sat cheek by jowl with a croquet lawn bearing the sign 'Footballers, please keep off the pitch'. It was occupied by elderly ladies wielding mallets which they'd sometimes use to return footballs. A bowling club was situated behind a couple of the goals and wayward shots (Alan Lee was the usual culprit) would send balls bouncing across the manicured lawn, scattering bowls and club members.

We had a great set of lads and I was pretty confident that we would be in the frame for automatic promotion at the end of the season. Some of the home games were difficult as teams tended to come to the Galpharm and shut up shop, but we were getting results and putting together an unbeaten run. Lee Clark took a lot of the training sessions himself, particularly in the days before a match and was incredibly animated on the touchline. He wasn't slow to let us know either at half-time or full-time if we weren't doing our jobs.

One game during this period sticks in my mind, a fourth round FA Cup tie at the Emirates. Some of the younger lads were nervous, but I was really looking forward to it as this was probably my last chance to play at a Premiership ground.

After going 0-1 down, there was a spell in the second half after we equalised when we dominated and had chances to take the lead. Then Cesc Fábregas came on as a substitute and called out in Spanish, 'This team are shit.' Joey Gudjonsson, who had played at Real Betis, spoke Spanish and confronted Fábregas, annoyed at his lack of disrespect. An unconcerned Fábregas just shrugged. A few minutes later Nicholas Bendtner went down very easily under the challenge of centre-half Jamie McCombe, leading to referee Mark Clattenburg awarding Arsenal a late penalty, and Fábregas gestured for Jamie to be sent off. Over the years I've had a few run-ins with Fábregas and particularly didn't like the imaginary card he was brandishing. I've never liked to see that.

At the end of the game, Fábregas refused to shake hands with any of us or swap his shirt. As much as I admire Cesc as a world-class player, I was disappointed by his arrogance and disrespect for our team, who in fact were very unlucky to lose 2-1.

In March I received a text from Giovanni Trapattoni telling me that I had been recalled to the squad for the European Championship qualifier against Macedonia and the friendly against Uruguay at the end of the month. From thinking that my international days were over, I could now see that the manager still felt I could do a job. Obviously I knew that my days in the green shirt were numbered so I was delighted to be back in and to continue my record run of competitive international appearances.

It was wonderful to be back with the boys and the match at the Aviva was important in that the 2-1 win made us joint leaders of the group. We were a couple of goals up in twenty minutes. Kieron Westwood was in goal for us and he produced a world-class save to give us all three points.

Soon after the end of the game, I contacted Lee Clark to inform him that I wasn't going to be involved in the friendly against Uruguay and that I could be available for Town's league game against Notts County the following afternoon. Lee was surprised but said he could do with me on the bench if I was up to it. I was really keen to be involved in the club's continuing press for promotion and so I left the Republic squad in the early hours of Sunday morning, had a quick sleep at home, and then joined the lads at the Galpharm. I didn't actually get on the pitch and wasn't sure how my body would have coped with two games in two days, but I any case I wasn't needed in our 3-0 win.

At the end of April we had a great 3-2 win at the Withdean, the last game to be played there before Brighton and Hove Albion moved into their state-of-the-art Falmer Stadium. It was quite an occasion as Brighton had already been crowned champions with four matches to spare. Before the game, we provided a guard of honour and Lee Clark embraced Brighton boss Gus Poyet and shook every hand in the Brighton dugout. Afterwards Albion were presented with the League One trophy. We remained third as Southampton also won at Brentford to stay ahead of us on goal difference, but were unbeaten in twenty-four league games – the best ever run in a single season.

An extraordinary 4-4 home draw with Brentford eventually saw us finish third in League One, five points behind Southampton and now facing a play-off semi-final against Bournemouth. In previous seasons eighty-seven points would have guaranteed us promotion but Southampton had finished the season in spectacular form, winning thirteen of their last fifteen games. But we were confident that we could finish the job and continue our own unbeaten run. Although I had been involved in winning promotion in my teenage days at PNE, these were my first play-off games. Of course I'd watched them on television and got caught up in the excitement, but it would be very different actually playing in such crucial matches.

The first match took place at Dean Court and I scored with a header from a Gary Roberts cross in the 1-1 draw. The atmosphere for the second leg was fantastic and we started well, playing at a high tempo. We led twice but were pegged back each time, being unable to kill the tie off with a third goal. It was 2-2 at full-time and each side added another goal to make the score 3-3. Bournemouth's Jason Pearce was shown a straight red, but we were unable to take advantage of our extra man and the game went to penalties.

During the game I kind of lost it, when, after clashing with one of the opposition and conceding a free-kick, I shoved referee Neil Swarbrick out of the way! I'd been angered by one of their lads having a got at me. I apologised straightaway and I have to admit I was lucky not to be dismissed and only receive a yellow card. Maybe my reputation of not normally being a hothead helped me on this occasion and so the ref gave me the benefit of the doubt. Anyway, I was still on the pitch and able to take part in the shootout.

As soon as the final whistle went, my mind went back to that night in South Korea. But by the time I had made the walk to the penalty spot, I was very confident that I would score. I'd missed one during the week in the lead-up to the game when we were practising penalties, but in a funny way that actually gave me more confidence. This time I knew exactly where I wanted to put the ball. It was a fantastic feeling seeing it hit the back of the net.

We had had a discussion among ourselves about who wanted to take a penalty after extra-time and those who felt confident put themselves forward. Also having Ian Bennett between the sticks, who had a bit of a history of saving penalties, gave us a good chance. And that's exactly what happened. We blasted home all four that we took and Ian's save from Liam Feeney, and another one that went over the bar, gave us victory.

The celebrations began immediately and soon the pitch was engulfed by the euphoric supporters. The scenes at the end showed how much it meant to us all. It was a wonderful occasion and something I'll always savour. At club level, this was one of the best nights of my career. The game had everything and it was all credit to both sides for really going for it. Even the experienced lads in the dressing room had not had many nights like that in their careers.

The play-off finals were usually held at Wembley, but because it had been selected as the venue for the Champions League final that season, the League One promotion decider was played at Old Trafford at the end of May. Once again I missed out on playing at England's national stadium!

The match was my fifty-second of the season, my thirty-first for Town and I still hadn't lost in a league game for the Terriers…until the play-off final when it all went belly up and our dreams of promotion ended.

The Old Trafford final was a terrible anti-climax after all our hard work. We just didn't perform as we could and, although it looked like we were heading for extra-time, Peterborough hit us with three late goals in seven minutes. It was our first defeat in twenty-seven league and play-off games. We'd finished third in the league, eight points clear of Peterborough and the scoreline was flattering to the Posh, but that was irrelevant – we were destined to remain in League One for another season.

Although it was hard to take that defeat, it was great to be playing every week and to be part of a team that was geared up for promotion and genuinely went out to win every game. I felt welcomed from the first day I walked into the club and there was no doubt that Huddersfield, despite being in the third tier, had rekindled my enthusiasm for the game.

I had hoped to be able to stay with Town for another season, but the loss at Old Trafford scuppered that plan. My contract with Hull didn't expire until the end of next season, but I thought I'd kicked my last ball for them and didn't believe I would get many first team opportunities as new players were already being recruited. I assumed I'd be playing my football elsewhere the following season, but didn't know where.

Soon after the disappointment of the play-off final, I travelled with the international squad to face Macedonia in Skopje. This was actually the sixth time that we had met in competition; it seemed such a coincidence that the two countries kept being drawn together and was an unfortunate reminder of the time that Macedonia had dashed our hopes of qualifying for the Euro 2000 finals when it seemed we were destined for Belgium and Holland.

Fortunately, these memories were soon dispelled when Robbie opened the scoring and became the first Irish or British player to reach fifty international goals, and he added to his tally to double our lead. We ran out 2-0 winners and so got the result that we needed to stay in contention for Euro 2012 qualification.

We remained in third position in Group B, tied on thirteen points with Slovakia and Russia.

I don't really have any specific recollections of the game other than the fact it was my sixty-sixth consecutive competitive match for the Republic. I wish I'd taken more note of the atmosphere, the action and the banter with the lads, and that my recollection of that game was stronger, but then I didn't know at the time it was to be my last ever game for the Republic.

But it also has to be said that I was also very much preoccupied with other matters. Because I had always given everything I could on the field, no one would have known that behind the scenes my personal life was in tatters. In the spring of 2011, Laura asked me to leave. I was shocked and couldn't believe what was happening. I stayed for a week, convinced that we could sort something out. There were no big angry scenes, but at the end of the week I knew that she was serious and that we had reached a crisis point. I moved into one of the club's service apartments for a couple of weeks.

We didn't talk about the long term but it was a very difficult, distressing time and I had no idea what was going on. The one thing that we did agree on was that Elsie and Isla should not have their lives disrupted or suffer in any way. The girls had to be made to feel secure and to know that they were still very much loved by both of us. To be near them, I moved into a flat in Stockport so I could see as much of them as possible.

By July, it was clear that the split was permanent and while I was in Belfast doing my coaching badges I found the situation just too much to bear. During one session I had to walk off the pitch – my head was all over the place and I just couldn't concentrate. One of the lads asked me what the matter was, but I couldn't tell him. It was totally unlike me to quit like that, but I couldn't concentrate or think clearly. I didn't know where my personal or professional life was heading and the future looked pretty bleak.

Chapter Eleven

Bowing Out

'All that I know most surely about morality and obligations,
I owe to football.'

ALBERT CAMUS

After all that had happened, it was important to have a proper break and so I took Elsie and Isla for a much needed holiday in Florida. It was strange and sad going without Laura, but the three of us met up briefly with David Weir and his family, which was great. I then returned to pre-season training with Hull but I knew my playing days there were numbered while Nigel Pearson was manager and I wanted to leave the club. At the beginning of August a six-month loan deal was struck with Derby County. I rented accommodation in the city, but kept my flat on in Stockport to be nearer to the family.

In August I was called into the Republic's squad for the matches against Slovakia and Russia the following month, but during a game of handball on the first day of training in Malahide I felt a niggle in my back. I didn't think it was serious so I finished the rest of the session. I got on the bus and headed back to the hotel, where I had a quick chat with the doctor. Although he tried to reassure me, I knew something was wrong. The following morning my back had seized up completely and I had trouble getting out of bed. I couldn't even walk, never mind run and I knew immediately that I couldn't possibly play in these games.

I was devastated. There was nothing I could do but pack my bags and head home, but I couldn't face saying goodbye to anyone so I waited until the lads boarded the bus to take them to the training ground and then I left the hotel. I really didn't want an emotional goodbye or a big fuss. I wasn't sharing a room – the one advantage of being one of the senior players – so I didn't even have to leave a note for a room-mate.

I caught a taxi to the airport. I felt absolutely gutted and I knew – I just knew – that this would be the last time I would be in the Irish squad. I did get a few texts from the lads saying, 'where are ya?', 'good luck', 'get yourself fit for next month', but deep down I knew my international career was over, even though I wasn't aware of the extent of the injury at the time.

Stupidly, ten days later, I played for Derby at Coventry City. My back hadn't really recovered and I wasn't fit to play, but I had a pain-killing injection beforehand. I managed to finish the game, but did my hamstring. I had never had any long periods of injury during my career, but it seemed that my age was now being to tell. I recovered enough to make my six hundredth career appearance against Portsmouth and, after the game against Peterborough at the beginning of November, we went on a club trip to New York. Big mistake. I could barely get off the aeroplane on arrival – my back had gone again and it was so bad that I couldn't even lie down for an MRI scan. I had started to feel discomfort on the car journeys between home and Hull and sitting on a plane for over six hours had exacerbated the injury.

My loan agreement with Derby County was terminated at the end of the month and I returned to Hull to have my injury assessed by the club medical staff. I'd only played ten games for the Rams. Nigel Clough was in charge and he was old school, just like his dad. I liked him. Another straight-talker, he could be harsh but he wanted his team to play football in the right way.

He gave a team belief and built team spirit and togetherness by varying the training routines with day trips and team-building exercises.

Despite the fact that I had been named in the twenty-seven-man squad for the European Championship qualifiers to be played against Andorra and Armenia, I had to withdraw. After victories in both those games, we had finished second behind Russia in Group B and faced a play-off against Estonia. I was officially available for selection for those games, scheduled in the middle of November, although I must admit I would have been struggling. Then I got a thirty-second call from Giovanni Trapattoni, which ended my Republic of Ireland career.

He told me simply in faltering English, 'You're not going to be involved but we will monitor you.' At least I think that's what he said, because, as I've said, communication was always a bit difficult. I suppose there was no easy way to tell me. It did hurt, but I didn't expect to be treated any differently as that's Trapattoni's way of dealing with players. But I knew that this was it. Funnily enough, I didn't feel bitter. I'd been given amazing opportunities over the years – to play once for your country was a dream I'd had ever since I was a kid...never mind 110 times.

The lads won the first game 4-0 in Tallinn so the second leg in Dublin was a bit of a formality. I got a phone call a few days before the game from Mary O'Brien of the FAI telling me that Trapattoni wanted me to be part of the celebrations as I had been involved in the group games. Fair play to him: it was a nice gesture from the man but I really didn't want to be there if I wasn't playing and my initial instinct was to refuse. Mary was, however, very persuasive and I agreed to go to Dublin.

Qualification was confirmed with a 1-1 draw, but I did feel a bit of a fraud as I hadn't been involved in the play-off games and it seemed a bit unfair on the players who had done the job against Estonia. It felt very awkward being in the dressing room as it didn't feel as if the celebrations had anything to do with me. I went through the motions with the lap of honour and I did have a few beers in a club with the lads afterwards, but I just wanted to get away and left on my own first thing the next morning. Looking back now, I'm a little disappointed in myself that I couldn't enjoy it more and appreciate that I was indeed part of the campaign that saw Ireland qualify for the finals.

I returned home but I was still in agony from my back. I had two lots of epidural injections before Christmas, which really didn't seem to make much difference, and then I saw a specialist, who confirmed that I had two prolapsed discs and told me that the only solution was to undergo surgery. It seemed that my back was in quite a mess.

I went under the knife in January and was told that I mustn't kick a ball for three months. Hull's physio, Liam McGarry, was great with me and helped a lot with my rehab and, while I was recuperating, Nick Barmby, who had now taken the reins as manager following the departure of Nigel Pearson, suggested that I could take on a coaching role. I could also do a bit of scouting for the club as well as reporting back on some of the Hull lads who were out on loan. In addition, I was responsible for managing City's reserve team. I was in charge for eight games and enjoyed the job very much, and talked to Nick about staying on as development coach. Unfortunately, Nick was sacked after making comments about the owners and lack of transfer funds. Steve Bruce was subsequently appointed and gave the coaching job to someone else! I was also really disappointed on Nick's behalf because I thought he had great potential as a manager.

In June, somewhat surprisingly I found myself in Poland for the European finals – sadly not as a player, but as a pundit, employed by the *Irish Daily Mail* and Radio Five Live. It was a bit strange to have to comment on lads who I had been playing with until recently and over many years, but I loved being there – apart from the defeats inflicted on the Irish team.

Group C was the group of death as far as Ireland were

concerned and being drawn with Spain (the eventual winners), Italy (runners-up) and Croatia resulted in us being beaten in all three group games. Despite this, the fans were absolutely brilliant and I was incredibly impressed by the Irish presence from the moment I arrived in Poznan Old Square. I was amazed at the sheer numbers and the passionate support throughout.

There was one incident with the fans that has now gone down in history. At a bar in Gdansk, and after a few lagers, I reprised my rendition of 'Ice Ice Baby'. What I didn't know was that Five Live commentator Conor McNamara filmed it and the uploaded it on YouTube. When I asked him why he hadn't asked my permission to upload the clip, he just said, 'You wouldn't have agreed.' Dead right. It's now had over 200,000 hits and unfortunately I'm often asked to repeat the rap!

I would have loved to have been playing but my only opportunity came in the media football match that took place at the Arka Gdynia Stadium, the Republic of Ireland's training base. My great mate Colin Young chipped the *Irish Star* goalie Mark McCadden from forty yards…and has been talking of little else since!

Before I had left for Poland, my contract at Hull had come to an end and I was now a free agent. I met with Barnsley's Keith Hill and Dave Flitcroft, who I knew from Preston, and was verbally offered a player/coach role at the South Yorkshire club. However, when I returned from the Euros, Dave rang to say that the Barnsley board had changed their mind and there would be no contract.

I then spoke to Coventry City boss, Andy Thorn, and was invited to train with the club. Carso was on the coaching staff, which made it more tempting, and at the beginning of July I joined them on a one-year deal. We went on a pre-season tour of Scotland and I made my debut against Dagenham & Redbridge in the League Cup and scored a late winner from the penalty spot. Two days later, I was given the team captaincy. I was really pleased, but also, I have to say, surprised. I thought I'd make about twenty appearances and work with Carso's development squad. But we were a fairly inexperienced team and my back was much better although it took longer to recover between games.

Unfortunately, Andy was dismissed at the end of August after six games without a win. Assistant manager Richard Shaw and Carso took over in caretaker capacities. Their first game in charge was a great League Cup win against Birmingham City before we travelled to the Alexandra Stadium for a League One game against Crewe. We hadn't played well and the game itself was forgettable but one incident in particular shocked me.

During the second half I went over to take a throw-in. We had been booed earlier on and insults were being hurled from the terraces. Then a Coventry fan shouted out, 'Kilbane, you deserve to have a handicapped daughter.' I turned around, furious, and told him to fuck off! I couldn't believe that someone could sink to such a despicable level and that he could dare bring Elsie into this.

It caused a stir and, afterwards, guess who had to express his regrets? A club statement was issued in which I said the following: 'Firstly, I want to apologise to all the fans who followed us to Crewe for the performance and the result. We want to be challenging in this league and that was simply not good enough and I can totally understand the frustration of our supporters. At one point, my own frustration got the better of me and I reacted to something one of our fans said to me. I wholeheartedly apologise and realise that, as club captain, I have a responsibility to conduct myself in a professional manner at all times and I have nothing but respect for the fans who have already travelled hundreds of miles around the country to support us this season.'

I insisted, too, that the following was added: 'If the supporter in question were to come forward I would be only too happy to meet him in person to offer an apology face-to-face because I am genuinely sorry for that reaction.' I was hoping that he would make contact with me because a face-to-face apology was the last thing that I was going to 'offer' him. He never did, of course, because some of these morons are very brave when hiding in a crowd, but not quite so courageous on their own.

The apology stuck in my throat, but I had to do it as it was deemed 'in the best interests of the club'. In reality, I would have done and said exactly the same thing to any 'supporter' had the situation been repeated.

Players will always get stick from fans and no one can deny that a certain amount of fan involvement and banter is part and parcel of the game, but there are clearly occasions when personal abuse becomes unacceptable. David Beckham was subject to extraordinary attacks in grounds all over the country following his sending off against Argentina in the 1998 World Cup. Even two years later at Euro 2000, England supporters were heard to chant, 'Your wife's a whore', 'We hope your kid dies of cancer' and 'We're going to kill your baby' following the 3-2 defeat by Portugal.

I have already mentioned the Eric Cantona incident at Selhurst Park. Although the Frenchman's response was spectacularly violent, I know there are some players who would have loved to have done the same thing when on the receiving end of such vitriol.

And, of course, it still goes on: in December 2012 Rio Ferdinand was struck by a coin thrown from the crowd when celebrating Robin van Persie's late winning goal in the Manchester derby. The FA responded with a statement, which read: 'We will work with the clubs and authorities to identify those responsible and support the strongest sanctions available, including life bans. We condemn any such acts and it is simply unacceptable that any player is exposed to injury in this way.' Despite this, you can guarantee that this behaviour will continue and players will just have to deal with it. Twitter has given greater access to players, but is also another outlet for fans to vent their frustration at players – and sometimes vice versa!

On 19 September, Mark Robbins was appointed as the new Coventry City manager, but, to be honest, by then I was really finding life difficult. I wasn't enjoying my football, the one activity I had always loved since I was a young boy. I was renting a bachelor flat in Solihull, Birmingham, and not seeing enough of Elsie and Isla. I was missing family life and feeling lost and miserable. Everything was up in the air and I was unclear about what the future held. I hadn't been in a good place for a long time and it was all getting on top of me. I was having trouble sleeping, had no motivation to get out of bed and realised that I had all the symptoms of depression.

I was very unhappy and knew I couldn't go on like this. I spoke to my good friend Paul Goodfellow, who contacted the PFA on my behalf. They were brilliant and put me in touch with the Sporting Chance Clinic, the charity founded by Tony Adams, where sportsmen and women could receive advice, support and counselling for any kind of problem. I had a number of therapy sessions, which I found very useful and put things in perspective. I was very grateful for the help.

Players are not robots – we are affected by personal and family matters. The general reaction to depression is not the same as a physical illness and there is still a stigma attached to it, not least in football where matters of the mind can sometimes be looked upon as 'swinging the lead'. When Stan Collymore admitted to depression while at Aston Villa, he faced crowds chanting, 'You're mad and you know you are' and wasn't helped by his manager, John Gregory's, response: 'How can you be depressed on £20,000 a week?' Depression has nothing to do with money and, of course, goes much deeper than financial security. Rio Ferdinand has recently talked about his own depression and thankfully the response has been a little more sympathetic.

Surprisingly, I wasn't dreading the end of my career, which is usually a desperately difficult time for footballers. It was actually the opposite – I had lost my desire for playing. My back, although improved, was never going to be perfect and I was approaching the age of thirty-six. The uncertainty of what lay ahead was causing me more stress than the thought of hanging up my boots. It suddenly became clear what I had to do and once I'd made my decision it was a huge relief. A great pressure had been lifted. I immediately felt so much better and more able to face the future.

On 8 December 2012, Coventry issued the following statement to the media: 'Coventry City have parted company with Kevin Kilbane after the club and the player agreed a mutual termination of his contract. Kevin has been away from the club for several weeks due to personal reasons and both parties have agreed that his contract can be terminated with immediate effect. The club, Kevin and the PFA have been working together to ensure the matter has been resolved in the interests of all parties.'

Altogether I made 612 league and cup appearances and played in 110 internationals. My retirement was now public knowledge and the reaction to the announcement really surprised me. Fans in Ireland and all my former clubs said some very nice things. Of course, there were one or two less flattering comments and my personal favourite was a tweet from a Sunderland fan that read, 'I thought he retired when he was playing for us.'

A week after my retirement was announced, I was surprised to read that I was about to be appointed as manager of Limerick! The club duly made contact with me, but it wasn't the right time. I wouldn't rule out taking on a coaching role in the future, but I didn't want to be away from the girls. I realised I might not get the same opportunity again but it wasn't to be.

By then I had already become involved in media work. I'd obtained a qualification in professional sports writing and broadcasting at Staffordshire University, completed further courses on the subject and was employed as a columnist for the *Irish Daily Mail*. I'd also worked as a pundit for RTÉ Sport and with Radio Five Live and Newstalk in Ireland while still playing. I'd always enjoyed the work, suddenly found myself in demand and now had the time to devote to it.

One of the first games I covered was at Goodison Park for Everton's match against Spurs. It was strange walking into the ground – a ground where I'd made a great number of appearances as a player – in a different job. Unlike my football career during which I seldom suffered from nerves, this was a different pressure and, although not my broadcasting debut, I realised that a lot depended on my performance for my future media work.

I appeared on Sky's *Soccer AM* and *A Question of Sport* and met Irish champion jockey Richard Hughes, which was a real honour. A week after retiring I was asked to appear on *The Late Late Show* in Dublin. Now *that* I was very nervous about as the show is such an Irish institution, being one of the longest running chat shows in the world, and especially as the other guests included the Dubliners, Domhnall Gleeson, Katherine Jenkins and Billy Connolly!

There have been a number of campaigns with which I have been proud to be involved over the years, including Show Racism the Red Card. English football has tackled racism well over the last twenty to thirty years, since the days when bananas were thrown at John Barnes and other black players, but we still have a long way to go, as a few disgraceful incidents last season resulted in banning orders. I fully support AC Milan's Kevin-Prince Boateng, who was so incensed by the racist chants in a friendly against Italian fourth division side Pro Patria that he picked the ball up and booted it towards the offending supporters before removing his shirt and storming off the pitch. His team-mates followed and the match was abandoned.

I do believe that the football authorities need to attach the same importance to ridding the game of homophobia as they do to racism. The PFA and football authorities are constantly tackling discrimination in all forms. In the late 1990s dressing rooms could be harsh places: if you looked at yourself in the mirror a few seconds too long, put a bit too much gel in your hair or wore any outlandish gear, you were going to get a lot of stick. I lost count of the number of times I was called bent, faggot, poof or gay boy because I was paying too much attention to my appearance when I was starting out at Preston North End.

Dressing rooms of today haven't changed that much, which is why it's still extremely tough for a player to come out as a homosexual. Ex-Leeds and USA international Robbie Rogers did just that and initially announced his retirement with immediate effect because he was convinced that the fans would make his life hell. Robbie has since bravely decided to return to playing with LA Galaxy.

In 1990 Justin Fashanu came out in an interview with the tabloid press, becoming the first prominent player in English football to do so. Many former colleagues spoke out against him and he also became the target of constant crowd abuse. Even his own manager, Brian Clough, who had signed Fashanu for Nottingham Forest, was supposedly outraged to discover that Fashanu was 'a bloody poof' and got him to train with the reserves. I suppose the point is that the whole of society has to change its behaviour as there is undoubtedly an element of discrimination in all walks of life.

Discrimination comes in many forms and, of course, having a daughter with Down's syndrome brings this home only too clearly. Nine years after Elsie's birth I feel very differently from those early dark days. Laura and I feel lucky that we have Elsie and although people sympathise with us when they find out Elsie has Down's syndrome, we don't feel that we need their sympathy. They only have to meet Elsie to see that she is such a vibrant, lovely girl and if we can educate them in some small way then it is making a difference. It's not that long ago that adults or children with Down's syndrome were routinely institutionalised and certainly excluded from mainstream society.

That's not to say we haven't had a few difficulties along the way. At the start we felt isolated and had to battle to get extra support for her at school. And, of course, we have some concerns for her future – she will always need some supervision to be able to live independently and I worry that with current public spending cuts things will be much more difficult. In May 2013, MENCAP identified about a hundred cases in which patients with learning difficulties have died after receiving poor care and estimates that over a thousand such patients die each year because of neglect by the NHS.

There was an incredible article in the *Lancashire Evening News* in May 2013 about a pair of identical twins, Arthur and Alfie Banks-Lowe, who were born with Down's syndrome. Their parents applied for Disability Living Allowance, which is the main benefit for disabled adults to help with the extra costs they face as a result of their disabilities.

Mr and Mrs Banks-Lowe were met with a bizarre response from civil servants at the Department of Work and Pensions; Arthur was accepted but Alfie was refused. The twins' mother commented, 'The boys are identical in every detail, they have exactly the same health issues, they need exactly the same care, yet one can get the allowance and the other can't. Arthur and Alfie need daily physiotherapy to build their weakened muscles. They both have identical heart and lung issues and eye problems, which all require frequent hospital visits. Two identical twins with identical problems shouldn't be regarded as different. It's ridiculous.'

The importance of being involved with Down's syndrome charities was never more clear to me than when, in January 2013, a father tweeted the DSA: 'My daughter was born in 2010 with Down's. I was 26 I don't speak about it in general. The fact that Kevin Kilbane is in the same boat makes me feel not alone...I also did not know that there were charities for DS.' This is why I have become a patron of the Down's

Syndrome Association and am involved with various charities. And, of course, the link with football continues. The Danny Mardell Knockout Football Challenge, which raises money for the Down's Syndrome Association, is now in its eighth year and the DSActive football programme is going from strength to strength.

A few years after Elsie was born I met with Christian Smith of the PFA, who had a young son, Dylan, with Down's. Gordon Taylor, the organisation's chief executive, allowed Christian time away from his commercial brief and allocated funds to contact football clubs to develop Down's syndrome teams. There had been teams of learning disabled footballers (Christian had worked in a 'world cup' while at Leicester) but there had never been teams just for children and adults with the syndrome. Christian spent time working with the DSA and clubs in their 'Football in the Community' programmes and also received financial support from Sport England.

The first tournament took place in 2011 with the help of a donation from the Premier League and Football Aid and gave players the chance to take part in what was for many their first competitive football tournament. It also provided the children's parents with the opportunity to come together and share their experiences and provided an ideal opportunity for disability coaches from all over the country to develop their skills and gain a better understanding of Down's syndrome football.

In May 2013, fourteen teams from the DSActive programme from all over England and Wales participated in the third annual Premier League's Down's Syndrome Football Festival. The tournament was made possible thanks to a donation from Football Aid and the free use of the West Bromwich Albion Foundation's brilliant facilities – so much better than when I was there! More than 150 players and 700 spectators made it the biggest festival yet.

It was a pleasure being a spectator and involved in handing

out the medals and I was amazed how much the standard of football has improved each year, a testament to the dedication of the parents, carers, coaches and, of course, the players themselves. It's brilliant that footballers with Down's syndrome can get to represent their favourite club sides, something a lot of young players don't have the opportunity to do. I'm excited to see just how far these players can progress; there's even talk of forming national sides.

A month before I ran in the London Marathon and followed in the footsteps of thousands of others, including Simon Beresford, who is, as far as I know, the only person with Down's syndrome to run the course. Having got out of the routine of daily training, I really enjoyed the running and am now hooked and plan to do few more marathons.

Coming into the last four miles reminded me of a scene at Poznan station during the Euro 2012 finals. There were dishevelled, weary-legged competitors all around me. As I tried to make my way to the finishing line, I had to run around the exhausted runners and somehow keep going. That last stretch was torture. My lungs were fine but the legs had gone and my head kept saying 'just pack up'. I knew if I stopped for just a second I would not be able to get going again. So I plodded on and the last eight hundred metres was the longest stretch of my life. But it was a brilliant experience. There were a few shouts of 'Zinedine' and 'Killa', which definitely helped. We raised nearly reached £10,000 for the Down's Syndrome Association. That eased some of the pain!

Another charitable sporting event in which I participated soon after was a match at Reading's Madejski Stadium to raise funds for the Team Army Sports Foundation and the Royal British Legion and to celebrate the Football Association's 150th anniversary. I appeared for the FA Legends team, managed by Roy Hodgson, in a match against a British Army side coached by Stuart Pearce.

We had some proper talent in the team, including Tore Andre Flo, Jan Age Fjortoft, Matt Le Tissier, Gary Neville and Jens Lehmann, and we ran out 4-2 winners. I wasn't surprised by the commitment of the Army team, who were really up for it, and it was pretty physical. There was a terrible two-footed lunge by one of the squaddies on Gaizka Mendieta, which could have broken both his legs. The ref, who I also think must have been in the services, just told us to 'Get on with it!' I was, however, slightly taken aback that our gaffer, the current England manager, took it quite so seriously and the half-time team talk was all about commitment and making sure we got the result! I wanted to have a free role but he told me the team had to keep our shape. I think this is the one time I ignored the gaffer...

I enjoyed playing, but the next day, when I could hardly walk, I realised that I'd made the right decision to retire from the professional game.

It's been an incredible career and, because I've been able to play in a number of positions and have stayed clear of injuries for the vast majority of the time, I've been able to take every opportunity that has arisen, particularly when playing for the national team

It has been a bit of a joke over the years that you just need to have drunk a pint of Guinness to get called up to the Republic of Ireland squad, but I think that a lot of the English-born lads in the squad have a strong affinity with Ireland. I've found that you can definitely be accepted by Irish-born players and fans if you're English-born, as long as you show complete commitment to the team. I think problems have arisen when players have reluctantly donned the green shirt after they had initially expressed a preference for England and then weren't picked. I chose, as others did, to play for Ireland at a young age and we made our intentions clear from the outset.

I'm grateful to all the clubs that gave me an opportunity to play professional football, but it's to the Republic of Ireland that I owe so much and where my heart lies. For me it's always, 'In Erin's cause come woe or weal'.

And now I think I can enjoy that pint of Guinness...

Acknowledgements

I'm very grateful for contributions from the following:

Chris Borwick, Kevin Campbell, Martin Clifford, Father Patrick Daly, Len Devey, Olaf Dixon, Ian 'Taff' Evans, Luke Flacks, Darren Griffiths, Declan Hanley, Chris Hutchings, Paul Jewell, Brian Kerr, John Leonard, Eddie Lewis, Colin Mackenzie, Dave Maher, Mick McCarthy, Paul McMenemy, David Moyes, Father G. Muir, Eric Nicholas, Father Paddy O'Donovan, Bobby Parkinson, Gary Peters, Ian Rigby, Christian Smith, Denis Smith, Steve Staunton, Alan Stubbs, Tommy Taylor, Fred Wilkinson and Simon Wright.

A special mention for all my family – especially Mum, Dad, Farrell and Geraldine. Without them I wouldn't be where I am today.

I am indebted to Johnny Fallon for all his guidance and continuing support throughout the years.

Thanks to my best mate Lee Carsley for the laughs and the tears, Paul Goodfellow for all his help and to Colin Young for his much valued friendship.

I am thankful to Paul Zanon and everyone at the Down's Syndrome Association for all their help and support they have given to our family.

For all FAI staff but especially, Adam Bux, Alan Byrne, Martin Byrne, Mick Byrne, Lenny Clark, Aisling Fennin, Tony Hickey, John Huntley, Alan Kelly, Mick Lawlor, Brian McCarthy, Ciaran Murray, Charlie O'Leary, Dick Redmond, Joe Walsh, Martin Walsh and Bobby Ward. A big thank you to the Irish fans and supporters of all the clubs I've represented.

To the staff at Aurum and copy editor, Richard Collins, for all his hard work.

Finally, I would like to thank Andy Merriman for his patience, time, effort and most of all friendship, not only in helping to write this book. I value the support you, Allie, Daniel, Sarah and Joel have given me.

Apologies to anyone I've forgotten!